PARENTING
FROM
A TO Z

PARENTING

FROM

A TO Z

AN ENCYCLOPEDIA
FOR LDS FAMILIES

Deseret Book Company
Salt Lake City, Utah

Library of Congress Cataloging-in-Publication Data

Parenting from A to Z : an encyclopedia for Latter-day Saint families.
    p. cm.
    ISBN 0-87579-298-7 (paperbound)
    1. Parenting–United States–Encyclopedias. 2. Parenting–Religious aspects–Church of Jesus Christ of Latter-day Saints–Encyclopedias.
HQ755.8.P3794   1990
649'.1'024283–dc20   90-39284
                                              CIP

Printed in the United States of America

10   9   8   7   6   5   4   3   2   1

CONTENTS

ACKNOWLEDGMENTS

We gratefully acknowledge the help of the following people, who prepared this book for publication. Each of them is an expert in his or her field, but more important, each is a successful parent, grounded in the gospel of Jesus Christ.

PROJECT COORDINATORS:
Roger K. Petersen
Ione J. Simpson

PLANNING AND REVIEW TEAM:
Janice J. Anderson
Thomas K. R. Baxter
Juel D. Gregersen
Scott R. Peterson

WRITING COMMITTEE CHAIRMAN:
Ivan Cornia

WRITERS:
Carole Reid Burr
P. Gary Esterholdt
Jack O'Driscol
Ronald L. Petersen
Adelia H. Rushforth
Kris T. Stone
N. Lynn Taylor
M. Gawain Wells
Lynda M. West

BASIC PRINCIPLES
OF PARENTING

PRINCIPLES OF PARENTING

Undergirding all principles of parenting is a single concept—that the sons and daughters of God are of infinite worth. The Psalmist said: "When I consider thy heavens, the work of thy fingers, the moon the stars. . . . what is man, that thou art mindful of him? . . . Thou hast . . . crowned him with glory and honour. Thou madest him to have dominion over the works of thy hands; thou hast put all things under his feet." (Psalm 8:3–6.)

We are literal children of God, our Heavenly Father. And by virtue of our being his children, our worth is inherent; it is within us at birth. Self-worth is not something we can build or acquire or earn while on this earth. It already exists, with or without our awareness. But it is something we must learn to understand and feel.

Our challenge is to be humble enough to recognize and graciously accept our self-worth, sensitive enough to feel it, faithful enough to believe in it, and wise enough to use it to serve God by serving others.

In Keeneland, Kentucky, there is an annual sale of thoroughbred yearlings. One yearling sold for ten million dollars. Why would a horse that has never run even one race be worth so much? The answer is that the buyer invested in the yearling's potential. Why did the buyer have such faith in that potential? That faith was surely based in part on knowing the yearling's ancestry.

Without the knowledge of our divine ancestry, we might not rise to our potential. If we know of our divine ancestry, however, and if we desire to fulfill the potential that that ancestry places within us, we can be blessed as our Heavenly Father intended.

3

The Lord has told us specifically how to fulfill our divine potential, and how to encourage our children to do the same. Jesus said, "I am the way, the truth, and the life." (John 14:6.)

Each child we receive into our home comes with an individual assignment and measure of creation to fulfill. It is an important measure, for during that child's earth life he or she must accomplish much, both personally and for the kingdom of God. The gospel of Jesus Christ and loving parents will assist the child in fulfilling this measure and understanding his or her worth. These influences will help the child discern between the doctrines of man and the teachings of Christ, and arm him or her with the faith to be in the world but not of the world.

Feelings of self-worth can come to a child who is led and taught, but the process of understanding is not automatic. It begins at birth, as parents embrace the children entrusted to them. Then, as children mature, there are several growing steps through which they pass.

First, a bond is created between children and those who care for their physical needs. Children begin to value the comfort and physical protection provided for them, and they value those who provide it.

Second, children begin to recognize that they also have value to their parents. This bonding is essential to the child's sense of well-being.

In a third step, children begin to recognize things that belong to them as having value. We sometimes call this the selfish age. But it passes.

Finally, if parents will believe deeply in this principle of worth, a fourth step happens in the life of the children: they will begin to see their true worth. As they see themselves through the eyes of those who love them — particularly their Heavenly Father — they will recognize the great worth they have had all along.

True peace comes only when we begin to understand this, when we start to live the commandments of God in some degree of fulness. Henry Thoreau said, "Whatever the human law may be, neither an individual nor a nation can ever commit the least act of injustice against the obscurest individual without having to pay the penalty for it." One reason for this is that inherently all people know of their worth to God, and that of other people as well. Happiness can never come to a person who is violating the knowledge of a person's worth.

As children mature they will naturally begin to feel what they are, unless they are distracted by false signals from the world. Often the failings of parents are passed down upon the heads of children, and the children begin to read their worth from what they see happening around them. The Doctrine and Covenants, however, clearly states: "Every spirit of man was innocent in the beginning; and God having redeemed man from the fall, men became again, in their infant state, innocent before God. And that wicked one cometh and taketh away light and truth, through disobedience, from the children of men, and because of the tradition of their fathers. But I have commanded you to bring up your children in light and truth." (D&C 93:38–40.)

As parents who have embraced the gospel of Jesus Christ we must be aware of the tactics "that wicked one" uses to take away light and truth. We must be mindful of the commandment from God to bring our children up in the gospel light.

But "Knowledge alone of gospel truth is not sufficient. We must live by the truths we know. Our children may sing 'I Am a Child of God,' but if we do not treat them according to that truth, they will not feel its meaning. Parents must affirm their children's worth as children of God *regularly* and *consistently*." (*Teach Them Correct Principles*, Family Relations Sunday School Course Manual, 1987, p. 112.)

Consider the following example: Three-year-old Sally knocked over a glass of water on the family room table. The little waterfall was already cascading to the carpet when she looked up toward her father. Having heard the telltale sounds, he turned around. Instead of a harsh look that meant, "What did you do that for?" Dad's face had a look that was soft and urgent. He said, "Sally, quickly, can you bring a towel from the kitchen to mop that up?" Like lightning, Sally raced to the kitchen and back. Her father helped her wring out the wet towel, and together they rubbed the soaked carpet a second and third time.

Suppose the glass had been filled with grape juice instead of water? Would Father have acted the same way? Spilled water, some would say, is an easy thing to handle, but grape juice— that's another matter. Can we as parents treat Sally as a child of

God, affirm her worth whether she makes simple mistakes or major errors?

"THAT YE LOVE ONE ANOTHER"

Sometimes when children rebel and blame us for their troubles, when they refuse to abandon their self-destructive behaviors, or when they run away from responsibilities, we as parents take offence. We are angry or hurt and begin to do to them what they are doing to us. We begin to punish their irresponsibility by withdrawing our responsible love. However, to give hostility back to hostile children is hardly what the Savior would suggest. Such behavior does not instill in children the desire to be Christlike and the confidence that, with his help, they can become so.

Even though some family members may not live by correct principles, parents should continue to love them and to invite and entice them to do good. This means neither accusing the child of being worthless nor excusing or indulging any wrongdoing. The key to follow is the Savior's counsel: "A new commandment I give unto you, That ye love one another; as I have loved you, that ye also love one another." (John 13:34.) To love as he loves will enable us to do all that is required to show our children their ultimate worth, and that the gospel of love and repentance is the only way for them.

SEEING OUR CHILDREN AS THE LORD SEES THEM

One of the greatest deceptions the evil one puts on children to affect their understanding of their worth is the admiration of the world. It is the measurement of success by the standards of glamor, academics, athletics, appearance, position, and possessions. Even the family can mislead a child by emphasizing the world's standards. Such standards have a tendency to frustrate the child, who often utilizes precious energy trying to fulfill someone else's measure, not his or her own. Worldly standards often teach people to esteem themselves rather than God, and to become unrighteously independent rather than dependent on Christ.

If we (or our children) fail to see ourselves as the Lord sees us, we tend to judge ourselves by others' expectations. We see ourselves measured against other people, instead of as individual children of God. By such standards it is inevitable that some will excel and others will fail, simply by virtue of the temporal gifts they were given at birth. Eventually this causes a preoccupation with self, self-consciousness, self-centeredness. Such concern with self causes what the world calls low self-esteem. Typically, people who are overly concerned with personal esteem will punish themselves for being less than others. But those who understand that all people are first and foremost children of God, and that only God's evaluation of them ultimately matters, are free of temptations to place themselves above or below others. God himself will grant his children all the abilities and strengths they need to please him and fulfill their earthly missions. Any road to self-esteem is a false road, unless "every man esteem his brother as himself." (D&C 38:24.)

In summary, consider these ten principles of parenting:

1. No family striving for celestial success can find it without basing their family's actions on a *sound spiritual foundation*. Basic principles include knowing that we are children of God, that we lived with him before coming to this earth, that life is sacred and that it has purpose. As children of God we must be obedient, praying and listening in faith for the promptings of the Holy Ghost—the messenger from the Father and the Son. Any person desiring to succeed as a parent must understand that the Spirit makes all the difference.

2. All children must have *nurturing and love*. These are basic human needs. Without them children wither and recede as surely as tender plants wither without sun, soil, and rain.

3. We need to understand that there are many different *styles of parenting*. No one style is right in all cases. All of us have different assets and liabilities. Some families have traditional homes—father, mother, children. But others have homes with only a single parent; sometimes children are alone. Sometimes men and women are alone without the hope of children.

Whatever situation we find ourselves in, whatever the experience or background we come from, God knows where we are. He is aware of all the struggling, and it is all for a purpose. He wants us to return to his presence.

4. *Parenting is a learned process*. Wherever we find ourselves today, we can do better tomorrow. We can study, pray, and seek help to qualify ourselves for the task of parenting. We never learn

solely from books. Experts can help, but only if we practice the techniques recommended and prayerfully find the ones that are right for us.

5. There are many prevailing *myths* that can affect parenting. These need to be swept out the door with other useless waste. The notion that only a few people will make it to the celestial kingdom is a myth. It makes some people say, "Why try?" The fact is that Father in heaven never sent any of us here doomed to failure. All can fill the measure of their creation, and men and women were created that they "might have joy." (2 Nephi 2:25.) The fruit that Nephi tasted from the tree of life filled his soul with joy (1 Nephi 8:12), and all were invited to come to that tree. Doctrine and Covenants 76:67 says that the inhabitants of the celestial world will be "innumerable," and Revelation 7:9–10 says that the host is to be "a great multitude, which no man could number." Clearly the celestial kingdom is for many, many people.

Another myth is that good parents have only righteous children, or that converts to the Church are somehow inferior to those born in the covenant. The truth is that all are God's children, and share the hope of returning to him. (See Romans 8:16–17.)

Another myth is that if people are righteous, they will have children. Some very special women from the scriptures were barren (see 1 Samuel 1:11; Luke 1:36), but the Lord knew their state and was well aware of promises made to them. He will not neglect any righteous person's desires, whether in this phase of our existence or the next.

Also, a temple sealing does not guarantee a happy marriage any more than a mission guarantees that a man or woman will make a good marriage partner. The temple and missions are important, even vital—but they of themselves mean little if the participants' heart is not right before the Lord.

Finally, some people build their lives feeling that if they are righteous they will prosper monetarily. Often this is true, but Job's experience should teach us all that the Lord will try his Saints. (See also Mosiah 23:21.)

6. Another great need in parenting is for *consistency with flexibility.* Children especially have a right to expect their parents to be predictable. This greatly enhances the security of the home. Like animals in a pasture, children usually have to try the fences.

When they realize that the fences will be consistently strong, they usually settle in and enjoy their experience within the family rules.

Family rules, however, should not be so inflexible that the child is hurt. A farmer who deliberately fences his pasture with an electric wire carrying 220 volts will soon lament the fact, as he sees his animals dying from the shock.

The words *discipline* and *discipleship* come from the same root. When we understand that we cannot force our children into the kingdom of God, we have learned a great lesson. Disciples of Christ must discipline themselves if they are to return to their Father; no one else can do it for them. All a parent can do is gently persuade and calmly direct.

7. All children, and even parents, need to have *confidence* instilled in them. They need to believe that they can succeed in spite of any and all obstacles. By avoiding comparisons and expressing confidence in children individually, parents can give them a new perspective of their eternal journey. All are not given the same gifts, but all can succeed.

8. Help your child *form values and attitudes* that are productive. These serve as beacons on uncharted seas; they give constant direction into safe channels. Model correct values and attitudes; let your children learn from righteous parents.

9. Remember that God gave all people their *agency*. They may not all have *freedom* yet, but no one can deny a person the power to choose the right. Even a person in the tightest prison cell has choices. Children must be taught that the power to choose was the central issue in the war in heaven. Satan can never win his battle because agency was declared long ago to be vital, fundamental to proper existence. In like manner, agency cannot be restricted or withheld from children. Their freedom can be circumscribed, but their agency cannot.

10. Free *communication* will often solve many problems before they get out of hand. When people are talking to each other, progress is generally being made. Guide the communication toward free expressions of love. Even older children get a thrill from the words "I love you," and when they say those words themselves, a moment of hope emerges. The scriptures say "God is love." (1 John 4:8.) Communicating that love to one another is the same as loving God.

DEVELOPMENTAL STAGES OF CHILDREN

People once believed that children were just tiny adults, and that they should act and think the way grown-ups do. The passage of time, practical experiences, observation, insights, and studies have taught us that children go through particular developmental stages as they mature from infancy to adulthood. Traits, needs, abilities, and behavior differ somewhat in each stage. Knowing what to expect will better prepare parents to understand their child's behavior. And when parents have an understanding of normal growth and development patterns, they can guide their children to have positive and joyful experiences as they mature.

The following brief summary outlines some general characteristics common in each age group, with particular attention to how these stages affect gospel learning. It should be remembered that a child's rate of development is a very individual thing. Parents should not expect every child to do everything at exactly the moment suggested by a book.

INFANTS—BIRTH TO ONE YEAR

From the very moment of birth an infant's uniqueness, personality, and divine qualities can be seen and felt. As parents love and nurture their baby, these characteristics will become gifts and assets to the child for the rest of his life.

At no other period of time will a child's growth and development be so rapid. During the first month infants are adjusting to eating and sleeping routines. They will gradually learn to focus on faces and objects, and may begin to smile at these at about six weeks. Baby's coos during the first few months will change to babbles, grunts, growls, giggles, laughs, and even "Dada" and "Mama" by the seventh month. And by the end of the first year the infant may even be saying a few short sentences, though many normal children don't talk this much until they are two. Throughout the first year, children's attention span and awareness increase, and they are constantly watching and taking in the world around them. They go from turning toward sounds they hear to reaching out to the sound to walking to the sound. Birth is a miracle, and infancy is the continuation of that miracle. At this stage, depending on how well his or her needs are met, the child's attitude of trust or mistrust toward the world will emerge. Normal nurturing care consistently applied will result in a sense of trust for others.

TODDLERS — ONE TO THREE YEARS

Toddlers can walk, climb, crawl, and run. They enjoy pushing and pulling things. They like to take things apart, but have difficulty putting them back together! They are busy and active and yet tire easily. Most toddlers are usually not toilet trained until they are close to three years of age. They are often able to speak in sentences, although their most-often-used words are *no* and *mine*. The use of such words indicates that children are beginning to separate themselves from their parents, a process that will ebb and wane as the child becomes an adult. Rather than be threatened by such signs of independence, parents should view these thrusts as a normal and desirable process.

Toddlers love stories, especially about themselves, and they love songs and fingerplays to be repeated over and over to them. They are curious and love to explore every pebble, hole, and cupboard they can find. Toddlers usually play alone or alongside others with little interaction. However, by age three they will want to play with other children in a more cooperative play. Toddlers do not usually understand the concept of sharing and taking turns—this is why so many tears and arguments arise in play— but they will get better at this as they turn three. It is more effective to distract or redirect toddlers than to try to reason with them. Although most religious concepts are too abstract or difficult for toddlers, they can begin learning to be reverent, to pray, and to listen to simple stories about Jesus and Heavenly Father and the beautiful world they created.

EARLY CHILDHOOD—THREE TO EIGHT YEARS

Active seems to be the best word to describe children from ages three to eight. During these years they will steadily increase in their large and small muscle coordination. They love to walk, run, skip, jump, race, climb, and throw and kick balls. Games of all sorts are a favorite activity. With so much energy to spare they will often be noisy, restless, boisterous, and sometimes aggressive in their play. By about five years of age they are having less conflict in their play because they are turning their interests more to others and away from themselves. At six and seven, boy and girl activities are beginning to differ and there is less play between them.

Children in this age grouping are anxious to please adults, and they seek for their approval, love, and praise. They may also cry easily and burst out at situations or people when troublesome feelings, fears, or anxieties arise.

These children are innocent and pure. They are interested in simple gospel truths, such as prayer and obedience. They have great faith and a love and admiration for Heavenly Father and Jesus. They are teachable and are growing in their awareness of what is right and wrong. Seven-year-olds enjoy learning and practicing gospel principles and look forward to being baptized and receiving the gift of the Holy Ghost.

LATER CHILDHOOD—EIGHT TO TWELVE YEARS

Eight-year-olds are on their way to becoming responsible people. They have a clear idea of right and wrong. In the eyes of the Lord, eight is the age of accountability. Children this age are teachable and need the help of family and teachers in expanding their knowledge of Heavenly Father and Jesus.

The years from nine to twelve are important ones for peer relationship. Children now enjoy being with a group and feeling "in" with their peers, and peers begin having a great deal of influence over them. At this age, girls are usually maturing faster than boys. Boys and girls differ more than ever in their personalities, characteristics, and interests. Boys like to be with boys and girls like to be with girls. And girls are becoming very aware of their appearance at this age.

This is a very productive age. These are the "adult" years of childhood, preceding the storminess of adolescence. Some children become very independent and enjoy doing things their own way and learning from their own experience.

Children in later childhood are influenced by the testimonies of others and are ready to learn more complex doctrines of the gospel. They are striving to gain their own testimonies. Girls are preparing to learn about the joys and responsibilities of womanhood, and boys are preparing to learn of manhood and to receive the priesthood. This period is also a time when children become aware of their adequacy, so it is especially desirable for them to feel a reasonable degree of competence in their pursuits. Parents will want to structure school-related or household tasks that the child can feel success in doing.

EARLY ADOLESCENCE—TWELVE TO FIFTEEN YEARS

During the adolescent years boys and girls change physically in dramatic and significant ways. They usually grow taller, broader, and heavier. Many experience some frustrating awkwardness and embarrassment with their new growth and development. Girls usually mature a year of two before boys (sometimes even as early as age ten or eleven; a girl's menstrual cycle can begin this soon). And boys' voices become deeper and more masculine.

Perhaps more than at any other age, adolescents are extremely self-conscious. When they are critical of themselves they think others must be also. When they are admiring of themselves they think others should be also.

Much of the behavior of adolescents can be understood as it relates to their fears and concerns. This is a time of worry and pain for many youth. They worry about their physical appearance, school failure, family relationships, and physical harm. They tend to rely heavily on their peers, and peer pressure is very intense at this age.

Some teenagers have particularly strong tendencies to assert their own individuality. They may rebel or defy parental authority, but if given opportunity and support as they learn, they will come to respect adult counsel.

Younger teens are beginning to show an interest in the opposite sex, although they usually have a whole gang of friends to associate with. They want to appear grown-up and are often resolving to do better. They are seeking to find out "who they are." Adolescents are usually truthful, concerned about fair treatment of others, and constantly trying to arrive at the right decisions by themselves. They thirst for knowledge and are receptive to gospel teachings. They continue to grow in their faith and testimonies.

LATER ADOLESCENCE – FIFTEEN TO NINETEEN YEARS

Later adolescence brings its own set of fears and concerns for youth. They continue to worry about school failure, physical appearance, and peer acceptance. Added to these is worry about the future – their security and vocations. Boys think about their preparations to go on missions as they approach age nineteen.

By now, most youth have matured and nearly completed the physical growth and development so dramatic during the teen years. Many enjoy an improved relationship with their parents, feeling that parents are more satisfied with them. They continue to need and want their independence.

Adolescents vary greatly in their maturity, especially in relationships with peers and parents. Some may be uncomfortable with the opposite sex and have little interest, while others are talking of marriage. This is an important time for parents to teach and help prepare youth for enjoyable and appropriate dating, courtship, and marriage experiences.

Later adolescence usually brings a more peaceful time in the lives of youth. They feel self-confident, and many have discovered their special talents and abilities. Others still continue to search for who they are and what they want out of life. Parents' love, listening, and gentle guidance can continue to help these youth find peace in their lives. It is important for youth to feel independent and self-reliant, but they also need to know the great importance of relying on the Lord to help them be led to fulfill their own unique purpose and the measure of their creation.

PARENTING SKILLS

Being a parent is never very easy. Many of us feel inadequate as we realize how little training and preparation we have received for such an important job.

The following parenting concepts and skills, briefly introduced here and emphasized throughout this manual, can help parents learn to solve specific problems facing their famiy and to guide their children in ways consistent with sound child-development principles and gospel truths. By cultivating these skills, and striving to be guided by the Holy Ghost, parents can increase their joy and understanding of their important role in the lives of their children.

LISTENING TO LEARN AND UNDERSTAND

For parents to have any positive, lasting influence on their children, they must learn to understand them. And one of the most important ways we can come to know and understand other people is by listening to them—to their ideas, their fears, and their joys. Being a good listener does not mean we must agree with everything being said; it only means we try to understand. It means trying to see things from the children's point of view—to understand why they feel the way they do—without judging or evaluating them. When a child comes home and says, "I hate Mark!" the evaluating parent will say, "Why, of course you don't hate him. You love him, and you shouldn't talk that way!" The parent who is listening to learn and understand will say, "You sound like you're upset with Mark about something," and will encourage the child to express feelings. If we take the time to pay attention

15

to our children and to listen to them when they want to talk about something, we are saying, "You are important to me." We need to put down the newspaper, shut off the TV, or cut the telephone conversation short to place our first priority with our children as we listen with our eyes, ears, and hearts.

Another important aspect of listening to learn and understand our children is to be sensitive to the promptings of the Holy Ghost. Parents need never go through parenthood alone, for the Lord is there to give guidance and direction to those who seek, ask, and listen for it. Through Him we will learn to better understand our children. "And the light which shineth, which giveth you light, is through him who enlighteneth your eyes, which is the same light that quickeneth your understandings." (D&C 88:11.)

When a child needs discipline, that is the time to guide and direct him. But when a child needs to be understood, that is the time to listen.

EXPRESSING LOVE, CONCERN, AND AFFECTION

Every infant, child, and adult needs to be nurtured with expressions of love, concern, and affection throughout life. This is nourishment to the body and the spirit. Children begin to feel loved and secure when their basic human needs of food, shelter, and clothing are met. And then come the deeper needs of feeling loved and accepted by those around them. These needs are met as parents verbally and nonverbally express sincere love to their children. How wonderful it would be if all children could hear "I love you" from their parents' lips every day! Another valuable expression of love is sincere praise. Christ must have felt his Father's love each time our Father in heaven introduced him with the expression, "This is my beloved Son, in whom I am well pleased." (Matthew 3:17.)

Affection can be expressed in many ways, but one of the most significant is through a soft and gentle touch. A pat, hug, or kiss, sitting or rocking on a lap, squeezing or holding a hand, all say, "I love you." We also show love and concern for our children by listening to them, by spending time together in work, play, learning, and worship, and by talking to them about our feelings regarding each new aspect of their lives. Our children will know that we care if we are there for them.

GIVING SPECIFIC CREDIT AND RECOGNITION

When parents give specific credit and recognition for something a child has done, they build their child's self-confidence and reinforce the positive behavior. This encourages the child to repeat the recognized behavior again. Here are some examples of specific, effective compliments:

"John, I really appreciate your cleaning the garage. It looks great and now I can get the car in easier."

"Wow! Your room really looks nice! Thank you for vacuuming the carpet. I feel so much better when the house is clean. I'm wondering how you feel. Doesn't it feel good to see your room looking like this?"

"Robbie, thank you for folding your arms. You are all ready for prayer."

When we fail to give children credit for what they have done, and always demand more, we make them resentful, dependent, and inadequate. They will lack confidence and self-assurance. If we give children jobs around the house that they can do successfully by themselves, we will have opportunities to acknowledge them for their accomplishments, no matter how small. We need to let our children know that we notice what they do and are pleased with their endeavors.

DEVELOPING COURAGE IN CHILDREN

As the children of Israel prepared to go to battle against their enemies, the Lord spoke to them and told them not to be afraid, "for the Lord thy God is with thee." (Deuteronomy 20:1.) The Israelites took courage and faced their unknown trials. Parents can help develop a deep and abiding courage in their children by teaching them to put their faith and trust in the Lord, and by encouraging them to take appropriate risks as part of their development. Such risks may include taking part in a roadshow, accepting a leadership position, giving a talk, making a new friend, or saying a prayer in Primary. Children's confidence will increase as their parents teach them they have a Father in heaven who loves and cares about them.

Daily prayers, priesthood blessings, family home evenings, personal testimonies, example, scripture study, fasting, and family and individual discussions with children can all emphasize the power of a loving Father in heaven who will take away fears and fill hearts with courage. "For God hath not given us the spirit of fear; but of power, and of love, and of a sound mind." (2 Timothy 1:7.)

SENDING CLEAR AND EASILY UNDERSTOOD MESSAGES

The apostle Paul said, "For if the trumpet give an uncertain sound, who shall prepare himself to the battle? So likewise ye, except ye utter by the tongue words easy to be understood, how shall it be known what is spoken?" (1 Corinthians 14:8–9.) Paul's counsel has great value for parents. If we speak with uncertain messages, how can our children understand our intent? Messages are sent both verbally and nonverbally. Sometimes we send messages that contradict each other, and this creates extreme anxiety and tension in children. An example of this would be the parent who preaches honesty but engages in a dishonest activity. Other unclear messages come when parents are not supportive of each other. One parent may give a different message than the other, and then instruct the child not to tell the parent. The resulting torn loyalties are very stressful to children.

It is important for the healthy emotional development of children that parents say what they mean and mean what they say when giving guidance and direction.

USING LOGICALLY RELATED CONSEQUENCES

The more closely a consequence is related to a person's behavior, the more effective it will be in influencing change. Consequences are usually classified into two major categories: natural consequences and logical consequences. When you run out of gasoline while driving, you suffer the natural consequences of not having filled your gas tank. You cannot blame anyone but yourself, and the consequence will probably be effective in influencing your behavior. In the future, you will watch the gas gauge more closely!

Natural consequences have often been used by the Lord to chasten his Saints. God forbade Adam and Eve to eat of the tree of the knowledge of good and evil and said if they did they would surely die. (See Moses 3:15–17.) In allowing Adam and Eve to experience the natural consequences of their behavior, our Father in heaven set an important example for parents. Sometimes, wise parents will counsel their children against certain practices and then allow a disobedient child to experience the consequences of his or her own behavior.

Sometimes natural consequences are too slow acting or too serious to be effective in child rearing. Allowing a child to play in the street or to experiment with drugs could result in dangerous and serious natural consequences. We want children to learn from their mistakes *before* it is too late.

Logical consequences are set up by parents to guide children away from inappropriate behavior when natural consequences are not practical. A child who plays in the street, for example, might be confined to the yard or house for a time. If bad manners are used, the child is removed from the table (or has food taken away). If the child neglects to come home on time, he or she forfeits the opportunity to go away from home the next time. Threats and warnings are usually ineffective or even counterproductive. Swift, firm action is very effective.

Logical consequences must be closely related to misbehavior so that the children can see the relationship between the two; otherwise they may perceive their parents as vengeful and angry people. Also, logical consequences are most effective when a parent remains warm and calm while firmly dealing with the child. Be confident that the consequence fits the offense and do not argue with the child about it. Be firm with yourself as well as with the child. Always be positive. End with an encouraging statement.

REWARDS AND PUNISHMENT

Too often, in child rearing, parents pay attention to only the annoying and offensive behaviors of their children. The walls may echo with: "Stop doing that!" "Why do you always cause trouble?" "Can't you remember anything?" "Don't!" Children and adults do need guidance to eliminate unacceptable behaviors. But even though punishment may work, rewards are much more effective in changing inappropriate behavior.

Guidance is more effective when it focuses on what *can* be done rather than on what *should not* be done. Many times, just by ignoring negative behavior and rewarding good behavior, parents can help the negative behavior diminish. As parents pay attention to positive behavior the children's reward will be a feeling of self-confidence and the joy of knowing that their actions are acceptable to others.

Ideally, punishment is used to discipline and guide children when they misbehave and a logically related consequence cannot be found. But, at times, parents use punishment as an outlet of their own anger, frustration, and impatience. Punishment then becomes a weapon rather than a teaching tool.

Punishment might include such things as fining children, separating them from others, restricting their activities, or making them do something they do not like to do. For these forms of punishment to be used constructively, they must follow the misbehavior immediately. When possible they should be used in concert with logical or natural consequences.

Parents should always explain clearly to a child why he or she is being punished. Punishments should be used as little as possible or in conjuction with rewards because they are less effective than rewards for reinforcing positive behavior.

The scriptures say: "Verily, thus saith the Lord unto you whom I love, and whom I love I also chasten that their sins may be forgiven, for with the chastisement I prepare a way for their deliverance in all things out of temptation, and I have loved you." (D&C 95:1.) The Lord clearly states that caring enough to chasten and correct is an expression of love. Parents should correct their children with love and firmness in a way that will "prepare a way for their deliverance in all things out of temptation." This is using punishment constructively.

RECONCILING DIFFERENCES

Conflicts are inevitable in families. Each person's uniqueness and the gift of agency make differences of opinion and actions a normal and healthy result of human interaction. No two people can exercise their agency without sometimes having conflicts and differences. However, the Lord has directed that these must be resolved before we enter his presence. (See 3 Nephi 12:22–24.)

Reconciliation requires communication that leads to understanding, which in turn leads to unity: "Teach one another . . . let every man esteem his brother as himself. . . . I say unto you, be one; and if ye are not one ye are not mine." (D&C 38:23–24, 27.) Differences can be resolved by talking together and sharing feelings; listening to each other's point of view and coming to an understanding of these views and the problem; planning solutions together through brainstorming, studying, and praying for inspiration; agreeing on a plan and implementing it, and eventually evaluating the progress being made. In due time, love will increase and happiness will permeate the home as these principles of peacemaking are practiced. Winning an argument is not worth destroying a relationship.

Children are constantly bombarded with frustrations, failures, discouragements, and negative experiences that eat away at their self-confidence and feelings of worth. Parents can help their children regain confidence and happiness by listening to them, encouraging them to express their feelings, giving affection, and voicing genuine love and concern for them. All of us need someone to lean on for support, even when our mistakes and failures are of our own making. The Lord taught that there is a time to reprove, and then a time afterwards to show forth "an increase of love toward him whom thou hast reproved, lest he esteem thee to be his enemy." (D&C 121:43.)

When children have erred or failed, they need love and support. Then, feeling loved and valued by others, they can concentrate on the tasks at hand instead of using all their energy to justify their ideas and actions. They are also more open to suggestions from others and better able to learn from their own mistakes.

ORGANIZING A LESSON

It is hoped that the information in this book will be helpful not just as a resource for parents trying to remedy their family problems, but also as supplementary lesson material for church callings or family home evenings. The following suggestions may help you plan and organize the material into lessons. The important thing to keep in mind is that "the basic goal of teaching in the Church is to help bring about worthwhile changes in the lives of boys and girls, men and women. The aim is to inspire the individual to think about, feel about, and then do something about gospel truths and principles. Great teaching involves knowledge, attitudes, and action." (Teacher Development Basic Course, Administrative Manual [Salt Lake City: The Church of Jesus Christ of Latter-day Saints, 1970], p. 3.)

EVALUATE THE LEARNER

Give prayerful thought to the learners, whether an entire class, a single child, or your whole family. Why do they act the way they do? How do they feel about the world, and, more importantly, how do they feel about themselves? Parents must be specialists where their own children are concerned; teachers must know and understand their class members. After determining the needs of the learner, evaluate the level of his or her understanding based on age, background, readiness to learn, and so on. Students react and interpret things in the light of their past experiences. Remember that just as you can't expect a man to run and jump to the top of a ladder, it is too much to expect the learner to leap immediately to the ideal level, or even to your level of knowledge or conviction. You must begin at the student's present level and work from there. You cannot skip the step-by-step procedure without creating frustration and discouragement and probably losing your cause.

Know that each person is unique, and acknowledge their differences. All are children of God, and no two are alike. For this reason, they do not all learn alike. Some learn best in a social environment; they are not comfortable if they can't talk and relate. Others relate to facts and figures. Everything must be in order. They like to learn systematically, a little at a time. Still others are controllers and like to take charge. They learn best when they have something to do, such as worksheets, games, or other activities. Others have to discuss and interact. They need to see the whole picture to start with, and to discuss the possibilities up front.

Nevertheless, there are certain ways in which all people are alike. All share some of the same basic needs: love, attention, recognition, feelings of self-worth, security, agency, and so on. As a teacher, you can appeal to these similarities.

USING OBJECTIVES

Select one main idea from the article you are using, keeping foremost in your mind what you want to teach and why you want to teach it. Write this objective out. For example: "Family members will begin to understand and cultivate reverence at home, thereby enriching their relationship to the Lord." A good lesson covers one idea, organized and illustrated.

Prepare adequately. Prayerfully study the principle you are planning to teach. We can't give anything away until it is ours. Ask yourself, "How can this principle be transferred to real life and made meaningful to the student?" Prepare an outline listing main supporting ideas. Remember that Heavenly Father will help only after we have done all we can do.

Teach as the Savior taught. He used examples the people understood, demonstrating what he meant. He related the unknown to the known, making vivid comparisons. He used repetition to stress the importance of the lesson. (See John 21:15–17.) He taught with respect and courtesy, lovingly caring for those he was teaching. His lessons were simple and direct. Note how many times he answered a question with a question, causing the learner to think.

Constant lecturing is not effective. Involve each student intellectually and emotionally by discussing real life problems to which he can relate. Use questions and discussions, sincerely inviting their comments and interacting with them to encourage, not to offend. Listen! Can a teacher who doesn't listen be any more effective than a doctor who does not listen to a description of symptoms or watch for other clues? Without listening a teacher cannot accurately diagnose or understand the problem. Vary your presentation. Use worksheets, games, videos, and so on.

SOME BASIC PRINCIPLES TO REMEMBER

The Spirit supersedes everything, including technique. Prepare to teach with the Spirit by living righteously and praying earnestly. Repent when necessary. Let your primary goal be helping your class member or child. If you teach by the Spirit you will build your student, never belittling or tearing down another.

Be an example of the things you teach. The teacher's character radiates a powerful influence.

Evaluate your teaching experiences. Measure what has actually been learned. Seek feedback. Observe facial expressions, posture, interested or uninterested responses. Always take problems to their conclusion. Never leave the child or class member dangling. Love them enough to see problems through to the end.

SECTION II

AN ENCYCLOPEDIA OF
PARENTING CONCERNS

ABORTION

Abortion reveals a contradiction in many people. They would weep and grieve for those who die, and they would pray for those whose lives are in jeopardy. They spend large amounts of money to preserve the lives of critically ill infants. Yet many of these same people give little thought to the termination of life in the womb, before birth.

The Lord has declared, "Thou shalt not kill," then added, "nor do anything like unto it," (D&C 59:6.) We have been strongly counseled by Church leaders concerning abortion. The following is from President Spencer W. Kimball:

"My brothers and sisters, I want you to know that abortion is wrong. We counsel girls and women never to consider having an abortion. We also counsel our doctors and nurses not to perform nor assist in performing abortions. We admonish parents and priesthood leaders to firmly oppose this revolting and evil practice. Anyone who is a party to abortion, including someone who might influence a girl to have an abortion, is an accomplice to a grievous sin, and stands in great need of repentance. Such persons should be called to account by their priesthood leaders.

"Now, I know that in some cases some so-called experts and others try to make abortion seem proper. Many young people, and even some parents, have been confused and misled. Many others feel that abortion is wrong, but may not have had all their questions answered about it. May I discuss some of these questions.

"One question applies to the consequences for a person who

27

has had an abortion, or who has been a party to one. As far as the Church is concerned, the consequences are serious indeed. Repentance for such a grievous sin is not easy. An absolutely necessary step is confession of the sin to one's bishop, who can help along the road to repentance. Members of the church guilty of being parties to the sin of abortion must be subjected to a proper court of the church, as circumstances warrant.

"Another question has to do with whether persons who have had an abortion can be forgiven, and how they could repent fully after such a serious sin. To every forgiveness there is a condition. The bandage must be as wide as the sore. The fasting, the prayers, the humility must be equal to or greater than the sin. There must be 'sackcloth and ashes.' There must be confession of the error to properly constituted authorities of the Lord. There must be restitution and a confirmed, determined change of pace, direction, and destination. Conditions must be a new consecration and devotion to the living of all of the laws of God. In short, there must be an overcoming of self, of sin, and of the world.

"When persons can honestly say that they have done all of these things, then they may plead with the Lord for mercy in the hope of forgiveness.

"Some people raise the question of the expectant mother's health in conncetion with abortion. There may be a very rare circumstance requiring life-saving surgery or treatment that may result in the loss of an unborn child. But such cases are rare and unusual. Even in situations such as these no decision should be made without divine confirmation following earnest prayer and consultation with the bishop.

"Occasionally the question of pregnancy by rape will be asked. Medical evidence indicates that this is an extremely rare situation. But regardless of how the pregnancy was caused, abortion would greatly compound the wrong. An unborn baby must not be punished for the sins of his father. Letting the baby be born and placing him in an adoptive home would surely be a better solution for an unfortunate situation.

"Now let us consider the question of abortion in cases of possibly defective babies. No one, save the Lord himself, has the right to decide if a baby should or should not be permitted to live.

All human life is sacred. One of life's most Christian opportunities is to work with those who have handicaps.

"And, while handicaps are a part of the imperfect world in which we now live, in the resurrection there will be no blind eyes, no deaf ears, and no crippled legs. In eternity there will be no retarded minds and no diseased or injured bodies. In the eternal perscpective, such infirmities exist but for a moment.

"Yet, some people would play the part of God and deny mortality to helpless children within the womb. And many that may be thought to be afflicted will be born without a blemish.

"Often the question is asked, 'What should unmarried parents do, then?' One of the most important things they should do is to seek help from their parents and their bishop. Loving parents and an understanding bishop can help them as they begin the vital process of repentance. They can then help the young unwed parents make eternal decisions.

"Whenever possible, unwed parents should marry and build a home. When this is not possible, adoption through Church Social Services is preferred so that the infant can be sealed to loving, eager parents in an eternal family. A baby needs a family—a father and a mother. The Lord intended for babies to have a family and for families to be eternal.

"When a young man and woman create life by sinful behavior, the very least they can do to begin their personal atonement is to preserve the life of their child, whether or not they place the infant with adoptive parents.

"Another important thing each unwed parent must know is that abortion would only compound the problem, both here and hereafter. Abortion should not even be considered as a possible choice.

"All of us should remember that the same God who cannot look upon sin with the least degree of allowance is a merciful God, who loves us enough to have sent a Savior, His only Begotten Son, to atone for the sins of the truly repentant.

"Should there be any situation where questions have not been fully answered, you should consult with your bishop who with the stake president could consult with the First Presidency. The Lord loves us all, and is kind and merciful." (*Church News*, March 27, 1976, p. 6.)

As young people grow and learn, parents need to teach a reverence for life, the eternal plan of families, and the sacredness of having children, and how men and women become co-creators with Heavenly Father. "And all thy children shall be taught of the Lord; and great shall be the peace of thy children." (Isaiah 54:13.)

Children should be taught to understand and gain control of their physical desires and bodily passions. One father, cautioning his son as he approached the dating age, pointed out how the practice of necking and petting could lead to the sin of unchastity. Unchastity could lead to pregnancy. Then he asked his son, "What if the girl chose to have an abortion? Would this major sin be only on the head of the girl?"

Some parents panic at having a daughter pregnant or a son who has fathered a yet-unborn child out of wedlock. With sorrow and selfishness they imagine what will happen to the family name and reputation. "What will people say? How can I face my friends?" This attitude is selfish and not helpful to those needing counsel. A better approach would be to consider how these young people will feel on judgment day instead of how their neighbors might react.

As parents counsel a child who is in the process of deciding what to do, they could (as President Kimball has) point out some alternatives: marriage, adoption, or even single parenting. Never should they advise or suggest, however, that abortion is a choice to consider. Some may choose to take advantage of a program where girls are placed in loving and supporting Latter-day Saint homes during their pregnancies. When the baby is born, it is adopted by a Latter-day Saint family, where it will be nurtured and loved, thereby providing a great source of joy to the adoptive parents. Giving a baby to a home where it will be wanted should bring comfort to any young mother caught in difficult circumstances.

Some parents may have a daughter or a son who, in spite of counsel to the contrary, chooses to be party to an abortion. The parents will experience grief and disappointment, but they will also need to deal with their child's inevitable pain and devastation. Youth who have made abortion their choice have the consequences to live with—feelings of guilt, loss, despair, unworthiness, hopelessness. These children need parents who are not condemning, not judgmental, but loving—who will offer hands to hold onto and arms to embrace. (See 3 Nephi 14:1-2.)

The parents themselves may also need help. They may need to talk about their feelings. Church leaders and family members can be of invaluable service.

As is the case with any grievous sin, the personal repentance required in cases of abortion is not an easy path to travel. Repentance cannot be forced on another, nor can any mortal do it for another. Parents can teach the repentance principle and process, and continue to love and to show their love, but children still have agency.

Innocent life, however, was not sent by the Father to be destroyed by man.

ADOPTION

There are many examples in scripture as well as in modern life of happy, successful families formed by adoption. Remember the infant Moses—scripture tells us that "Pharaoh's daughter took him up, and nourished him for her own son." (Acts 7:21.) Adoption can be a joyful experience and can provide the opportunity of parenting to couples who might otherwise have missed this blessing.

Some people say adopted children have more problems. Much of the research that has been done on adopted children is based on studies of children who go for therapy, and indicates that adopted children are not as well adjusted as their nonadopted peers. However, a recent study by Richard Detweiler, Ph.D., and psychoanalyst Kathlyn Marquis of Drew University (*Growing Together*, Region II Children's Services Div., June 1987) on a "normal" population of 167 teenagers, 46 of whom were adopted as infants, showed that "adopted kids were significantly more confident, felt more in control of their lives, and viewed their parents as more nurturant, comforting, predictable, concerned and helpful, than did the nonadopted counterparts." They continue, "Our research shows that adoption is a boon to both child and parent . . . the adopted may be different, but they differ by being more positive—not more negative—than their nonadopted peers."

Adopted children come from a different genetic background than their adoptive parents. These differences may involve not only physical appearance but also talents, interests, and temperament. Parents should acknowledge such differences, cultivating the child's unique abilities while trying to understand and deal with characteristics that at times may appear troublesome.

Adoptive and biological parents encounter far more similarities than differences in raising their children. Most parenting challenges arise from the developmental stages that every child experiences. Adoptive parents may be inclined in times of parent-child conflict or stress to attribute such behavior to the adoption. Becoming aware of the stages and usual challenges in normal growth and development will be helpful for both parent and child.

Although there are many similarities between adoptive and biological families, there are differences. It is important that adoptive parents recognize, accept, and deal with these differences. Such acknowledgment will result in more relaxed communication between husband and wife as well as between parents and child, and will result in better adjustment to the adoption. The following are issues you may wish to consider:

INFERTILITY

One of the most important challenges to be addressed by many adoptive parents is their feelings regarding their infertility. It is important for the good of all concerned that these feelings are resolved. It is normal to feel anger, guilt, frustration, and even shame when first discovering one's infertility. If the man is infertile he may begin to doubt his masculinity. The woman, if she is the infertile person, may feel inadequate. Actual mourning will follow this initial discovery. Resolution occurs over a period of time. When the couple is able to talk about their infertility to family, close friends, or an adoption counselor without feeling ashamed or apologetic, they are ready for adoption. This does not mean that they will be free of their feelings of sadness about their infertility, nor that they will not still hope the problem can be resolved, if that is a possibility. There is need for concern, however, if the person's sense of competence is based on the ability to reproduce. Professional counseling might be helpful in such cases. Many communities have organizations where couples with similar problems come together to discuss and resolve their feelings. Frequently, association with someone who has had the same experience is helpful.

"SUPER" PARENTS

Adoptive parents should recognize that they do not have to be "super" parents. Circumstances surrounding adoption, such as the long waiting time and the interest and excitement of family and friends when the baby finally arrives, focus unusual attention on the event. This may cause parents to feel the need to be perfect in the eyes of others.

If the new baby is unusually stressed with colic or has other problems that keep parents up night after night, they may find it difficult to feel immediate affection for the child. This may lead to feelings of guilt as well as upset schedules and tiring days and nights. The parents will need to remember that they are normal people with a normal baby and will have the same stress and frustration as other parents.

Bonding does not necessarily take place instantly, whether the child is adopted or born to the parents. It will take place as there is interaction between the child and parent. As the parents nurture, care for, and protect the infant, the bond develops. Love and acceptance form the basis for stability and productivity in a child's later life.

HANDLING QUESTIONS

Occasionally well-meaning relatives and friends unthinkingly contrast adoption with giving birth, suggesting the superiority of biological over adoptive parenthood. Adoptive parents might anticipate, discuss with each other, and determine answers for such comments, keeping in mind that inquiries are usually friendly and not meant to be hurtful.

The child may likewise be subjected to curiosity, questioning, and even teasing by peers. Parents could rehearse appropriate responses with their child, helping him or her to respond in a nondefensive way.

Whether your child is adopted is not something everyone

needs to know. Family and close friends will be aware and will rejoice with you, but bringing it up frequently, either to the child or to others, is not in the child's best interest. One set of parents, who were able to give birth to two children after having adopted others, often introduced their first children as "our adopted children." Even though their intent was good, it singled the children out as being different, and they felt less a part of the family.

TALKING WITH YOUR CHILD ABOUT ADOPTION

Many adoptive parents regard the "telling" process as a challenge about which they would like more knowledge. Each set of parents must choose the way and the time to talk with their child. Following are some suggestions:

David Brodzinsky, Ph.D. ("Adoption Report," North American Center on Adoption, Volume 7, no. 4., Fall 1982) says there are two separate steps in the child's comprehension of the adoption—the "telling" and the "understanding." The telling is the parent's responsibility, and the understanding is the child's responsibility. Do not make the mistake of thinking that your child has a full understanding just because he or she has been told once about being adopted.

Most adoption authorities and literature recommend telling the child when he or she is between two and four years of age. Generally children love to hear the story about their birth and adoption, about the finalizing of the adoption, the sealing, and how the family felt. Though they will not understand the full meaning, the early telling permits the children to be acquainted with the word adoption in a positive way, as parents recount the anticipation, the receiving of the child, and the joy the child has brought into their lives. It will help establish a relationship based on honesty. The longer parents wait, the greater the chance someone else will tell the child first.

During the elementary school years children may respond to their adoption less positively than they did earlier. What is happening is that their knowledge is increasing faster than their emotional ability to handle it. At this age the child may become particularly concerned about "why people adopt children," and "why my parents gave me up." A child may fantasize about birth parents and the possibility of being reclaimed them, or may lash out in anger with, "You're not my real mother."

It is important at such times not to feel crushed or to take the child's comments personally. The child should be allowed to express feelings and taught that those feelings are normal and that you understand them. He or she also needs answers, insofar as you are able to give them.

The best time to give information is when the child asks. Parents need to sit down together and determine what they want to tell their child and when. A good rule of thumb is to give only information relating specifically to the child's questions at the time. Adopted children need to know something about their birth parents and how they decided to place the child for adoption. Such a decision is usually made out of love for the child, a feeling of responsibility for the child's welfare, and a desire to give the child the advantages of a better home. If children have no information about their birth parents, they will be more inclined to fantisize about them.

If the child never asks or talks about the adoption, be sensitive to the possibility that he or she may be fearful of approaching you. Perhaps the child is worried about hurting your feelings, in which case you may need to take the initiative in detemining whether or not the subject is of concern. Many adoptive parents never experience the circumstances mentioned above. Either way, you can be assured that the actions of your child are normal.

An eight-year-old girl, upon observing a neighbor lady's pregnancy, asked her mother about it. When she was told that their friend would soon give birth to a baby, the child broke into tears and said to her mother, "I wish I had come from your tummy." Her mother gathered her in her arms and said, "I wish you had, too, but another mother who cared for you very much carried you inside just for me." Together they wept for what obviously could not be. It was a hard but good experience for both mother and daughter as the mother again explained that Heavenly Father has two ways of sending children to families, and talked with her daughter about how much they wanted and loved her.

In all families, relationships change as children grow into their teens and early twenties. During these years it is especially important to acknowledge the difference between adoptive and biological relationships. Children who are adopted are biologically and genetically unrelated to the adoptive parents, and come to them through a social and legal process more like a marriage than birth. Such children actually have two sets of parents.

Tests of independence and of your affection are common as the child's understanding of adoption increases. These tests often take the form of discussion about the child's "real parents." Acknowledge that it is normal for a person to wonder about things, and that while others are related biologically, you are the child's "real" parents.

As children mature and change – going to college, filling out forms requiring background information, getting married – additional questions and concerns about their origin may arise. Your ability to enter into these discussions without becoming upset will help meet your child's need to know. The more comfortable you are with the adoption, the more readily the child will accept the circumstances. Being able to communicate to the child that you are comfortable and that it is all right to have an interest in his or her birth parents gives strength to your relationship.

WHAT IF YOUR CHILD WANTS TO SEARCH?

Some parents are afraid that their children will go in search of their origins. Interestingly, if there are two adopted children in a family, it is not uncommon to find that one will have no interest in knowing about his or her heritage, while the other one wants to know.

In the past few years agencies have given more background information about the newborn to the parents when the baby is given to them. Frequently this information is sufficient to satisfy the child's interest. As young people reach their late teens, and particularly prior to marriage, they may desire to know more. This is a good time to give additional information if you have it. If you do not, it might be a good idea to go with children to the agency from which they were adopted to see if they have nonidentifying facts. Your willingness to help lets the child know that his or her needs are important to you, and that you are willing to tell what you know and help find out more.

Many states now have laws specifying that when adopted children reach the age of majority, agencies are required to give nonidentifying information to them. Also, an increasing number of state legislatures are passing registry bills, allowing adoptees and birth parents to place their names in a registry, if they desire. When a child reaches the age of majority, if both parties have registered, arrangements may be made to put them in touch with one another. State laws vary as to how this is done and whether or not there is direct contact between children and birth parents.

Studies show that usually a search for heritage is not related to any lack of love for adopted parents or desire to find a new set of parents. Rarely do adopted children actually want to know or see their birth parents. Jacqueline Horner Plumez (*Successful Adoption—A Guide to Finding a Child and Raising a Family*, Harmony Books, 1982) reports that in Scotland, where adult adoptees can apply to Register House for their original birth certificates, over a ten-year period an average of only 1.5 adult adoptees per 1,000 requested such information.

One young woman at age sixteen started asking about her birth mother. Her mother told her that she had no additional information, but that when the girl became of legal age, the mother would help make an appointment with the agency from which she had been adopted, and together they would find what they could. Mother and daughter did, in fact, go to the agency on the girl's twenty-first birthday and were given nonidentifying background information. This was a satisfying experience for the girl as well as for her mother, who had initially felt threatened by her daughter's interest in knowing about her heritage.

A special blessing that accompanies adoption in the Church is the opportunity of having the child sealed to the parents in the temple to form an eternal family. A feeling of security, peace, and belonging accompanies this experience. One well-taught five-year-old was heard to say to his nonadopted cousin, after going with his parents to have their newly adopted eight-month-old brother sealed to the family, "We've just been to the temple and had Jakey sealed to all of us, so now we're a tied-together forevermore family." Adoption is a beautiful experience, bringing joy to parents and children alike.

AGGRESSION, EXCESSIVE

Aggressiveness is found in varying degrees in every child. Being aggressive in a positive way means to go forward striving to succeed, even in the face of obstacles and difficulties, without hurting or infringing on the rights of others. Being aggressive in a negative way involves acting destructively, often ignoring the rights and feelings of others in order to get what one wants.

The typical overly aggressive child is a high-energy child who is constantly stirring up trouble: pushing, shoving, hitting, tripping, and perhaps even kicking and biting. In the course of growing up, most children will exhibit some of these aggressive forms of behavior, but the overly aggressive child is always expressing himself or herself this way and has the same kinds of behavior problems at home, school, and church. These children are often labeled with such words as "bossy," "bully," "mean," "tough," "rough," "intimidating," and "destructive." They are usually disliked socially, and often even their own families have trouble enjoying them when they are around.

SOME CAUSES OF OVERAGGRESSION

1. Stressful events or situations. A traumatic or stressful event, personal concerns, and family troubles can often disturb a child enough to provoke destructive behavior. Such events as a death in a family, marital problems or divorce, identity problems, rejections by friends, a change of residence, a loss of something important to the child, a new baby, or school or work problems cause tension in the home. Parents' most effective response to these situations is to help their children understand what has happened and to help them express in words what they are feeling. To help prevent or minimize the trauma associated with stressful events or situations, communicate in a nurturing atmosphere of love and honesty—before the event, if possible, or very soon after it.

2. Unfulfilled needs. All children have the basic needs to be physically nourished and cared for, but just as important are their needs to be nourished with love and attention. They need to feel that they are people of worth. If, for whatever reason, children do

not feel they have had these needs met, they may act out their frustration aggressively. The behavior may seem irrational to others, but the child is merely saying, "Hey, look at me! Please help me! I'm unhappy!" The more desperate the child is, the more intense the behavior will be. Parents will need to pour forth time and love to understand what needs are not being met. Often a great deal of patience will be required, because the aggressive behavior may not disappear overnight even though the child's needs may seem to be met.

3. Environmental influences. Sometimes children behave aggressively because they are imitating someone popular at school or on television or movies. This kind of behavior usually occurs suddenly, rather than as an ongoing pattern. Parents might ask themselves, "Has our child learned this from someone?" If they feel this is the case, they may need to exercise better control over what their children are watching or reading or who they are associating with. Parents need to explain to their children why the aggressive behavior is not acceptable even if people on television or at school engage in it.

4. Lack of proper teaching and training. Sometimes children act aggressively because they do not recognize that their behavior is inappropriate. They may not have been taught how to handle their anger and frustration in appropriate ways. Just telling children not to act a certain way may not be sufficient. They need to be given suggestions of healthy ways to vent their anger:

"Punch the pillow, not Jenny, when you feel like hitting someone."

"We do not kick, Sherrie. Tell Janet *with words* why you are angry."

"When you feel like screaming at someone, take three deep breaths first, and then tell them in a calmer voice why you are upset."

Young children will need to be reminded often, as they mature, of some healthy ways they can express their frustrations, but if parents are consistent in the reminders and suggestions they give, most children will eventually be able to use words to express anger rather than aggressive acts.

An important aspect of teaching these skills is the example that parents set for their children. Children may be confused when their parents tell them not to yell, hit, or push, and yet they see their parents venting their own anger this way. In this situation, the parents become an "uncertain trumpet" whose call is not clear. "For if the trumpet give an uncertain sound, who shall prepare himself to the battle? So likewise ye, except ye utter by the tongue words easy to be understood, how shall it be known what is spoken? for ye shall speak into the air." (1 Corinthians 14:8–9.)

Parents may also encourage aggression in their children by being too permissive, failing to discipline and guide children when they are disobedient, uncooperative, or aggressive in their behavior. Without consistently reinforced rules and guidelines in a family, many children will act out their feelings aggressively.

Fathers may unknowingly promote aggressive behavior by teaching their sons to "be tough." They may encourage this toughness by the way they dress and play with their children.

CASES OF OVERAGGRESSION WITH SPECIAL CONCERNS

1. Bullies. Bullies can be any age, but they are often older children who are intimidating and hurtful, both physically and verbally, to other children. Underneath they are usually insecure and anxious and in need of love and acceptance. They are often unable to get acceptance in normal ways, so their bullying allows them to boss and gain power over others. They may not be liked, but at least they are not ignored. They are lonely children with social inadequacies.

Parents can help children overcome bullying tendencies by giving them lots of genuine affection, love, and firm guidelines for their behavior. Teach them there is a difference between their feelings and their fists. Discourage their unacceptable behavior by teaching them that you will not allow bullying and that others do not enjoy being with them when they behave like this.

Point out positive characteristics about the bullying child that make him or her likable to family and friends. Help the child find ways to gain respect and recognition from others through positive behavior and activities, whether in sports, a developed talent or skill, an acquired knowledge of a certain subject, or improved social skills. Invite one friend over at a time so the child can learn to form friendships in a normal way. Enlist the help of friends and family in giving the "bully" lots of positive reinforcement for behaving in a socially acceptable manner.

2. The sadistic child. The sadistic child is one, five years of age or older, who appears to enjoy inflicting real torment on other children or animals. This child takes pleasure in causing pain, and may actually torture or kill animals for amusement. This form of behavior is quite rare, but most often it indicates deep-seated emotional or mental problems. Loving discipline and guidance are not enough to help sadistic children; they will also need professional help and therapy.

3. The hyperactive child. Hyperactive children have an attention deficit disorder (A.D.D.), which means they are unable to focus their attention and control their behavior in ways that are expected for children their age. Some of the symptoms of hyperactivity are that a child is restless or overactive, disturbs others, has a short attention span, is easily distracted, cries often and easily, has temper outbursts and dramatic mood changes. This child may need some professional diagnosis and help. Special guidance techniques, prescribed medication, and changes in diet will often help. And especially, parents can touch their child's life with their love, compassion, and understanding of who their child is and what he or she can become. For more information on this topic, see *Attention Deficit Disorder* in this volume.

Parents need to recognize that some fighting and aggressiveness is normal in the growing-up process. It may be a needed entertainment or release for children to wrestle and fight; mats, boxing gloves, or a safe place to tussle may be helpful. When sibling rivalry and quarrelsomeness is a problem, redirecting, guiding, or separating those involved may be sufficient measures to take. But when the aggressiveness becomes too constant or too destructive, parents will need to look for reasons and take careful action.

ALCOHOLISM

Not always, but for the most part young members of the Church who partake of alcohol differ from young people outside the Church (and from most adults) who partake. These young people in the Church know that drinking alcoholic beverages is wrong in the eyes of Heavenly Father, and many can quote section 89 of the Doctrine and Covenants better than their parents. The difference is that they do it in spite of knowing it is wrong.

For the most part these young people are not yet serious drinkers, but their dabbling with alcohol—beer, wine, or hard liquor—should be quickly dealt with by parents. Initially, alcohol use may appear to be fun, an adventure in tastes and feelings, a new vista of experience, which the young usually do not view as long-term or ominous. They may try alcohol simply to please their friends, or to alienate themselves from past acquaintances who have somehow hurt them. Also, if parents have pushed abstinence heavily, stating that they have never used alcohol, young people may delight in entering a realm never experienced by their parents, who have given the impression that they know everything. Or they may want to be like the glamorous movie or television stars they see drinking.

Like many drugs, alcohol may seem to make difficult things easier and stressful situations more relaxing. Asking for a date, conversing with the opposite sex, or just relaxing with friends may seem easier after a few drinks. But parents and youth should remember first that God has given a clear commandment not to drink alcoholic beverages. Usually one's first exprience with alcohol or other drugs is pleasant. The drinker experiences immediate feelings of well-being and euphoria. As the effects of the drug are neutralized by the liver, the youth returns to normal, with no ill effects. The youth then questions the teaching of parents and the Church against the use of alcohol and other drugs, and is more easily enticed to use alcohol in the future.

As the liver becomes more efficient in detoxifying consumed alcohol, more of the drug is needed to achieve the desired effects. This is referred to as tolerance, an early stage of dependence.

As people continue to use alcohol regularly, they will eventually begin to suffer ill consequences, such as feelings of inadequacy, guilt, and loss of self-esteem. They then turn to alcohol to find relief from these feelings. Now the youth discovers futility, using drugs to escape the pain caused by drug use.

Wise parents, although they must act in some way, will do

well to remember that a can of beer is less serious than lost virtue, and drinking a glass of wine is easier to repent of then stealing an automobile. At the same time, parents should be cautious not to minimize the can of beer, as it may be a symptom of more serious problems. Even though alcohol may lead to grosser sins, when dealing with youth it is best to react only to the current situation.

Both youth and adults seem to have an almost insatiable desire to be "free." Alcohol is one substance that gives the illusion of freedom—freedom from earthly restraints and realities. Agency, however, is the true freedom our Father in heaven gives, and it fully comes only to those who obey his will and follow his commandments. Alcohol is a poor substitute, particularly as it has the potential to lead to total dependence or "slavery."

Alcohol has widely different effects on people, and a tremendous danger lies in this fact. A group of young people who decide to experiment with alcohol may all be able to resume their normal activities—but some, or even one, may not be able to. Some youth may have a greater disposition to become physically and psychologically dependent on alcohol. This dependency often leads to rebellious behavior, which in turn may lead to loss of freedom, impaired judgment, clouded values and standards, loss of normal inhibitions and self-control, and hampered performance. Dependency usually also means academic problems, juvenile delinquency, and even sexual promiscuity. Generally, parents and youth have no way of knowing what the long-term effects of a few drinks will be.

Again, youth should not be given exaggerated examples of degradation, death, or the debilitating effects of alcohol. As they observe society they see few genuine alcoholics, but they do see many adults using alcohol with few apparent side effects. Some of these people may be their heros. Children need more realistic explanations of reasons for abstinence, and here the teachings of the gospel will help.

The Word of Wisdom is the commandment of our Heavenly Father. It was given long before the adverse effects of alcohol were proved in the laboratory. We need not rationalize or justify it, nor do we need volumes of man's evidence to accept its precepts. Abstinence can best be taught to children by teaching them pure obedience to our Father's commandments, and dependence on his love for his children and the guidance he provides. Through this obedience, and only through it, can young people be assured that the possible destructive effects of alcohol will not happen to them.

HOW TO HELP A CHILD AVOID THE USE OF ALCOHOL

1. Set the example in the home. Parents have great impact on children. Their attitude will usually be emulated by the children. Be consistent. Set a standard of abstinence from alcohol and drugs. Note that even over-the-counter and prescription drugs can be abused.

2. Teach children the real reason for not partaking of alcohol. Teach them to say things like, "I don't use alcohol because it isn't good for my mind and body." If they are tempted to drink and drive, teach them the very real — even horrible — consequences. Friends, even drinkers, who are confronted with this information will generally help youth to stand by their beliefs.

3. Help children decide in advance to avoid temptations. "Making our commitments before the moments of decision arise and deciding how we will keep those commitments can help us endure to the end and gain eternal life." (Carolyn D. DeVries, *Ensign*, October 1981, p. 73.)

4. Help youth, especially teens, learn to make gracious refusals in such a way that both host and guest may feel comfortable. For example, in many social situations a simple "No, thank you," is sufficient.

5. Watch your child's friends. You can't easily pick friends for your youth, but you can usually weed out the really bad influences just by talking the problem through with your child. Usually children are much better at the reasoning process than we give them credit for.

HOW TO HELP YOUTH OVERCOME ADDICTION

1. Be there. A drinker needs the family's love to overcome an addiction. However, be careful that your love is not contributing to a cycle of dependence. If you are providing the child with food, shelter, and money, allowing him or her to use this available cash on alcohol — this simply prolongs the dependence. At times the

concept of "tough love" requires that those who are addicted be allowed to suffer the consequences of their acts.

2. Remember that this is not just your son or daughter, but a literal child of God, having worth far beyond this present moment. Accept and love the child even though you abhor the distasteful act of drinking. Separate the person from the behavior.

3. Find out where your child is getting the alcohol, if possible. In many situations where youth experiment with alcohol, the law of the land forbids it because of age. Parents are justified in helping to close down illegal outlets, including friends, accommodating or devious adults, or even other family members.

4. Encourage church attendance. Youth who know it is not proper to drink may want to stop attending church. This can only harm the child further. Never suggest or imply that children should not attend church because they have been involved in drinking. Partaking of or participating in the preparation of the sacrament is a personal situation, which should be addressed at an appropriate time, such as in family home evening or in a father's or bishop's interview.

5. Determine as soon as possible if professional help is needed. Much pain can be avoided if non-drinking family members will get help early, both for themselves and for the drinking loved one.

6. Seek guidance from the Holy Ghost through prayer. Alcohol problems are so varied that any single solution would hardly apply to every case. Pray with the faith that comes from righteous living. "Behold, I say unto you that whoso believeth in Christ, doubting nothing, whatsoever he shall ask the Father in the name of Christ it shall be granted him; and this promise is unto all, even unto the ends of the earth." (Mormon 9:21.)

(SEE ALSO DRUG ABUSE)

ALLOWANCES

(SEE FINANCIAL RESPONSIBILITY)

ANOREXIA

(SEE EATING DISORDERS)

ANXIETY DISORDERS

Feelings are the colors we add to the experiences of life. All our memories are individually painted with the bright and warm hues of happy moments and darkened with the greys of painful times. And, like a child learning to use crayons in a coloring book, we begin life using a few bold colors that cover the whole "page" and move toward more varied and subtle shades. Yet every one of us wants to be the one who chooses the colors and does the painting. We want to be in control of our feelings.

Anxiety disorders in their various forms are particularly frightening because they are experiences in which feelings appear unbidden and grow when we are trying desperately to get them to subside. When people develop phobias — extreme and unreasoning fears — they are usually afraid of being afraid, more terrified of the uncontrollable feelings in themselves than they are of the situation.

FEARS AND PHOBIAS

Searching for patterns among children's anxiety difficulties suggests several kinds of problems: phobias, fears of separation, excessive avoidance of strangers, a more general overanxiousness about many things, and a condition related to anxiety called tics. As mentioned, phobias are persistent, extreme, and unreasoning fears. A person may have a phobia about a class of animals, such as snakes or spiders, or about a situation, like flying in an airplane or being in closed, dark places. Following is an adult's description of a phobia of dogs that he developed as a child: "When I was six years old two dogs attacked me as I tried to cross through 'their' yard on my way home from school. I was petrified, unable to run, or yell, or do anything but stand there backed up against the fence with them barking and growling. Luckily the owner of the home heard them and called them off. Even though I wasn't hurt at all, I was deeply shaken by the sheer terror I felt.

"For many years afterward I wouldn't walk or ride my bike in neighborhoods where I knew there were dogs. If a dog surprised me, barking, I felt paralyzed by fear, unable to do anything but stand terrified, staring at the dog."

Phobias are often initiated when a person encounters a frightening situation and is surprised by the intense feelings of fear. Thereafter he or she might feel anxious just by anticipating another similar experience, and usually attempts to avoid the situation, creating even stronger reactions if and when the event is repeated.

Fears of separation seem to represent anxieties of a child about being separated from his or her parents. One nine-year-old, for instance, began calling her mother from school several times a day to make certain her mother was safe. At about the same time, she stopped going to friends' homes to play or, especially, to stay overnight. Finally, she became so fearful that she would have severe stomach pains in the mornings and have to stay home from school. When her parents studied the situation, they realized that their daughter's fears were related to the sorrow of a classmate whose mother had recently died of an illness. Of course, more mild versions of separation fears also occur. Many children may suddenly become afraid of going to sleep, wanting to sleep with Mommy and Daddy.

Avoidant fear is the term used to describe the situation of a child who is persistently frightened of strangers, of any social situation where interaction is required with someone outside the family. The child may become tearful and upset about even trivial interactions with strangers and may cling excessively to parents.

A child experiencing general *overanxiousness* displays excessive worrying and generally fearful behavior about many aspects of life, without a focus on a specific situation. Such children may worry constantly about future events such as examinations, or doctor's appointments, or the possibility of injury. They may spend a lot of time worrying about completing chores or about being included in peer groups. Often overanxious children are very concerned about their competence and what others will think of their performance.

TICS

Tics are body movements, vocal sounds, or muscle twitches that are repeated again and again in an identical pattern. For example, a seven-year-old boy experienced a tic (which his parents called a "nervous habit") of clearing his throat frequently, which disturbed his school class. Another boy squinted his eyes and blinked rapidly when he was feeling under pressure. In many cases tics represent a brief physical means of expressing and relieving tension and anxiety.

It is important to remember that most children experience some unreasonable fears and even tics that appear and diminish with time as a normal part of development. Fear of the dark, fear of nightmares, or early childhood fear of separation from parents, for instance, are frequently experienced anxieties that most children overcome successfully. One may ask how a parent determines which fears are serious enough to become concerned about. One answer must be directed toward the degree to which anxieties are interfering with other normal activities. When fear of separation from parents makes a child unable to tolerate their being gone from home for an evening, it has gone beyond a normal phase. Another answer may be that some fears that are appropriate at one stage are of significant concern if they persist into another stage. A fear of being kidnapped, quite common at age four or five, is of more concern in a child of eleven. And a third answer deals with the intensity and extent of the fears. Anxieties that are intense enough to cause unreasoning fear are sufficient reason for concern. The extent of the fear is determined by the degree to which the child thinks about it during times when the object of fear isn't present, or alters his or her life to avoid encountering the situation.

WHAT CAN PARENTS DO?

1. Help the child talk the problem out. The child needs to talk a lot. Rational discussion during calmer times can help ease the problem away.

2. Parents must remember that their own fears and apprehensions will be communicated to their children and sometimes heightened. Therefore, it may bless their children's lives for them to face the struggle of overcoming their own fears. In that regard,

the blessings of personal righteousness can do much to help all of us. Even unreasonable fears can be affected as a person draws close to the love of God. Paul the apostle spoke of this blessing to Timothy: "For God hath not given us the spirit of fear; but of power, and of love, and of a sound mind." (2 Timothy 1:7.)

3. It is most important that parents of the anxious child be themselves unafraid of his or her difficulties. Because the child's fears are "silly" and "there's nothing to be afraid of," parents are apt to demonstrate either a lack of understanding and patience or, conversely, their own anxiety about the child's fearfulness. Most children know that the fears are silly, too, which makes it all the more frustrating and threatening that they can't control them. They know that they continue to feel the anxieties in spite of their parents' assurances that nothing will happen. The net effect of their parents' impatience is to increase their anxiety and their sense of being trapped in the problem. On the other hand, a child who detects parents' anxiety about his or her fear may think, "If Mom and Dad are afraid of this problem I have, it must be worse than I thought."

Parents need to be able to show the child their acceptance of his or her difficulties as a problem that can be solved, one that the child can face with them being optimistically cheering from the sidelines. In that way the child can take courage from their confidence.

4. Similarly, tics are sometimes overcome by the same expression of love and confidence. In addition, parents may discover the causes of tension and distress and work to eliminate those sources.

5. Although some children experience anxieties so extreme and pervasive that they require professional help, many can be helped by mild, repeated exposure to the feared situation with the support of loved ones. This is a deliberate use of the naturally occurring processes that help children overcome normal fears. Most parents don't even notice their children overcoming their fears of the dark, for instance. If they want a light left on when they go to bed, the parents leave it on. Over time the children are naturally exposed to enjoyable or calming experiences in darkness that teach them to be unafraid, and they take pride in their sense of growing mastery.

Parents must sometimes take an active part in helping a child overcome a specific fear. They must plan for ways to help the child face the feared object or situation gradually and with encouragement. Children experiencing separation anxiety, for example, may need to have their parents work up to being gone for an entire evening by leaving for just a few minutes, returning to reassure them and show pride in the children's ability to handle their feelings, and then leaving again for a longer period, and so on. Parents need to convey that they accept the child's fears, love the child regardless of those fears, and have confidence in the child's ability to gradually overcome the anxieties.

6. A most important element in helping a child is to try to understand the reason for the fearful behavior. In the situation described earlier about the child and the dogs, the person's phobia was clearly the result of a terrifying experience with dogs. Knowing that, his parents may have helped him very effectively by buying him a puppy. As the puppy grew, the boy's understanding of dogs and their behavior would grow and his anxieties diminish.

On the other hand, the child who developed stomach pains each morning before school wasn't afraid of school—she was afraid that her mother would disappear the same way the mother of her friend had. In this case, the mother could directly reassure her daughter of her love and of the probability that she, the mother, was not going to disappear. This is a process of desensitization to the fear. The mother might even take the child to school, and be sure to be home when she arrives after school.

7. The blessings of the gospel can be a significant source of reassurance for a child and, indeed, for all of us. Heavenly Father's love and support for our growth and his understanding of our immaturities is there for all of us to recognize. Sincere prayer, alone and with parents, will bring the child Heavenly Father's help to face and overcome fears, as shown by his scriptural reassurance:

"Fear not to do good, my sons, for whatsoever ye sow, that shall ye also reap; therefore, if ye sow good ye shall also reap good for your reward.

"Therefore, fear not, little flock; do good; let earth and hell combine against you, for if ye are built upon my rock, they cannot prevail. . . .

"Look unto me in every thought; doubt not, fear not." (D&C 6:33–34, 36.)

(SEE ALSO EATING DISORDERS; STRESS)

ATTENTION DEFICIT DISORDER

Elder James E. Faust said: "With a prayer in my heart for understanding, I speak today concerning parents of children with special problems. I do so because I am persuaded that these extraordinary challenges are, as the Savior himself said, that the works of God should be made manifest' (John 9:3). How these challenges are met can often be the expression of the very essence of the Gospel of Christ." (*Ensign*, November 1984, pp. 54, 58–60.)

One of the groups of children with special problems spoken of by Elder Faust is that group experiencing hyperactivity, or, as it has more recently been named, attention deficit disorder (A.D.D.). It is so called because the essential features of the condition seem to be that the children are unable to focus their attention and control their behavior in ways that one might expect for children their age. Listed below are the primary symptoms, from a checklist often used in diagnosing the problem:

1. Is restless or overactive, excitable, impulsive.
2. Disturbs other children.
3. Fails to finish things started.
4. Has short attention span.
5. Is constantly fidgeting.
6. Is inattentive, easily distracted.
7. Insists that demands be met immediately; is easily frustrated.
8. Cries often and easily.
9. Changes moods quickly and dramatically.
10. Experiences temper outbursts, explosive and unpredictable behavior. (See C. K. Conners, "Symptom Patterns in hyperkinetic, neurotic, and normal children," *Child Development* 41 [1970]: 667–82.)

Many, but not all, of these children will have specific learning difficulties.

Although we don't know exactly how or when the difficulties begin, the best information to date suggests that problems can be observed early in the child's life, perhaps by three years of age or younger. Most hyperactive children aren't identified, however, until school age. This is because of the demand at school for controlled and consistent behavior. Boys are much more apt to experience the problems of attention deficit disorder than are girls, the ratio being about ten to one.

Symptoms of attention deficit disorder are sometimes mimicked by other problems, such as hearing losses, allergic reactions, and severe emotional stresses.

Sitting still or concentrating is nearly impossible for the child who can't hear well enough to understand what the teacher is saying. In the words of one mother: "We've learned from this that a child who is *being* a problem usually *has* a problem. The parents' role is to find out what the problem is and then help him with it. Problems won't just disappear—there are no quick solutions—but getting to the source can begin a slow healing." (Pat Cowley, *Ensign*, September 1984, pp. 44–47.) Getting to the source of the child's problems requires the direction and confirmation of Heavenly Father. Parents' stewardship for their children entitles them to a sensitivity to needs that even a doctor or school guidance counselor cannot duplicate.

Now, to consider treatment. If the child is hyperactive, one treatment that may be considered is the use of medication prescribed by a physician. This is an important decision that should be weighed prayerfully, because there may be some negative side effects from the medication. On the other hand, a carefully chosen and monitored medicine may permit the child to sustain attention and "settle down" in a way that would have been impossible without it.

There is much that parents and teachers can do to create a helpful environment for children suffering from attention deficit disorder. Here are some suggestions:

1. Set up specific time periods for waking, bedtime, homework, playtime, and so on. A consistent time schedule with predictable

events will help the child relax. If changes in routine are necessary, explain them to the child ahead of time so they can be anticipated.

2. Set up clear and concise family rules. Again, consistency is the key. Help children learn what can realistically be expected of them, and let them feel the reward of appreciation and warmth as they meet the expectations.

3. When behavior gets out of control, the child's environment or feelings may have become too stimulating or distracting. Remove the child into isolation in a quiet place for a short period of time, perhaps five to ten minutes. This will help him or her regain control.

4. Give instructions that are simple, clear, and short. Ask the child to repeat them back. Divide complex tasks into smaller parts.

5. Provide the child with a personal "special" quiet place, free from distractions, in which to do homework or quiet work.

6. Try to reduce the stimulation level by having the child play with only one child or one game at a time. Remove needless background noise, such as the radio or television.

7. Keep a diary of foods eaten and effects, if any, on behavior. As mentioned, allergies may sometimes produce reactions similar to hyperactivity. Some common allergenic foods are chocolate, tomato products, wheat, sugar, milk products, and peanuts. Also note any strong reactions (such as headaches) to fumes from perfumes, detergents, gasoline, or other distinctive smells.

In addition to the management suggestions above, it is vital for parents to be aware of the emotional effects upon the child of the behavioral difficulties. Unfocused, extreme behavior will likely expose the child to the exasperation of teachers and rejection by hoped-for friends. Therefore, an additional area of concern must be this child's sense of self-worth, of belonging and being treasured in the family. The following suggestions can help you foster a positive self-image in your children:

1. Help children to recognize and accept that they may have problems with some school subjects or athletic activities. We all have areas of strength and weakness. It's a part of being human, and Father in heaven has given us struggles and weaknesses so that we may learn to rely upon him, and through him, become strong. (See Ether 12:27.) It may help to describe for children some areas of difficulty in your life. They need to know that things

aren't always easy for you, either, and that perhaps you still struggle with some things, but that you are learning to work around them. Try very hard to communicate to your children that you accept their problems, that you are unafraid of them, and that together, with Heavenly Father's help, you can work them out.

2. Look for ways for your child to clearly receive your affection. For some, the straightforward expression of love is uncomfortable; thus, you may want to find different ways of letting the attention deficit child know how much you love him or her. One father, in mock sternness, demanded of his daughter, "Who do I love?" He teasingly forced her to admit that she was the one loved, and then with the same pretended sternness he said, "And don't you ever forget it!" Sometimes a favorite, shorthand message of love such as three quick squeezes of the hand will serve as a reminder in times when longer or more obvious communication is impossible.

3. Help the attention deficit child's brothers and sisters also develop an understanding and compassion for him or her. They should know that you recognize that sometimes things are difficult, but that the child is worth it, and your loyalty to all your children will never waver.

4. Look for and help children develop areas of success upon which they can stake a sense of self-worth. One five-year-old managed to lose almost everything: keys, tools, purses. His redeeming quality was that he seemed to be the best one in the family to find things that were lost, even those he hadn't misplaced. This attention deficit child was proud to be the "finder," the one especially called upon when something was lost, and he would work with great energy to find the misplaced object.

Your image of your children may be the most important gift you can give them. They cannot help but look at themselves through your eyes. Sometimes the difficulties and frustrations can become overwhelming, and we get too close to our problems. Feeling that our attitudes aren't appropriate, we punish ourselves with guilt, or perhaps angrily attempt to justify our bad feelings. Yet we still feel helpless to do more than suppress or disguise those emotions.

King Benjamin, as recorded in the book of Mosiah, teaches us that the Lord will help us change our hearts more effectively than we could through guilt or harsh demand upon ourselves:

"And again I say unto you as I have said before, that as ye have come to the knowledge of the glory of God, or if ye have known of his goodness and have tasted of his love, and have received a remission of your sins, . . . I would that ye should remember, and always retain in remembrance, the greatness of God, and your own nothingness, and his goodness and long-suffering towards you, unworthy creatures, and humble yourselves even in the depths of humility, calling on the name of the Lord daily, and standing steadfastly in the faith of that which is to come. . . . If ye do this ye shall always rejoice, and be filled with the love of God, and always retain a remission of your sins; . . . and ye will not have a mind to injure one another, . . . and ye will not suffer your children that they go hungry, or naked; neither will ye suffer that they transgress the laws of God, and fight and quarrel one with another, and serve the devil, who is the master of sin, or who is the evil spirit which hath been spoken of by our fathers, he being an enemy to all righteousness. But ye will teach them to walk in the ways of truth and soberness; ye will teach them to love one another, and to serve one another." (Mosiah 4:11–15.)

Through our devotion, the Savior can and will change our hearts. He will bless us with the requisite love, vision, compassion, and patience to bless all our children's lives. Through this spiritual process the attention deficit child can achieve a high degree of success.

BABIES, NEW

There are few moments as thrilling in life as when parents cradle their newborn infant in their arms and realize that they have been part of the miracle of creation and birth. One new father described his feelings this way: "As my wife relaxed between contractions in the labor room of the hospital, I found myself marveling at the magnificent technology available to protect her and this arriving little spirit. All of the sterilized instruments and electrical monitoring humbled me, realizing how much man had learned about making the process of giving birth safe for my loved ones. Thirty minutes later I watched the nurse cradle my new son and begin washing him off. As I watched his arms and legs kicking, and his little lungs giving power to a healthy newborn howl, I could only grin sheepishly behind my surgical mask and cry. Here was the miracle! No one checked and calipered those little fingers to see if they were the right size, no machine adjusted his heartbeat and breathing. 'Father in heaven,' I thought, 'Thou art God, and how grateful I am to know of thee and praise thy name.' "

As Latter-day Saints we rejoice in the knowledge that we are sons and daughters of a loving Father in heaven, and that he has bestowed upon us the sacred privilege of parenthood. We are partners with God in the plan of salvation. We bring each new spirit to earth to give it a physical body and a loving environment in which to dwell. The birth of a child should bring overwhelming joy and complete humility.

The future almost always looks bright and beautiful for expectant parents, and they usually have a song in their heart as they prepare the nursery or go looking for the tiny things to outfit their baby. But shopping for booties is only a small part of preparing for a new baby. Consider also the following:

1. *Mother's and baby's health.* Mothers need to see a doctor early in pregnancy and follow the advice given concerning diet, rest, and personal care. Many women say they feel their best at this time and attribute it to the fact that they are eating nutritious meals and taking good care of themselves.

Understanding the growth and development of the baby during pregnancy can be rewarding. Several books and pamphlets have been published on the subject, and most hospitals offer classes to help parents prepare.

The term of pregnancy is also a good time to look for a pediatrician.

2. *Home environment.* The best start you can give a new baby is the feeling that the world is a clean, safe, and loving place to live. You can find many suggestions in child development books regarding clothing, furnishings, and supplies that are needed for new babies. In addition, talk to other parents and find out how they prepared. Create a spirit of love and harmony as you get ready for the baby. Husbands and wives will draw closer to each other and the Lord as they prayerfully discuss what kind of home they

want their child to be raised in, and share their feelings about their different roles as they care for the new baby.

3. *Supporting each other.* The months of waiting for a baby can be intensely emotional and confusing. Everything is felt deeply. Husbands and wives may be filled with questions. Joy, fear, and worry seem to combine into a general excitement. A pregnant woman may feel self-conscious about bodily changes such as weight gain; she will need to be loved and reassured by her husband. Husbands, at first, may see only the added expense. If they take part in the preparation, these fears and anxieties are greatly reduced. It is important for both parents to voice their feelings and to listen to each other. This way good communication develops. Also, each parent has specific roles. Parents should talk to each other and determine what roles are most appropriate for each of them. As a couple works together to prepare for a new baby a bonding will develop between father and mother as well as between parents and baby.

Remember that this new baby will change your life and the lives of its brothers or sisters, whose needs have not changed. Often a new baby demands and gets a disproportionate amount of the parents' attention. When this happens the other children will invariably react. One five-year-old was heard to remark to a cousin about the same age, who had just had a new baby come home, "Just you wait, Lacy, pretty soon you'll get shoved out of the way like I was."

4. *Fatigue.* A new mother often will be very tired. Some experts say that mother should sleep when baby sleeps. New mothers sometimes have unrealistic expectations about what they can accomplish in a day; they should take care not to overplan, especially at first. Willingly accept help from family and friends.

5. *Changes in routine.* Parents and baby will be getting to know each other during the first few months. Allow your schedule to change; become involved in caring for the baby's physical needs and develop bonds of love through cuddling, kissing, rocking, singing, and playing with the baby.

6. *New emotions.* At times mothers experience the "baby blues" or feelings of depression. This happens as the body and mind try to adjust to the new demands of motherhood, and as hormonal changes take their toll. At the same time, many parents

become anxious about finances. Each spouse needs to feel loved, supported, and understood by the other in these new roles. If the depressed feelings persist, professional help might appropriately be sought.

With all the joy accompanying your new addition there will also be a very real awakening as to how much work a baby is. Babies may be demanding, hungry, wet, and totally unappreciative of all you are doing for them. They may cry often. If the vision of blissful parenthood vanishes at 3:00 in the morning as you are still walking, bouncing, standing, and sitting in hopes of finding the magic position to stop baby's crying, remember that the joy and frustrations of parenthood are all part of the same package— a priceless gift from our Father in heaven that he has entrusted to your love and care. The inestimable worth of these little ones is highlighted in the Book of Mormon: "And he spake unto the multitude, and said unto them: Behold your little ones. And as they looked to behold they cast their eyes towards heaven, and they saw the heavens open, and they saw angels descending out of heaven as it were in the midst of fire; and they came down and encircled those little ones about, and they were encircled about with fire; and the angels did minister unto them." (3 Nephi 17:23–24.)

BACK TALK

It is an unhappy home in which a child is never allowed to express his or her feelings. But it is also an unhappy home in which the child is permitted to express those feelings with rudeness and disrespect. The aim should be to teach children to share their opinions without irrational and impulsive behavior, to create an atmosphere where good judgment and love can rule. A child's back talk usually brings nothing but uncomfortable feelings to all involved. Even the child who feels justified in his or her thoughts and actions generally experiences guilt and shame for a tirade; parents usually feel anger and resentment or a sense of failure. Onlookers are embarrassed to be witness to such rudeness, and they lose, to a degree, respect for both parent and child. Back talk is harmful to all.

To some it may seem natural for a child who disagrees with the direction given by parents and other authority figures to talk back. We need to understand that it is not natural. It is a hasty act done in anger, an act based on impulse rather than mature consideration. It takes teaching to get a child to act otherwise. It takes time and diligence, patience and love.

The greatest success in eliminating back talk comes with an early start. In early childhood a child is laying the foundation for his future happiness or misery. Later both nature and society will demand obedience, and home is the best place to develop it. Parents who say to a child, "Don't talk back to me," and then accept the back talk, are teaching that child that such behavior is permissible. Those parents are sowing seeds of disobedience that will bring pain later. Brigham Young said, "How necessary it is for mothers, who are the first teachers of their children and who make the first impressions on their young minds, to be strict." (*Discourses of Brigham Young*, compiled by John A. Widtsoe [Salt Lake City: Deseret Book, 1975], p. 206.) Today we use the words *firm* and *consistent*. We must understand that we can be strict and still be loving and kind.

If when children are small both parents teach consistently and firmly that back talk is not permissible, it will be largely prevented by the time the children reach adolescence, when correction is much more difficult. Parents might say, "Don't talk back. We can never let you do that. Tell us in reasonable words and tones what you are trying to say, and we will listen."

Children will have a tendency to ask "why?" when they are told to do something. Often parents will mistakenly consider this back talk rather than a genuine inquiry. Parents should always be willing to give an explanation that the child can understand.

If the child continues to refuse to cooperate, the parents can place the child in a "time out" room to calm down and think things over. Usually there is no need for punishment, but rules in the home must be obeyed, and "No back talk!" should be a most important rule in every home.

In teaching our children to respect us, we have a commandment from our Heavenly Father to consider. He has said, "Honour thy father and thy mother." (Exodus 20:12.) Honoring means showing respect, reverence, and veneration. Parents have been given a special role by our Heavenly Father, which is enough reason to bring honor to them. They bring children into the world, they take the responsibility of caring for them, and they teach them to live the laws of God. Adoptive parents should be honored and respected the same as any other parent.

A father should make it clear, leaving no doubt, that children may not talk back to their mother. If the mother allows it when the father is not around, she is doing a great disservice to both father and children, not to mention herself. If the father allows back talk, he is shirking his position as presiding authority in the home.

In recent years there has been a theory among many parents that permissiveness is the way to bring up children in love. As Dr. Haim Ginott says, "Afraid of losing his love, they [parents] dare not deny anything to the child, including control of the home. . . . Children exploit it (this control or power) mercilessly. They become tyrants ruling over anxious parents." Parents are, he says, "afraid of damaging my child for life." (*Between Parent and Child* [New York: Avon Books, 1971], p. 90.) Such youth are led to believe that all their problems are the result of what their parents did or didn't do. Their parents were too strict or too indulgent. They made the children work too hard or didn't give them enough to do. They domineered or they didn't care what happened to the children. These youth don't think their parents "deserve" their respect. They feel justified in whatever they turned out to be. They don't seem to realize that such thinking goes against one of the basic principles of the gospel: We are free to choose how we act, and we are responsible for our actions. (See 2 Nephi 2:27.)

Parents will earn the respect and honor due them by respecting their children and by conscientiously holding them to high standards, even when it would be easier not to. They don't earn it by letting children do anything they want to do, and they especially don't earn it by allowing children to talk back. The story is told of an American couple in Europe who were having dinner at the home of a doctor. They were impressed by the courtesy and esteem shown the grandmother who was part of the family. The doctor seemed surprised when they mentioned it. His reply was, "God used parents in creating us. We cannot dishonor them without dishonoring God."

Parents need to be careful that their own behavior does not contribute to the problem. As the old saying goes, "Behavior is caught, not taught." Emotions are contagious. If parents allow themselves to become out of temper and excitable, it is unreasonable for them to expect calm, acceptable behavior from a child. The first step in fostering an atmosphere of respect is to be good-natured parents.

Avoiding the temptation to respond to rudeness in kind becomes particularly difficult for parents of teenage children. Even children who have heretofore been compliant and courteous may shock their parents with their adolescent behavior. The parents are alarmed to find this once sweet child now rebellious and rude. Their first reaction may be an overreaction. They may lose their own self-control and add to the problem. It is important for a parent to realize that adolescents are experiencing changes physically, psychologically, and socially. They are wanting more control over their own lives, and they see their parents as interfering and bossing. A certain degree of resistance to parental authority is natural. Teenagers need, and must be given the chance, to express their feelings. But again, this must be done without rudeness or disrespect — on either side. As parents show understanding and unconditional love, they should also in a kind way express their own honest opinions so children will have a clear idea of the standards and values expected. Parents can and should insist on adherence to family rules. It is helpful to take the time to talk one-on-one, with calmness and courtesy, and never give up when the child shows no change in feelings. This stage will pass, and the way parents handle it will truly make a difference in the end, even though there may be no signs of success at present.

DEVELOPING SELF-MASTERY

Among the greatest rewards of teaching children not to talk back is knowing that children are learning the art of self-control. If a parent can teach a child self-restraint and self-mastery, that child will develop confidence and learn that true happiness comes from being in harmony with rules of honorable social conduct. Being a law unto oneself will bring only misery.

President David O. McKay said: "Another thing which a child should learn in the home is the matter of self-control. Home is the best place in the world, for he submerges himself for the good of another; he controls his temper, and that is where the father should control his, and mother should control hers, and the child will grow up in an atmosphere of self-mastery. When he gets out into society and meets with his playmates . . . he must find himself master of himself on the playground as he is in the home. . . . Unhappiness in the child's life, as in the adult life, springs largely from nonconformity to natural and social laws." (*Pathways to Happiness*, compiled by Llewelyn McKay [Salt Lake City: Bookcraft, 1957], p. 117.)

Dr. Victor B. Cline expresses it this way: "The ultimate aim of discipline is to free the person from the irrational and impulsive side of his nature—not to repress or tyrannize him, but rather to give him powerful habits of focus, direction, work, and good judgment, adding up to great personal power. Good discipline produces strength, not weakness; creativity, not banality; responsibility, not self-indulgence. It can also produce the character out of which the capacity to love and sacrifice can emerge." (*How to Make Your Child a Winner* [New York: Walker and Co., 1980], p. 121.)

As with most discipline problems, back talk is easier to prevent than to correct. If there is already disrespect shown in the family, if bad habits need to be corrected, the remedy is a bit harder— but it isn't impossible. The cure will just take more time, patience, and perseverance. Understanding, kindness, and love are still important secrets of success, but do not forget those other important ones: firmness and consistency.

When the correct atmosphere has been created in a family council or family home evening, the parents might admit that they have been a bit lax and have permitted some damaging behavior to creep into the family. Having firmly stated that back talk and disrespect are destroying their family relationships, they can insist that they can no longer allow it. Parents can let the children suggest what might be the results if the practice is permitted to continue. When all have recognized how detrimental the behavior is, parents can call for a discussion on ways to eliminate it, again considering the necessity of having rules and of abiding by them.

Parents should explain to the family that anything well done (even courtesy) takes practice. Piano playing, athletics, public speaking, or anything in which they want to be proficient has to be diligently worked at. Parents and children will help each other. Reminders and methods of punishment can be decided upon as a family. If the children have a part in making the rules, they will be more apt to live by them. Parents have the final say—but they, too, must abide by the rules.

When children (or parents) slip occasionally or even frequently at first, a gentle, cheerful reminder may be all that is necessary; but a call for a quiet discussion will probably be needed. Habits are habits. Remember the suggestions given for preventing: (1) be an example of mature behavior; (2) do not overreact; (3) show self-control as you expect the child to show it. Children will test parents at intervals. Often they provoke parents or teachers purposely to get them to lose self-control. Parents should be on their guard and remain consistent.

Eliminating back talk is a giant step in teaching self-discipline, which in turn is a giant step in (1) creating a loving home, (2) enjoying success in the vocational field, (3) having and keeping worthwhile friends, (4) spreading peace in the world, and (5) preparing for eternal life. Parents must strive diligently, prayerfully, faithfully, and persistently to prevent or rid their families of this destructive habit.

BED-WETTING

Bed-wetting is not something that a child wants to do, and no child should be punished for wetting the bed. Wet sheets, interrupted sleep, and other inconveniences that accompany bedwetting can be frustrating to the parent and humiliating to the child. Yet, never should parents sacrifice the dignity of their little ones. Acceptance of the child who has this problem is critical, and it is absolutely necessary that the child feels loved and accepted by parents, no matter how often he or she wets the bed. Before progress can be made toward a solution to this problem, parents must understand that even in such matters as these our Heavenly Father wants us to show love and patience towards our children. The Savior said: "And whoso shall receive one such little child in my name receiveth me. But whoso shall offend one of these little ones which believe in me, it were better for him that a millstone were hanged about his neck." (Matthew 18:5–6.)

Children can be offended and embarrassed by the way their parents respond to their bed-wetting. If they sense their parents' irritation with them, they may begin to feel they can't do anything right. If the parents accept this problem as an opportunity for growth, this attitude will allow all involved to handle the challenge properly.

There are several approaches to handling bed-wetting problems. You might prayerfully consider each suggestion before deciding which may be best for your child. Children may wet the bed just because they are still quite young and their bladders are still small. Many children need diapers at night well past their third birthday. A child who goes to the bathroom every couple of hours during the day and always wakes with a wet diaper in the morning most likely is simply not ready to stay dry at night.

Maturing physically is an important factor in a child's staying dry. Parents can be comforted in the knowledge that nighttime accidents are common until around five years of age, and may be natural even until around seven years of age — especially in boys. Don't be in a hurry to decide your child has a problem. What the child needs is expressions of love, support, and positive encouragement. Assure the child that he or she will eventually be grown up enough to remain dry all night. The following suggestions may help you and your child to have a positive experience during this maturing process.

1. Help your child develop the habit of always going to the bathroom before getting into bed at night. It is better not to overemphasize that this precaution is to prevent the child's wetting the bed. Just state it matter-of-factly; make it a part of the bedtime routine. You might say, for example, "Johnny, after you go to the bathroom, we will say our prayers and then you can choose a book for our bedtime story."

2. Make bedtime a relaxing time. Some children, who by

nature are a little more anxious than others and sometimes seem to "fight life," may sleep hard. In the morning it may look like they had a fight with the bed covers! These children may have bed-wetting problems and will need to be soothed into relaxing at bedtime.

3. You may wish to put a plastic covering on the mattress to protect it. Some children may want to continue to wear plastic pants or diapers at night, but do not force this on a child who objects.

4. Try limiting the number of drinks a child has before bedtime, but don't make a child go to bed thirsty. Arguments between parents and children over this can have the effect of making the bed-wetting a bigger problem.

5. Teach your child about personal cleanliness—washing hands and body and wearing clean, fresh-smelling clothing.

6. Be sensitive to the child who is embarrassed about bed-wetting; convey your love, your knowledge of that child's worth, and your confidence that he or she will eventually be able to stay dry throughout the night. Build your children up and make sure they know you are proud of them. Name specific things that they do well, giving reasons why you are proud of them. In fact, give lots of positive encouragement and praise throughout this period of maturing.

7. Teach your other children to show love and consideration for the child who is striving to overcome bed-wetting. Emphasize that no family member should tease or make fun of that child.

Two five-year-old cousins loved "sleeping over" with each other. The one little fellow started wetting the bed and had a hard time explaining why he would no longer spend the night with his cousin. The mother of the other little boy explained, and the next time he invited the cousin he told him in a sweet way that he knew that he had to wear a diaper, but "we will both wear one." This permitted the two to remain close, and eased the tension for everyone.

8. If your child is invited to sleep away from home at a relative's or friend's house, it is your responsibility to inform the relative or the parents of the friend about the child's bed-wetting. Plan with your child to minimize situations that may be embarrassing.

Frequent bed-wetting in a child over six may be due to some physical problem. Take the child to a physician to determine if such a physical cause exists. The doctor may be able to give some helpful suggestions.

Many times a child whose bed-wetting is related to a physical problem may also have accidents during the day. One sensitive mother who was helping her child to overcome this problem spoke with the teachers at school. She made them aware of the child's situation and asked them to allow the child to go to the bathroom as often as necessary without questioning or embarrassing the child.

If an older child does not have a physical problem that is causing the bed-wetting, or if the bed-wetting suddenly occurs when a child has usually been dry at night, the problem may come from stress, tension, or anxiety in the child's life. A new baby in the family, separation from family members, divorce, a hospital stay, a move, school, death of a loved one, fatigue, sickness, or overexcitement can cause a child to revert to bed-wetting. If there is an obvious situation causing stress, a parent can talk to the child about what is happening, listen to his feelings and words, give him love and assurance that all will be well. Parents should teach children that our Father in heaven knows and loves them, that the Lord will help them as they pray for help. Perhaps a priesthood blessing could be given during this time to give the child comfort and patience. "Whatsoever thing ye shall ask the Father in my name, which is good, in faith believing that ye shall receive, behold, it shall be done unto you." (Moroni 7:26.)

If you are not aware of something obvious that may be causing stress in your child's life, but the child is still wetting the bed, give loving time and special attention to that child, focusing on dicussing feelings. Help your children to feel "safe" in the family, to realize that you are "on their side" and that they can depend on your love, strength, and calmness to help them through hard times. Pray for personal inspiration as to what you might say or do to help your child overcome present anxieties. *Focus on the child's feelings and not on the bed-wetting.* Draw as little attention as possible to the problem unless your child asks for specific help with it.

A child who wets the bed day after day can become a real

challenge to the parent who has other children to care for as well. If the child is old enough it may be wise to give some of the responsibility for caring for bedding or clothing to him or her. This should not be done as a punishment, but as a way to help the child see that Mother may need some extra help. One kindergarten child who had problems at school was given the responsibility of checking each night to see if he had clothes for the next day. He notified his mother upon arriving home from school, and frequently put clothes in the washer. As part of his responsibility he would help with folding the family wash and carrying it to the different bedrooms. Children may be given the responsibility for stripping their beds, putting the linen in the washer and dryer, then helping with putting the bed back together again. Whenever possible, children should take some responsibility for caring for themselves in this way. Making it a part of their work assignment, and not a punishment, will keep it in proper perspective.

Parents should take solace in the fact that time and working together will resolve the situation. A child wants to resolve the bed-wetting problem every bit as much as the parent does. Never should shame or fear have any part in solving the problem. This truly can be an opportunity for growth and learning: the child's learning self-control, cleanliness, confidence in self, and the overcoming of problems in a positive way, and the parents' learning to love and accept their child even when there are frustrating and inconvenient problems to deal with. As one mother said: "It is worth washing the sheets daily, and with love, if it preserves my child's self-worth. We can conquer this together!"

(SEE ALSO TOILET TRAINING)

BUDGETING

(SEE FINANCIAL RESPONSIBILITY)

BULIMIA

(SEE EATING DISORDERS)

CAREER PREPARATION

(SEE PLANNING FOR THE FUTURE)

CHASTITY

(SEE SEXUAL PROMISCUITY)

CHEATING

Ernest L. Wilkinson, a former president of Brigham Young University, said: "If you are tempted to cheat, remember the charge of Karl G. Maeser: 'My young friends,' he said, 'Place me behind prison walls—of stone ever so high, ever so thick, reaching ever so far into the ground—there is a possibility that in some way or another I may be able to escape; but stand me on the floor and draw a chalk line around me and have me give my word of honor never to cross it. Can I get out of that circle? No, never! I'd die first.' " (Brigham Young University Devotional Assembly, October 15, 1957.)

Honor and integrity are attributes all parents hope for in their children. Yet, frequently young people are dishonest, compromising the teachings of their homes. When they discover this, parents usually become disheartened, and they often take impulsive disciplinary measures before assessing the situation accurately.

Cheating (getting something by dishonesty or deception) may be a symptom reflecting a need in a child. Perhaps it is a need for assistance, a need for social acceptance, a need for attention. Some children would rather be seen negatively than not be noticed at all.

Most young people are aware of the commandment, "Thou shalt not steal." Few students, however, relate cheating to this commandment. They are willing to cheat in school, but would be appalled at the thought of taking something from a store, or from a friend's locker. Yet cheating is a form of stealing. People who cheat take something (i.e., a grade) that does not rightfully belong to them.

Children cheat, of course, for various reasons. Some do it simply because it seems a "cool" thing to do, and creative cheating (outsmarting the teacher) is clever and entertaining to friends. Such cheating is usually done during the teen years when peer approval is most important. During this period, most adolescents feel that reporting cheaters to school authorities is disloyal. Primary school children, in their innocence and desire to please the teacher, are usually more eager to report a cheater. College students will sometimes respond differently because they seem to comprehend the ramifications of cheating for all concerned.

Returning to President Ernest L. Wilkinson's comments: "If you see someone committing a robbery, do you think you are a good citizen if you do not report that person to the police? If you should see someone stealing an automobile, would you be a good citizen if you sat by and made no report of it? If you were competing for an engineering job and you saw that your competitor cheated in examination by going to some book and copying from it, would it be fair for you to sit by and not report the wrongdoing of the other person? It is equally wrong for you to sit by in a class and permit someone else to cheat, when your comparative grades are going to be based on your relative performance in that examination.

"If, in private and public life, we did not report the wrongdoings of others, there would be a complete breakdown in law enforcement. May I suggest, therefore, that you have the same student responsibility in your school classes as you do civic responsibility."

Parents should be very concerned about what motivates their child to cheat. Usually it is simply lack of preparation. A child who has procrastinated assignments fears humiliation, and is usually too fearful to admit it to the teacher. Parents should consider the following questions before taking action:

1. Is my child accepted by me, just as he or she is, as being of great worth?

2. Is my child's class too advanced? Do we need to find a tutor? Is the teacher effective? Is the teacher aware that some basic concepts need to be reviewed?

3. Can I as a parent spend more time helping my child with homework? (Many parents do not show the patience necessary to work with their children. The children sense the parents' frustration and read it as a disappointment in them as people. Such discouraged children have a tendency to give up, which can actually compound the problem and damage relationships.)

4. Does my child understand the gravity of cheating, not only of participating in it but of letting it continue in his or her classroom? Have I taught that letting someone else copy his or her work makes my child a participant in cheating? Does my child understand *plagiarism*?

5. Do I consider my child as an extension of myself, or can I appreciate his or her individuality and own set of attractions and academic potential? Do my expectations put too much pressure on my child? Can I appreciate the differences in my children and help them individually fulfill the measure of their own creation?

6. Am I aware of what my child can realistically accomplish? Do I focus on what I want the child to learn and feel in the learning process? Regardless of grades, do I believe that this child has great worth and much to contribute to the family and society?

Some parents may find consolation in the fact that many great scholars and leaders were not outstanding students in their childhood. Many in fact, caused great concern for their parents and teachers. Sir Winston Churchill's father considered him so "dull" that he doubted whether Winston could ever earn a living. Churchill failed the entrance exams to Sandhurst twice and was taken out of Harrow so that he could study with a tutor. Giacomo Puccini, the Italian opera composer, was described by his first music teacher as having "no talent." Thomas Edison's teachers described him as "addled"; his father thought he was a "dunce," and his headmasters warned that Edison "would never make a success of anything."

Patience, love, approval, and time seem to solve a lot of concerns and take care of a lot of parents' apprehensions about children. Meanwhile, children need to be aware that cheating is not a way out of problems; it compounds them.

Parents need to examine their own conduct to see if they may also be cheating in subtle ways. Observant children will transfer the example to their own lives, including their school work. Such things as driving hard bargains, avoiding income taxes, dishonesty in the payment of church offerings, not following traffic laws, disregarding handicap zones and fire lanes, lying over the phone or having the child tell "white lies" for them are all cheating. Children usually adopt the standards they live with as their own.

Parents should look carefully at the policy on cheating in their child's school. On an elementary school level, the teacher should handle each situation on an individual basis. On a junior high and high school level, a policy should be encouraged that is consistent in every class and gives the teachers the support they need to enforce discipline. The policy should be one that every teacher and student fully understands and that is also presented to the parents for their approval and support.

There should be a stigma attached to cheating, and the school itself should take a stand for integrity. Honesty should be the standard for all students. Athletic events, elections, and tryouts should be conducted so that honesty and sportsmanship are emphasized. Standards for participation should be clearly outlined and understood by the students, and enforcement should be consistent and fair to all. It must be remembered, however, regardless of school policy, that the responsibility for teaching and resolving these problems belongs in the home with loving and patient parents.

What, then, might parents do with a child they have caught cheating? With love unfeigned, reason with the child. Ask what has really been accomplished by cheating. Is the child truly an "A" student, was the game really won, or has the child taken something that doesn't belong to him or her? (It is also important not to emphasize grades over learning.) Isn't there greater satisfaction when rewards result from our own effort? A child's success will depend more upon a reputation for honesty than upon a reputation for brilliance.

Once parents have assessed the situation (with the help of the questions outlined earlier), they have the opportunity to lead the child through the repentance process. First must come the admission and recognition. Second will be the restitution (redoing the work, sacrificing the grade, being eliminated from the team). Better study habits could be agreed upon with a clear understanding of what is at stake. Reinforce the standards with firmness, but show absolute love for the child. Remember that children are here to learn and grow. They are "becoming," not already "arrived." The time will come when they will do what you want because they know you love them, not because you force them. These experiences can bring parents and children to a mutual respect for one another, especially as they witness in each other sincere efforts to improve.

CHILD ABUSE

When Jesus was asked by his disciples to describe who would be the greatest in the kingdom of heaven, he called a little child to stand beside him. Here in the child's innocence, trust, and freely given love the Savior demonstrated the kind of person he wants us to become: "Except ye be converted, and become as little children, ye shall not enter into the kingdom of heaven.

"Whosoever therefore shall humble himself as this little child, the same is greatest in the kingdom of heaven." (Matthew 18:3–4.)

We are told by the Savior that angels dwelling in the presence of the Father watch over these children. (See Matthew 18:10.)

It is little wonder, then, that just hearing of child abuse produces shock and outrage in us. We recoil at the thought of a child being abused in any way.

Child abuse is a much larger, more complex and painful tragedy than most realize. There are many causes that contribute to such abuse. It is important to remember that the healing power of the gospel, coupled with appropriate care from compassionate individuals and professionals, can greatly help both the abuser and the abused child, freeing them from the pain and sorrow they may feel. Carefully structured treatment programs have met with considerable success in treating abusing families. As a community of Saints we must let neither our anger at someone's abuse nor our guilt, if we have been abusing, keep us from overcoming the problem. For the sake of the children we must get help quickly.

Child abuse falls in several different categories. Although these

types sometimes occur together, varying causes may lead to separate effects.

Physical abuse, of course, refers to the circumstance in which
an adult inflicts physical injury upon a child.

Neglect occurs when a child is not given adequate love, supervision, or attention. Proper food, clothing, shelter, education,
and medical care may be lacking.

Sexual abuse is the use of a child for sexual stimulation or
gratification. (*See* Sexual Abuse of Children.)

Verbal abuse refers to consistent emotional indifference, rejection, or verbal punishment. It may be particularly devastating
because parents often do not feel guilty when they hurt children
with words or feelings. The children's sense of guilt or being
rejected, their inability to please or feel loved may be constant,
something from which they cannot escape.

Emotional abuse is usually present with all other forms of
abuse and is potentially the most harmful, but the most difficult
to identify and correct.

CAUSES OF CHILD ABUSE

1. Some incidents of abuse come from people so selfish or
unrighteous that they have little desire to change their ways. They
justify their acts, deceiving themselves. Indeed, the Savior pro-
phesied that, in the latter days, "because iniquity shall abound,
the love of many shall wax cold." (Matthew 24:12.)

2. Physical and emotional isolation from relatives or other
caring and supportive people increases stress, leaving a parent
with a feeling of having no place and no one to turn to for relief.

3. Personal stress is usually a factor in abuse, in the form of
financial pressures, a poor job or none at all, health problems, or
severe marital difficulties.

4. Some parents may feel overwhelmed and helpless to deal
with a particular child, and lash out in anger in moments when
they feel inadequate.

5. Sometimes victims of child abuse have some physical or
behavioral problem that makes them more difficult to parent.
Infants born prematurely or colicky babies who cry excessively
are more stressful in and of themselves. Similarly, children strug-

gling with physical handicaps or hyperactivity may be more annoying or exasperating than other children.

6. Parents may themselves be experiencing severe emotional
difficulties that distort their perceptions of their children and their
responsibilities to them. Women experiencing major depression,
for instance, may feel that they are unable even to get out of bed
to care for their youngsters.

7. Finally, abusive parents may have been abused themselves
as children. *That does not mean, however, that parents who were
abused as children will become abusers.* Many parents have had
to struggle with and overcome such difficult beginnings. However,
when people are under considerable stress, they may revert to
earlier patterns of behavior that they learned as children.

It is important for all parents to remember that there is a
great deal of difference between an isolated incident of lost temper
where harshness is used and the occurrence of repeated and frequent abuse. While not minimizing the effects of any abuse, we
should realize that parents sometimes punish themselves unduly.
Children are remarkably resilient, and part of their purity comes
in their ability to quickly and truly forgive. Parents must similarly
forgive themselves.

HELPING ABUSIVE PARENTS AND THEIR CHILDREN

If abuse is severe, one of the most important acts we can
perform for both parents and children is to *report the abuse immediately to both ecclesiastical and legal authority.* In many states
it is a civil offense to be aware of abuse and not report it. Moreover,
in spite of the family crisis that it occasions, calling attention to
the problem is often the critical first step in overcoming it. The
children must be protected against further abuse, and the helping
forces can then be mobilized on behalf of the entire family.

We can do much to establish a caring community where
support acts as a great preventive measure against stress for parents. Joy Evans says, "Perceptive and friendly people can provide
a frustrated parent with this type of support by doing such seemingly simple things as listening to the individual's problems, taking him or her to lunch occasionally, or helping with yard work."
(*Ensign,* April 1984, pp. 58–61.)

The very structure of our Church programs, such as home

teaching and visiting teaching, welfare resources, and priesthood quorums, exists to bless people's lives in ways that will prevent abuse. As we are "willing to bear one another's burdens, that they may be light; yea, and are willing to mourn with those that mourn; yea, and comfort those that stand in need of comfort" (Mosiah 18:8–9), we will have done what we can best do to make abuse in any form unthinkable.

If members of the Church provide foster care for children who have been abused, they may need the gifts of the Spirit to guide them. These children may require months, even years, of corrective experience to overcome the trauma. Research shows that, as a group, abused children are more likely to have problems in school performance, social difficulties (especially with fighting or its opposite, shyness), and a general inability to trust anyone. Establishing that fundamental willingness to rely on others takes a long time, and often occurs only after many trials. Sometimes because the only relationship such children have known is an abusive one, they may even try to provoke the foster parents into abusing them again.

Abusing parents can take positive steps toward helping themselves. First, parents must face the possibility that they may be acting abusively. This may be very difficult, especially in cases of emotional abuse, which often consists of nothing more than words. But words said in anger or disgust, with the intent to hurt or "teach those kids a lesson they will never forget," can be harmful.

Identifiable elements of such emotional maltreatment may be:

1. *Rejecting the children*, communicating to them that they aren't wanted, loved, or accepted.

2. *Ignoring the children*, communicating to them that somehow they aren't important enough to deserve attention.

3. *Terrorizing the children*, wherein the parent berates and verbally assaults the children or destroys beloved possessions or hurts pets, creating an atmosphere of fear and tension.

4. *Isolating the children*, preventing them from developing normal social relationships, unduly restricting them over long periods of time. (See James and Anne Garbarino, "Emotional

Maltreatment of Children," *National Committee for Prevention of Child Abuse*, 1986.)

Like physical abuse, the precursors of emotional maltreatment may have come from childhood, such as growing up with a father who was never pleased with the children's performance, or a mother who imposed constant and long-lasting guilt on the children for relatively normal irresponsibility, or a parent who consistently told the children in some way that they were no good. Children who believe and accept such negative definitions of themselves may grow up to believe that their children are behaving the same way, thus deserving the same treatment.

Sometimes, parents must face the possibility that they are experiencing stress or emotional problems greater than they can handle, and that their children need more support or protection than they can presently provide.

The next step is often equally difficult—to ask for help. But it is essential. An understanding bishop and loving Church members can help by decreasing one's sense of isolation, giving some respite with children when extreme stress is felt, or bringing to bear the welfare resources of the Church for financial aid, employment, or even professional counseling. The experience of being abused as a child carries aftereffects long into adulthood. Some of these may require the assistance of professionals who are trained to help unwind the threads of the emotional knot created years ago.

Finally, through the healing power of the gospel, a man or woman can truly be "born again," be washed clean of the entrapping history of early childhood abuse, and set free of the compulsive rage that besets the abuser. President Ezra Taft Benson spoke of this process in specific reference to child abuse:

"We must earnestly desire a righteous and virtuous life. . . . There are some . . . who must pray until they, too, have 'a wicked spirit rooted' from them so they can find the same joy. Attaining a righteous and virtuous life is within the capability of any one of us if we will earnestly seek for it. If we do not have these character traits, the Lord has told us that we should 'ask, and ye shall receive; knock, and it shall be opened unto you.' (D&C 4:7) . . .

"He expects us to be like Him. He expects us to demonstrate

the fruits of the spirit in our life which are 'love, joy, peace, long-suffering, gentleness, goodness, faith, meekness, temperance.' (Gal. 5:22–23)." (*Ensign*, November 1983, pp. 42–44.)

Thus, we have a promise from a prophet of God that through an awareness of our faults, sincere and patient striving for the gifts of the Spirit in our lives, and the healing power of the Savior's atonement we may be free of our deepest and most feared tendencies.

CHORES

(SEE HOUSEHOLD CHORES)

COMPETITION

(SEE IDENTITY; JEALOUSY; SIBLING RIVALRY)

DATING

For young people the prospect of dating is filled with anticipation and excitement. It is a time to be prepared for and a time to be shared and enjoyed. And it can be a time for parents and teenagers to come to know each other better.

Dating is filled with wonder and fantasy, mixed with fear and apprehension. It is a time for youth to venture from the security of the family circle, to form new relationships. It is a time for parents to be patient, loving, and available – and, usually, worried. They will spend a lot of time on their knees seeking guidance from Heavenly Father for inspiration – for themselves and for their children.

When a young boy and girl first have an attraction for each other, it may be awkward and confusing. "What should I say?" "How should I act?" "I wish he would call." "I hope he won't!" "Why can't I date before sixteen? Everyone else does!" "Ten

o'clock is too early." " 'R' movies are all right. I would be embarrassed to tell him I can't go." "How can I ask her to the dance
when she has only smiled at me once? What if she turns me
down?" "How much should I spend?" "I don't know what to
talk about." "I would like to kiss her, but I am afraid of what she
would do." "Why only double date, when we would like to be
alone?" "My parents are too strict. Why do they have to wait up
for me to come in; don't they trust me?"

Hundreds of thoughts and questions like these may present
themselves when the dating years arrive. Both parents and youth
would do well tó prepare. It will make the process smoother and
more enjoyable.

For some, the dating experience may not be too difficult. Some
young people are very social. They interact with peers and adults
comfortably. However, for most the process is strained, and the
fear of rejection sometimes seems not worth the risk.

Parents should know that, although young people are subject
to many influences outside the home, usually parents have the
most lasting influence. Following are a few suggestions to help
parents with teens through the dating years:

1. *Listen to them.* Set aside enough time to be with your
teenagers when dating time approaches. Listen to their concerns
and share some of your own experiences. Young people almost
always fear rejection, especially where the opposite sex is concerned. Listening that is nonjudgmental, understanding, and total
may be the best gift of love parents can give. Youth will not,
however, share their feelings honestly unless this pattern of communication has been set early, long before the dating years.

Your waiting up to hear about their evening will encourage
your young people to be home on time. But more than that, it
will help them to know of your concern for their welfare. Late in
the evening, when the phone has stopped ringing and the other
family members are in bed, is a good time to share, listen, and
laugh without interruption. It's also a time to detect problems
and stresses that may have developed.

One mother who had established the habit of waiting up for
her daughter confessed that sharing her daughter's experiences
made her feel young again and happy that they could sweetly and
privately share their feelings. Another mother said that never is

her son a better friend than at night after coming in from an activity. "By the time we go to bed we both know how much we love each other," she said.

2. *Help them.* Many young people do not have confidence in their personal appearance. Help them with personal grooming and hygiene, and be patient with their selection of clothes. Now is the time to emphasize the fun of dressing stylishly but modestly, too. Adolescents may need help with skin care, hair styling, or makeup. Maturation processes vary widely, and youth are often distressed with the blotches that appear or the shapes that do not appear. Often their maturation rate will determine their physical abilities and their subsequent adjustment in school groups. Listening, consoling, holding, and just being there for these difficult adjustments is vital.

3. *Prepare them.* There are many kinds of activities that make for successful dating. Each one requires different kinds of preparation.

Discuss with your teenager proper manners: how to greet at the door, to put on a coat, to walk on the right side of the sidewalk, to open the car door; how to order at a restaurant, use proper table manners, and tip the servers. One mother had her son take her to a restaurant, where she coached him on some of these things. At first he resisted the idea, but later he was very grateful (plus he got a great meal). Every family library should contain a book on creative dating, party planning, and acceptable etiquette.

Practice asking for and accepting a date. You might also prepare for times when a date cannot be accepted. Think of some ways of turning the asker down while still maintaining both people's dignity and not hurting feelings.

The hardest part of any date is the conversation. One college-age girl said, "It's easy: just ask them about their mission, and the conversation is set for the evening." Of course, the high school student doesn't have this option. Conversing with the opposite sex can be difficult at first. Maturity usually solves this problem, but a few suggestions may help: Have your teenager find out something about his or her date before the evening comes. Hobbies, activities at school, or family are good conversation beginners. Rehearse conversations with your teenagers. Teach them to talk about things besides themselves: events, school, the other person. Effective conversations often begin with open-ended questions that are broad and general: "What's happening?" or "How's your day?" The other person can then choose what and how much to say.

Teach youth to listen for "free information." This is information that goes beyond the question asked. It is an indicator of interest, and usually of trust as well: "My day was great, except I am worried about an algebra test. The teacher is cool, though, a lot better than my English teacher." Build upon this new information, trading comments. Be willing to offer free information about yourself. It shows trust when information is given that has not been specifically requested. Caution: avoid name dropping, gossiping, or speaking negatively about other friends.

4. *Teach them.* The leaders of the Church want youth the world over to have positive social experiences in their dating years. President Spencer W. Kimball counseled young men: "One can have all the blessings if he is in control and takes the experiences in proper turn: first some limited social get-acquainted contacts, then his mission, then his courting, then his temple marriage and his schooling and his family, then his life's work. In any other sequence he could run into difficulty.

"When you get in the teen-age years, your social associations should still be general acquaintance with both boys and girls. Any dating or pairing off in social contacts should be postponed until at least the age of 16 or older, and even then there should be much judgment used." (*Ensign*, February 1975, p. 4.)

Recent research validates the wisdom of this counsel. A survey of 2,200 high school students from three western states showed the following conclusions: Ninety-one percent of all who began dating at the age of twelve were involved sexually by the time they had graduated from high school; 68 percent were sexually involved if they had started dating at fourteen; 40 percent of all fifteen-year-olds were soon sexually active after beginning dating. The figure, however, drops dramatically to 20 percent if youth do not begin dating until age sixteen. In one year there is a significant difference in one's ability to make commitments and live true to personal values. (Miller, McCoy, Olson, *Juvenile Adolescent Research*, Vol. 1, 1986.)

Some youth who are eager for the dating experience may pressure their parents to compromise and permit dating before age sixteen. All their parents' explanations may fail to satisfy them. The consequences are far removed from their thoughts, and life seems innocent and uncomplicated.

Throughout life, however, there will be many times when we do not have all the answers or a clear understanding as to why the Lord directs the way he does. Faith is something we must begin to exercise at a very young age. As Bishop Vaughn J. Featherstone has said:

"Now, my dear young friends, the Lord doesn't always tell us why. We simply get direction and sometimes have to trust. Often your parents will not be able to tell you why they feel you shouldn't date until you are 16: the bishop cannot give you all of the reasons. All they know is that they feel at peace in their heart with this decision and that is probably the greatest answer that can be given. Follow their counsel, obey your parents, and know the decisions you make in this very serious matter will have eternal implications." (*New Era*, February 1975, p. 9.)

5. *Limit them.* One of the great deceptions of the adversary is that the gospel of Jesus Christ is restrictive and filled with "Thou shalt nots." Actually, John 8:32 states: "And ye shall know the truth, and the truth shall make you free." The restrictions that the gospel imposes are not designed to take away agency; they are a formula for preserving freedom. In truth, freedom actually comes with limitations.

Foul lines and goal posts provide athletes with freedom to play the game according to rules. If the rules didn't exist, only chaos would result. Chaos is never freedom. In time youth learn to appreciate family rules and inspired direction. Some may resist for a short period, but as they test and experiment with realistic limitations they soon come to appreciate them. Especially do they come to appreciate the counsel of inspired leaders.

One sixteen-year-old boy said: "It's a lot easier to get off the hook by complaining to your friends, 'My parents won't let me,' than to admit, 'I don't want to.' "

Another young girl stated: "At first I thought Alan's parents were too strict, but now I am grateful that they insisted he be in by ten on week nights and midnight on weekends. We always leave when we still want more, more conversation, more of each other's company. We haven't exhausted the evening. I am rested for work the next day and dating only twice a week I find I anticipate our next evening together. His phone calls aren't too long, so I can still get my homework done. I hate it when a boy doesn't know when to go home. I run out of things to say."

There must be some limitations to keep youth physically and spiritually safe. Parents should encourage double dating and group activities. Youth will be happier if they choose friends whose values are similar, and attend only those activities that are wholesome and meet Church standards. They should be taught to avoid physical involvement such as passionate kissing, petting, and necking.

6. *Instill in them courage.* Dating takes courage—courage to go into the unknown, and courage to risk oneself socially. The world often accepts standards that the young people of the Lord's kingdom cannot tolerate or even expose themselves to. Everywhere there are social drinking, drugs, and unacceptable entertainment. For the Holy Ghost to be an influence in the lives of our youth, they must have the courage to heed its promptings and be true to their values. Joseph, in the Old Testament, faced a severe test of his courage. He "fled" when faced with temptation, and our youth must have the courage to do the same. (See Genesis 39:1–12.)

Very often, if one young person has the courage to withdraw from an undesirable circumstance, others will follow. One young man stood up for his moral beliefs at a party, and later on his friend responded, "I knew what he said was true and I am thankful he had the courage to express it to me. That night we both left the party. I don't know that I would have if he hadn't spoken with such conviction."

What does a parent do when children wish to date, but the opportunity never comes? This can be stressful and damaging to a young person's self-esteem. It may be some consolation to know that many young men who never dated prior to their missions find they are better prepared after their missions.

Social pressures often cause young women to feel unacceptable if they are not dating by a certain age. Even though this hurts, they should never drop their standards just to be certain they are dating. It is better to marry the right person at age forty than the wrong one at twenty. The Lord has promised that no worthy person who lives faithfully will be denied the full blessings of eternity.

DEATH, TEACHING CHILDREN ABOUT

Children can be prepared to understand death even before someone close to them dies. At the time of the death of a neighbor or acquaintance, parents might effectively use a family home evening to explain about the plan of salvation, talking in a very simple way about the premortal existence, the purpose of earth life, the spirit world, resurrection, and the Holy Ghost. Even the death of a favorite pet can be an opportunity to instruct and help the child understand that death is a time of separation of the body and the spirit. Elder Boyd K. Packer, in an *Ensign* article (July 1973, p. 53) titled "Behold Your Little Ones," explains death to little children: "Pretend, my little friends, that my hand represents your spirit. It is alive. It can move by itself. Suppose that this glove represents your mortal body. It cannot move. When the spirit enters into your mortal body, then it can move and act and live. Now you are a person—a spirit with a body, living on the earth.

"It was not intended that we stay here forever. Just for a lifetime. Little ones, you are just beginning your lifetime. Your grandparents and great-grandparents are nearly finished with theirs. It wasn't long ago that they were little fellows and little girls just like you are now. But one day they will leave this mortal existence, and so will you.

"Someday, because of old age, or perhaps disease, or an accident, the spirit and the body will be separated. We then say a person has died. Death is a separation. All of this was according to a plan.

"Remember my hand represents your spirit and the glove represents your body. While you are alive the spirit inside the body can cause it to work and to act and to live.

"When I separate them, the glove, which represents your body, is taken away from your spirit; it cannot move anymore. It just falls down and is dead. But your spirit is still alive. . . . It is important that you get in your mind what death is. Death is a separation.

"The part of you that looks out through your eyes and allows you to think and smile and act and to know and to be, that is your spirit and that is eternal. It cannot die."

Children equipped with this fundamental understanding will be better able to deal with the death of someone close to them. Following are some further suggestions for helping children increase their knowledge and cope with the circumstances surrounding the death of loved ones.

1. Invite children to participate in funeral arrangements. It is the unknown in death that frightens children, rather than the reality. You might take children with you to the cemetery to help pick out the grave site, or if a family member is already buried there, take them to the site and explain that this is where the deceased will be buried. They might go to the mortuary to help select the casket or the burial clothing.

Explain to children that the purpose of a funeral is to help the family and friends understand and be comforted about the death of the person who died. Explain what will happen at the funeral—the talks, the hymns, the viewing, and what will happen at the grave. Explain that many people may cry because they will miss the person who has died, but that even though everyone will be sad, the Spirit of our Heavenly Father will help.

A family of five young boys experienced the death of their five-month-old brother. At the viewing, while parents were being comforted by friends, the boys were sitting with other family members. The seven-year-old finally got up and walked hesitantly toward the open casket; several of his brothers soon followed. A thoughtful grandmother, sensing their need, lifted the smallest fellow so he could see, then asked them if they would like to touch their little brother. Little hands went out cautiously at first, then caressingly. One small boy said, "He's cold," and the oldest responded with, "That's because his spirit has gone back to Heavenly Father, and this is just his body."

2. Permit children to experience grief. There are stages of grief that most persons pass through when they experience a severe

crisis. Although these stages may not be as obvious with children, they nonetheless usually occur. A knowledge of these stages may be useful to parents in their own understanding and in helping children through their grief. The first stage is one of disbelief, of nonacceptance or denial. This is especially pronounced when the deceased has had no previous illness and is taken suddenly. The second stage is one of anger. Even a child may feel angry that a best friend or sister or parent has been taken. This may be followed by feelings of depression—of hopelessness, or of having been deserted. The final stage, acceptance, arrives when the child is able to think and talk about the experience realistically. This does not necessarily indicate a total recovery; the child may yet have more problems.

Throughout this grieving period, children should feel the love of significant family members. If one parent is grieving to the extent that he or she is unable to respond to the children's needs, a grandparent, older sibling, or other close family member or friends should be sensitive to those needs. Often when one parent dies the remaining spouse finds it difficult to think consistently of the children. Other family members should offer love and concern when possible.

Children should be allowed to cry and to express their feelings. There should be no effort to get children to "forget" their loss or to diminish it. They need to be encouraged to talk, not just be talked to. Sometimes a child may feel guilt and some responsibility for the death. A mother who was acting as a foster parent to an eight-year-old girl passed away while the child was in the home. This little girl had to leave the home because of the foster mother's death, but fifteen years later she was still carrying the guilt of feeling that she had contributed to her foster mother's death because shortly before the accident that took the woman's life, the little girl had disobeyed, and had been reprimanded for what she had done. Had she had the opportunity or been encouraged to express her feelings at the time, this heavy burden could have been lifted then.

3. Avoid explanations that are hurtful to the child. It is important to say the right things when telling children of a death. The information should be given by someone who is well ac-

quainted with the children and can talk sensitively but without showing extreme grief. Phrases to be avoided might include:

"Heavenly Father took Daddy because He loved him so much." This may cause the children to have contradictory feelings about their Heavenly Father.

"Your little sister was taken because she was too good to live on this earth." Children might feel that they are not as "good" as their sister.

"Grandpa is only sleeping." Children might fear going to sleep.

It is more assuring to a child to be told about death in a straightforward manner, and then to talk about how sad it is to lose that special person's companionship.

4. Watch for signs that the child is not adjusting. The loss of a sibling or parent or other loved one can affect a child quite deeply. One boy became fearful of the dark and of being alone in his room. His parents encouraged him to talk about his fear, and for several weeks his older brother slept with him and a small night light was left on through the night in his room.

Another child who had been an excellent student began failing in his classes and became a discipline problem after his mother passed away. The teacher was alerted to the situation in the home and a special effort was made by her and the father as well as his Primary teacher to get him to talk about his feelings. At such a time a child needs not only love and caring, but stability and loving discipline.

5. Encourage children to talk about their memories. Make opportunities to talk about the loved one who has passed away. Sometimes the best lessons are learned in informal talks when parents and children are snuggling together or when the parent is tucking the little ones in for the night. These need not be sad times. They can be remembering times of happy events that have occurred. At the funeral of a special child in a large family, a table holding three pictures of her—one when she was about six, another at age ten, and still another at age fourteen, her age at the time of her death—was displayed in the foyer of the church. On the table were little notes this sweet child had written to different family members at special times. This family will remember and

talk about Alecia and the joy she brought into their lives for many years to come.

Another family who lost their tiny brother had a birthday cake for him on what would have been his first birthday, and all joined in to sing "Happy Birthday" to Jacob. It helps to cherish the memory of the loved one. This develops a bond in the remaining family members and a connection with the hereafter that can give each family member a greater desire and determination to live worthy to be together as an eternal family. It is comforting to observe the ability of children to adjust to losses as they understand and are loved and given emotional support.

When children are taught that they are children of a loving Father in heaven, when they are taught about the plan of salvation and the Holy Ghost, they have a better understanding when a loved one dies. The death of a loved one is an occasion to strengthen their understanding of these gospel truths.

DEPRESSION

To many people in and outside of the Church, depression seems to be a disease or problem peculiar to our times. Yet David of Israel wrote: "How long will thou forget me, O Lord? for ever? how long wilt thou hide thy face from me? How long shall I take counsel in my soul, having sorrow in my heart daily?" (Psalm 13:1–2.) David's sense of helplessness in feeling unending sorrow is similar to the feelings of many today who experience depression.

Some individuals who are unacquainted with depression and its effects may think, "Why doesn't she just snap out of it?" or, "If he would just stop looking on the gloomy side of things, everything would work out all right." Part of the problem is described by the word *depressed,* and the conditions it represents.

Depression has several meanings, ranging from a mood to an intense psychological reaction. It may occur for many reasons, including the loss of someone or something loved, or it may be caused by a biological condition in which chemical imbalances exist in the brain. In the same fashion, then, appropriate treatment may range from a mere increase of love and support to medical intervention and medication.

We all struggle to recognize when a circumstance requires help. Spiritual discernment is particularly important regarding the needs of our children. Because they have more difficulty than adults in understanding and describing their feelings, we must seek the help of Heavenly Father to be sensitive to their needs.

Until recently, children were not considered to be vulnerable to depression, partly because children and younger adolescents express its effects in somewhat different and less recognizable ways. Because we now understand better the characteristics of depression in younger people, we can do more to prevent its occurrence or treat it more promptly.

RECOGNIZING THE SYMPTOMS OF DEPRESSION

Identifying depression is sometimes difficult because different symptoms may be indicative of the same condition. All of us respond to feelings in our own individual ways. One person, when hurt, may retreat and want to be alone; another may need people and want to talk it out, while a third may defend against the hurt by becoming angry, looking for someone or something to fight. Yet all three of these people may be responding to the same kind of hurtful experience. Over time, however, enough similarities have been identified in the recognition of depression to indicate patterns of behavior to watch for.

The following symptom characteristics have been taken from the work of Weinberg, et al., "Depression in Children Referred to an Education Diagnostic Center," *Journal of Pediatrics* 83 (1973): 1065–1072.

1. Depressed children will show various kinds of unhappy or discontented moods. They may feel sad, or lonely, or express feelings of hopelessness or pessimism. On the other hand, they may seem especially irritable and difficult to please. Events that earlier would not have caused upset, now cause crying or anger and frustration.

2. The children's feelings toward themselves will be strongly negative. They may talk about being dumb, or stupid, or ugly. They may feel they can't do anything right. They may express a desire to run away or leave home, to somehow escape from the

situation in which they find themselves. The extreme extension of these feelings is manifested in thoughts of suicide.

3. Children may have problems with sleeping: difficulties getting to sleep, complaining of unrestful sleep with many dreams, waking up early and being unable to get back to sleep, or difficulty in waking up in the morning.

4. School performance may decline. Teachers may notice that depressed children seem to daydream a great deal or are unable to concentrate. They may lose interest in school activities that formerly were important to them, and may look for reasons to avoid attending school altogether.

Older adolescents may become increasingly worried and "driven" about school requirements. This may increase until they are exhausted and physically ill. On the other hand, the pressures may provoke them to repudiate the educational experience and become cynical, hiding from their sense of failure to perform.

5. The children's interest in being with friends may decline. They won't want to be with groups, and will withdraw from social activity, even with close friends.

6. Depressed children may have an increase in bodily complaints, such as stomach pain, headaches, or backaches. They may lose their appetite and lose weight quickly, or become worried about problems with health and generally seem more listless and fatigued.

7. By contrast, children sometimes express their depression through aggressive behavior—being more difficult to get along with, quarrelsome, and resistant to authority. They may act out their frustrations by illegal or antisocial activities that sometimes seem calculated to hurt or embarrass parents.

Most children experiencing depression will not show problems in all of the above categories. In addition, it is important to keep in mind that in cases of depression the symptoms will have occurred fairly consistently over several weeks' time or more. Many children will experience moods that mimic more serious depression, but these moods seldom persist for longer than a few days. If parents see several of these characteristics in their child, they should seek the help of the Lord to search out the source of the difficulties and the necessary help.

CAUSES OF DEPRESSION IN CHILDREN

Having considered the presenting symptoms of depression in children, we will next address the issue of causes. What brings depression on? And how can we tell the difference between problems we can handle by ourselves and those that require the help of a physician, a psychiatrist, or a psychologist?

As might be expected, there are several possible answers. First, some children experience depression as the result of long-term stress, some threat to their sense of well-being. For instance, children for whom school achievement is very important may worry too much about assignments or tests, attaching their feelings of self-worth to grades or teacher praise. Other stresses may be linked to problems in the family, or desires for achievement in other areas of life. Over time, the effects of stress have a wearing and destructive impact upon the child's health that may be expressed in the experience of depression, as well as other health problems.

Some children are teased excessively in school. Just going to school day after day anticipating persecution and rejection is a significant stress that may result in depression.

Another related general cause of depression results from loss of loved ones or objects. Death of a parent, a divorce in the family, or even the breakup of a boy-girl relationship that has become important to the person can create the sense of helplessness in the face of hurt that is the seedbed of depression. Other times the loss is more symbolic than real. Adolescent children who feel that their parents don't listen to them, that they prefer younger brothers or sisters to them, may experience the same sense of loss. A third sense of loss, that of self-esteem, occurs as children develop patterns of thinking that hurt by predicting defeat even before attempts have been made to achieve. Children may also punish themselves unmercifully for minor mistakes.

Evidence suggests that, in some cases, the tendency toward depression is inherited. Theories derived from the research suggest that these depressions are caused by a deficiency in the substances that carry nerve impulses. Thus, in the same way that diabetics' bodies do not manufacture sufficient insulin, some depressed individuals experience a chemical imbalance that must be remedied by medication.

WHAT PARENTS CAN DO

1. *Be sensitive.* Parents must be sensitive to the experiences in their children's lives, particularly to what constitutes stress. This can be done only by establishing trusting communication lines between parent and child. In effect, the parent becomes an expert on his or her child by dint of years of interested listening, watching, cheering, consoling, and talking. Parents can then be sensitive to times when their own goals for the child may be creating stress instead of encouragement. They can recognize when a goal has become too important, too consuming, and perhaps too threatening to reach. One father noticed how discouraged his son had become about his Scouting progress toward the Eagle badge. Circumstances had created a situation in which the boy was now behind several other younger boys in Scout advancements, and the boy talked as if he no longer wanted to be active in Scouting. His father, perceiving that the complaining may have been coming more from his son's feelings of pressure and embarrassment than actual lack of interest, said, "Son, I don't know where it was ever written that a boy can't grow up to be a fine priesthood bearer without being an Eagle Scout. Maybe you can just enjoy the activities and participate with the troop. If you want to work on merit badges that's fine, but if you don't, that's okay too. We'll help you any way we can." The boy told his mother later that his father's comment had lifted a big weight off his shoulders.

On the other hand, there are times when loving firmness is vital in helping children face and overcome difficult tasks they would rather avoid.

2. *Listen to children.* Parents can pay attention to the words children use that describe the way they think about themselves in relationship to others. For instance, if the parent hears a lot of words that suggest distorted or negative thinking from their child, they can take steps to further understand what the child is feeling. Listening carefully and asking questions to clarify what the child is thinking will usually help parents learn what distortions may be occurring.

3. *Lead a healthy life-style.* Parents can help their children in a surprisingly direct way by helping them lead a more healthy life-style. The importance of exercise, fresh air, sunshine, a healthy

diet, and adequate, consistent rest cannot be understated. Because the cumulative effects of eating "junk" food or sleeping at irregular hours are not immediately noticeable, their gradually harmful influences upon a person's sense of well-being are often overlooked.

4. *Keep faith in yourself as counselor.* If parents have experienced depression in their own lives, or have other close relatives who have, they will be aware of its possible expression in the lives of their children. They must be prepared to accept without guilt that their children may face some of the same struggles with which they have been acquainted. They can know that it is within God's loving tasks for us to experience weaknesses so that, through our faith on his Son, we may be made strong. (See Ether 12:27.)

Finally, the two most important ingredients for parents in preventing or dealing with depression are, perhaps, the two most important ingredients in all of parenting: loving each other and loving God. President David O. McKay said: "The greatest gift which parents can give to their children is to love each other." The foundation of security and love that emanates from loving parents to their children will do much toward helping them recognize their own self-worth, which cannot be taken away by any loss. Sometimes, of course, it is a single parent who must communicate out of his or her sense of wholeness the love and acceptance that let children take confidence in their own worth.

Second, loving God and desiring to do his will assures the parents of the whispered guidance of the Spirit on behalf of their children. Inspiration sought for these precious charges can teach parents when to discipline and when to console, when to provide loving but firm expectations for performance and when to give the child equally loving "wiggle room" to relieve undue pressure. Moreover, as mentioned earlier, God will help parents discern when it is time to seek professional assistance. Alma was inspired to counsel his son Helaman: "O, remember, my son, and learn wisdom in thy youth; yea, learn in thy youth to keep the commandments of God. . . . Counsel with the Lord in all thy doings, and he will direct thee for good. . . . For just as surely as this director [the Liahona] did bring our fathers, by following its course, to the promised land, shall the words of Christ, if we follow their course, carry us beyond this vale of sorrow into a far better land of promise." (Alma 37:35, 37, 45.)

DEVIL WORSHIP

(SEE SATAN WORSHIP)

DISABILITIES

As parents, we want and hope for a great deal for our children. Though we may understand from a distance the blessings of adversity, we do all in our power to avoid it in our lives, and, even more to protect our loved ones from suffering. Yet suffering and adversity are inescapable and valuable parts of life in this imperfect world. God has willed it so, not because he loves us less, but precisely because he loves us and comprehends our hearts and needs so well. He knows of the opportunities for softened hearts, increased patience, and greater dependence on his Spirit that comes as we learn to accept and work with infirmity and weakness, sorrow and need.

Still, the initial shock and anguish of learning of a child's handicap can be almost unbearable. Elder James E. Faust describes the process poignantly: "The tearful concern, the questions about what the child will and will not be able to do are heartrending: 'Doctor, will our child be able to talk, walk, care for himself?' Often there are no certain answers but one: 'You will have to be grateful for whatever development your child achieves.'

"The paramount concern is always how to care for the person who is handicapped. The burden of future nurturing can seem overwhelming. Looking ahead to the uncertain years or even to a lifetime of constant, back-breaking care may seem more than one can bear. There are often many tears before reality is acknowledged. Parents and family members can then begin to accept and take the burden a day at a time." (*Ensign*, November 1984, pp. 54–60.)

What can parents do? To begin with, they can allow themselves to mourn. Our Father in heaven has not asked us to be so insensitive that we fail to feel pain from tragedy. A spiritual understanding may help give purpose to our struggles, but it will not keep us from experiencing earthly trials. Sorrow can have a healing, cleansing effect, helping us to accept and readjust our lives to the necessary coming changes. It can help us seek and receive the consolation and whispered reassurance of God to speed the healing process.

It should be added that handicapped children will usually provide their parents with a special source of joy. Mary Jane Hawkes wrote of her Down's syndrome child: "Sarah's short life broadened our understanding, increased our compassion. During her time with us we found ourselves thinking and speaking of her as 'our bright spot,' 'our little sunshine,' 'the light of our lives.' " (*Ensign*, June 1981, pp. 32–34.)

As adjustment begins, more mundane and practical issues will press for attention. However, it is always important to seek continually for spiritual promptings that comfort as well as instruct.

STEPS THAT CAN HELP

1. It is important that parents become "experts" on their child. This does not mean that they must study to become experts in the scholarly sense, but implies instead a combination of learning from written materials, listening and talking to parents who themselves are having similar experiences, and carefully watching their own child to learn to *know* him or her.

Every child is different, whether normal or disabled. Parents can become much more confident and "expert" in the handling of all their children by careful attention, by watching and observing them as they grow. They can then help design learning experiences specially geared to each child's progress. Joseph Smith said, "All the minds and spirits that God ever sent into the world are susceptible of enlargement." (*Teachings of the Prophet Joseph Smith*, compiled by Joseph Fielding Smith [Salt Lake City: Deseret Book, 1976], p. 354.)

2. Keep in touch with other parents who have children with similar problems. This can be of great comfort, providing compassion and predictability as tasks must be met. The support of someone else who "really" understands is invaluable in times of stress, and such support helps reduce the isolated feelings of dealing with problems parents of normal children do not face.

Established community centers for the developmentally disabled provide important information and moral support. These centers will be aware of resources available for training and rehabilitation. Frequently, programs of early stimulation will provide heartening gains that were not thought possible just a few years ago.

3. A constant and major challenge for parents of disabled children is to pace their expectations and demands for the child's progress. Like parents of normal children, they must ask, "Are we pushing too hard, expecting too much, or not enough? Are we not giving our child enough of the right experiences?" The difference, of course, between the respective situations is that parents of normal children have many more examples of children, teachers, and parents with which to compare.

4. Parents with disabled children should learn to provide security without being overprotective. Because of the birth defect or injury, parents often feel sorry for the child's extra burdens and are afraid to make demands on him or her. Here it may be important to remember an oft-repeated statement by professionals in the field. Disabled children are still children, and they are always more like other children than they are different. They will have the same desires to be held and loved and challenged, as well as the same fears of inadequacy. The elements of the expertness described above, in concert with earnest seeking of the Lord's direction, will guide parents in this critical task.

Like other children, children with special problems may become sensitive to means by which they can manipulate to get what they want. Thus parents must be aware of the phenomenon sometimes called the "tyranny of the weak." For instance, one child who experienced seizures learned that his parents were so fearful of reoccurrences that he could get his own way by threatening a seizure (that is, by becoming excited and upset). The behavior problems occasioned by his tyranny were becoming more serious than the possibility of seizures. In spite of their fears, these parents had to let their child become a child again by not responding to his threats; the child had to again become obedient and dependent upon his parents.

5. Very often parents must balance their concern for the disabled child with their concerns about other children in the family. Usually they are the parents of normal children, too. These chil-

dren have their own legitimate needs for attention and love. The family will undoubtedly make particular concessions for the disabled child, and the other children can be greatly blessed by their participation in this child's care, but the siblings must have a place in the family for their normal ups and downs as well.

DEALING WITH THE REACTIONS OF OTHERS

Many parents of disabled children express as one of their greatest fears the way other people will respond to their child. These fears may range from what other children will say, to criticism from other well-meaning parents, to professional suggestions for institutionalization. Perhaps the best counsel for this situation is demonstrated in the teaching of one father to his daughter who came home crying, hurt by the jeering of school children: " 'Sweetheart,' he said, 'what the children said about you is true, but it wasn't fair and it wasn't kind. You do have a hump on your back and some other serious problems. But that isn't your fault. It isn't your parents' fault or Heavenly Father's fault. It is one of those things that happen in this yet imperfect world. What the boys and girls said is true, but it wasn't fair and it wasn't kind. If all your life you will try to be more fair and more kind to others than some of them may sometimes be to you, then you will be happy, and your life will be full and useful.' " (Marion D. Hanks, *Ensign*, November 1976, 31–33.)

Parents can best help others deal with their child by being as open and forthright as possible. Experienced parents have observed that others respond best when they answer children's questions honestly without defensiveness, ask ward members for help, patiently explain the child's difficulties to teachers, and openly enlist everyone in the effort to help the child grow.

In considering the decision to institutionalize, the family should try to balance the drain of resources among family members. No one member of the family should try to carry the burden alone. In some situations institutionalization may be appropriate; in others it may be totally inappropriate. Institutionalization is a most difficult and heart-rending decision, for which study and professional counsel are important, but spiritual guidance is critical. As believing people who understand that it may be through the child's difficulties that "the works of God should be made manifest" (John 9:3), we would try to exert every effort of the family and the Church to keep the child in the home. However, there are times when the demands of the child's care so exceed the resources of the home that institutionalization is necessary. Consultation with local priesthood leaders may be helpful in coming to this determination. If after prayer the Spirit confirms the decision, institutionalization may be accepted with peace and equanimity. Parents may then seek to enlarge their child's spirit through their loving visits, their prayers, and their working with the institution to provide for the child.

Parents should be aware that the Church has exerted great effort to develop materials and resources for families with handicapped children. These may be obtained on request from the Coordinating Committee for Special Member Needs, room 2453, Church Office Building, 50 East North Temple, Salt Lake City, Utah 84150.

Finally, it is important to reiterate the question asked by so many parents and the Savior's answer as found in John 9:1–3:

"And as Jesus passed by, he saw a man which was blind from his birth.

"And his disciples asked him, saying, Master, who did sin, this man, or his parents, that he was born blind?

"Jesus answered, Neither hath this man sinned, nor his parents: but that the works of God should be made manifest in him."

As members of the Church, fellow-citizens in the household of God, all of us can be blessed to help to make his works manifest by our love and care of those less fortunate than ourselves.

DISRESPECT

(SEE BACK TALK)

DIVORCE

Divorce is not an action to be taken lightly or rushed into. Regardless of the circumstances, divorce has lasting effects on all members of a family. To undo a partnership and separate a family requires thought, prayer, and careful weighing of facts about the future. People usually suffer greatly before breaking up a marriage because there are so many investments and shared experiences, especially the bearing and rearing of children.

To justify a divorce, one must have pure intent. "For I, the Lord, will judge all men according to their works, according to the desire of their hearts." (D&C 137:9.) Unfortunately, there are some cases where the problems in a marriage are more serious than those that would result from a divorce. One partner may believe he or she has done everything possible to reconcile differences and provide a loving home, but one alone cannot create a healthy relationship. Even so, it is not easy to decide when a divorce will serve the best interests of the family.

A divorce brings a loss much like death, but can cause even worse pain because it is harder to understand and it has no closure. A divorce is seldom final, especially where there are children. Visitation, child support, income taxes, Church ordinances, performances, awards, graduations, missionary farewells and homecomings, weddings and receptions, births of grandchildren, family reunions, funerals, illnesses and accidents are some of the occasions that continually bring a divorced couple back in contact with each other. The deep emotional pain they suffered earlier will likely return whenever they are together again.

Most divorced people feel failure, resentment, and rejection and carry a great burden of guilt whether or not they were responsible for the breakup. They torture themselves with such thoughts as: "Could I have done more?" "Should I have done something differently?" "Were my standards wrong?" "Did I marry the wrong person?" "Can I trust my feelings and judgment again?" "Why doesn't my spouse love me anymore?" "How could my partner do this to me?" "I must be a failure, so why try?"

Dwelling on the past, which cannot be changed, will usually not help. The decision for divorce was made when all of the data available was fresh. It will not help to second-guess earlier decisions. The best that can be done is to move ahead.

FORGIVE AND FORGET

The first step in working through a divorce is to forgive and forget. "I, the Lord, will forgive whom I will forgive, but of you it is required to forgive all men." (D&C 64:10; see also D&C 98:23–48.) Self-pity and bitterness are cancers that must be controlled and removed. Divorced parents do better if they look forward, not letting the pains of yesterday destroy their tomorrows. Remembering the good they have learned, rather than the hurt, is a difficult, uphill climb. Divorced parents must gradually and steadily reorganize their lives and start putting their worlds back together.

A divorced parent can learn a valuable lesson from the oyster. When a bit of foreign matter enters the oyster's shell it causes an irritation. The irritation cannot be removed, so the oyster secretes a substance called nacre of mother-of-pearl. As thin successive layers of this substance surround the irritation, it is slowly isolated so that it no longer damages the oyster. As a result the oyster produces a pearl. The process is slow: Depending on the kind of oyster, it may take from four to seven years of repeated layering to make a pearl.

The divorced parent definitely has an "irritation" that must be dealt with. Pain, disappointment, guilt, and rejection will not disappear magically, but must be healed to enable the parent to carry on and to be a resource to the children. Like the oyster, all of us can produce a layer of hope with the knowledge that God loves us. We each have value and much to offer to family and friends. "The Spirit itself beareth witness with our spirit, that we are the children of God: and if children, then heirs; heirs of God, and joint-heirs with Christ; if so be that we suffer with him, that we may be also glorified together." (Romans 8:16–17.)

To start the healing layers around the pain three beliefs must be developed: (1) I have value, (2) I can make responsible decisions, and (3) there isn't any situation I cannot face, if I have Heavenly Father's help.

1. *I have value.* In most cases, feelings of self-worth are very low following a divorce. People may doubt their value, attractiveness, and judgment. Each person must regain a realistic perspective of his or her infinite worth in the eyes of God. It is important to turn to family members and close personal friends for genuine support and reassurance at this time. Following the death of a

spouse, much love and devotion are provided, but following a divorce one may feel deserted. As one person said, "Think of yourself as a whole—not a half looking for another half."

2. *I can make responsible decisions.* The responsibilities and decisions that face a divorced mother or father seem overwhelming. "How do I both provide for my children and care for them?" "Where will we live?" "Should Judy take gymnastics or dance lessons?" "Should I let Johnny go to the party?" "Who will help Sue get ready for her dates?" "Who will fix Brent's bicycle?" "How can I mend Tony's pants?" "Should I buy another car or have the old one repaired?"

These decisions don't have to be made alone. Assistance is available from the bishop, home teachers, visiting teachers, friends, and family, *but only when needs are clearly known.* One divorced mother persuaded her home teachers to stop coming on the last Sunday of the month to read from the *Ensign,* and instead to come on two Saturdays per month to play basketball with her ten-year-old son. This worked so well that the bishop assigned each priest in his quorum to be a big brother to a boy in the ward who had no father in the home.

A divorced mother must see to it that her children are not left out of church and school activities. For example, there are other fathers in the neighborhood who can include her boys in father-son outings, but this will not likely happen unless she asks for help. A divorced father can similarly provide for his children.

3. *There isn't any situation I cannot face if I have Heavenly Father's help.* Being a single homemaker, breadwinner, teacher, and guide to children is a big challenge. Emergencies and accidents can cause frustration and panic. But perhaps the worst problem is the loneliness. Flat tires, loads of washing, broken appliances, meals to prepare, dirty dishes, and no dates all combine to accentuate the loneliness. As the divorced person works through the first crises, self-confidence will return and troubles will lessen.

WHAT ABOUT THE CHILDREN?

As divorced parents progress in their own recovery, they are better able to deal with the needs of their children. Explaining divorce to children is very difficult. Regardless of the reasons for the divorce, children experience confusion, loss, and pain. They want to know why. "How can two people we love very much, not love each other?" "How can two people who have taught us to be kind, considerate, and gentle, fight so bitterly with each other and break up our family?" "How can our mother, who has been so mature and nurturing, suddenly be crying and in need of talking so much?" "How can our father, who has been rational and logical, be so emotional?" One daughter said, "I cried a lot, but many years later I learned to understand." A son said, "I felt worse than I have ever felt in my life, so I just tried not to feel."

Often children are caught in the middle as each parent tells them his or her side of the story. Children feel very uncomfortable and disloyal, whether or not they take sides. One young son whose parents were in the midst of a separation said, "I feel like the peanut butter in a sandwich being torn apart."

It is helpful when children can talk about their confused thoughts and their feelings. Parents may answer questions with this preface, "What I tell you is my point of view. Your father (or mother) has a different opinion. It is not your job to try to figure out or solve our problems with each other. Your job is to be our child and enjoy your youth."

Both parents should take great care not to use children as weapons to hurt each other. The children are not pawns on a game board; their needs must be considered very highly. Even though parents may be able to justify to the Savior their own behavior in the marriage, and their reasons for seeking a divorce, parents will never be able to justify offending their children in the process.

Children need to feel free to love both parents without being disloyal to either parent. They also need clear evidence that both parents love each child, even though the parents cannot get along with each other.

After a broken marriage, the mother usually has the primary responsibility of creating a home and rearing all the children. Sometimes the father has this role. In other cases each parent has one or more of the children. Custodial parents make many decisions alone, without the benefit of consultation and support from a marital partner.

The issue of custody is usually decided in the courts. It is not fair to require children to choose between their parents. An independent evaluator can listen confidentially, consider the feelings and desires of each child, and make recommendations to the judge. If the judge makes the decision, the children will feel blameless. The most common arrangement is for one parent to have sole custody of all children and the other parent to have visitation rights. The visiting parent can usually develop and maintain a very good relationship with the children. One visiting father, for example, felt that his relationship with his children was even better than it had been before, because now he structured the time to be with his children. Parents must be flexible in arranging visits so that they do not interfere with church, school, and other activities that are important to the growth of children.

Whenever possible, children should continue to enjoy a consistent relationship with both parents. However, in some the noncustodial parent doesn't maintain contact with the children, and perhaps does not provide consistent financial support. The custodial parent must be very cautious not to influence a hateful attitude toward the other parent. Children's self-worth can be quickly damaged as they come to hate that which is part of themselves. Comments such as, "Your dad doesn't care about you," or, "Your mother never was any good" can make deep and painful scars. A child can survive and even benefit from a divorce if the parents keep their differences to themselves and continue a positive involvement with the children.

Care must be taken that the visiting parent does not spend money on entertainment, treats, and gifts for the children, and then send them back to the custodial parent to do their household chores and schoolwork. Any efforts to play Santa, trying to buy a child's love, will backfire. Some parents are too permissive in their efforts to be liked by their children. Children do not need "buddies" at this time; they need parents who are mature, wise, and fair. Children need the security of structure and rules, even though they may complain about them.

Some children conclude they are to blame for the divorce. They may think, "Maybe I didn't help enough with the housework." "Maybe I teased and argued too much." "Maybe I didn't mind enough." Children need frequent reassurance that they are not to blame for their parents' problems.

Another normal reaction of some children during the first

year after a divorce is to believe they can get their parents back together. False hopes that parents will remarry can create considerable pain for both children and parents. Children may need help to express their private feelings. A parent might say, "It's okay to wish we were back together. I had hopes and dreams myself before the divorce. You would really like to have both of us loving each other and close to you, but it will not likely happen. It is okay to talk about it, though."

Another hurdle some children deal with is seeing mother with another man or father with another woman. The children may feel intruded upon or rejected again. Parents should consistently reaffirm their love for the children, prepare them for the parents' renewed social life and possible remarriage, and help them reconcile their feelings so that these do not interfere with meeting the parents' own needs for companionship.

In contrast, some children are anxious for their mother or father to marry again, and may often ask when it will happen. One mother said, "We are a special family, so we have to find a very special person to become part of our family."

Comfort for both parents and children comes from the Lord. "Whosoever shall put their trust in God shall be supported in their trials, and their troubles, and their afflictions, and shall be lifted up at the last day." (Alma 36:3; see also 2 Nephi 2:2; D&C 58:2–4.)

Being a divorced parent carries great responsibility, but with the help of others and of our Heavenly Father, parents can become equal to any challenge. Love for the Savior and Heavenly Father can make of one's life the pearl raised from "irritation."

DRUG ABUSE

When parents think of drug abuse, they normally think of drugs like heroine, "crack," or marijuana. It is, however, true that the most abused drugs are prescription and over-the-counter drugs.

Any drug used abusively is exactly what 2 Nephi 15:20 warns against: "Wo unto them that call evil good, and good evil, that put darkness for light, and light for darkness, that put bitter for sweet, and sweet for bitter!" Drugs often appear to give increased freedom, ability, awareness, and even euphoria. Almost always, however, their misuse results in physical or psychological dependence, or both. When used in combination with alcohol, they become potentially lethal. A recent study concludes, "Many mood altering drugs are prescribed. They include antianxiety drugs, sleeping compounds, antidepressants, and sedatives. Real danger arises when some of these drugs are combined with alcohol . . . even a small amount of alcohol taken with a mood drug can slow the brain to the point of coma or death." And alcohol mixed with some antidepressants "may send blood pressure soaring high enough to cause a stroke." (Dan Kaercher, "Health – the Uses and Abuses of Mood-Altering Drugs," *Better Homes and Gardens*, May 1983.)

Drugs, both beneficial and harmful, are readily available in society. Affluence combined with this availability provides a temptation that many young people can hardly withstand. Add the power of some media personalities, who are often guilty of popularizing the "fun side" of drugs, and we see why drug abuse is a real problem. The wide range of drugs available (heroin, marijuana, barbituates, hallucinogens, tranquilizers, and so on) promise to elevate one to realms of pseudosupremacy and even seemingly great self-worth. But the promises are all lies.

Church members should know that any unwarranted use of drugs is against the teachings of the Savior and Church leaders. The formidable consequence of AIDS (Acquired Immune Deficiency Syndrome) and other associated diseases makes drug abuse extremely dangerous. Between 17 and 25 percent of all AIDS cases are transmitted by needles not properly sterilized. (If parents suspect needle use, the child should be encouraged to take the AIDS test to determine if he or she is either a carrier or has contracted the disease.)

One early sign of drug abuse is excessive redness or a "glassy" look in the eyes. The drug user will often appear preoccupied, distant, far away. Sometimes large amounts of money will pass unaccountable through the young person's hands. If youth are selling drugs, the opposite may be true: they may possess large amounts of money and not be able to explain. Often drug abusers will stay out very late, and they have a tendency not to fulfill assigned responsibilities. They may also begin to appear quite unhealthy.

Why do young people turn to drugs? Every case is individual, of course, but some common factors are as follows:

1. Sometimes young people just want to test the laws of free agency, or they may just be curious. Sometimes rebellious feelings, peer pressure, and fun-seeking lead to experimentation.

2. A traumatic event in the family where the normal, preestablished routine is disrupted or abolished may create an atmosphere condusive to drug use. One family experienced an accident in which a son was killed and the father was severely injured. Recuperation was long and tedious. Whether one parent's total dedication to the other excluded needs of the children, or feelings of guilt weighed on family members, or pure trauma cried for relief, some members of this family turned to drugs.

3. Among the most common reasons young people abuse drugs is a feeling of just plain lack of caring from other family members. Being a "child of God" may not seem enough at a moment when love from an earthly parent is needed.

4. Inconsistency in observance of the Word of Wisdom by adults can cause a child to turn to drugs. Even while haranguing children about drugs, parents may be overcome with frustration, anxiety, pain, depression, and even insomnia. They themselves have been known to develop difficult drug habits. A child may then view this as an accepted method of coping with the world.

5. Unrealistic expectations that life should be very exciting, always glamorous, never dull or routine, may lead to frustration and disappointment. To some, drugs seem to alleviate these conditions.

6. Some young people turn to drugs to help them deal with the guilt they feel because of other transgressions, such as sexual sins. Immorality usually leads to feelings of being unworthy and unclean, and drugs may help obliterate those feelings, if only for a short time.

PREVENTING DRUG ABUSE

Young people from all walks of life become ensnared by drugs. There is no guaranteed success formula that parents can follow to protect their children—they have their free agency. But there *are* steps parents can take to minimize the power of the temptations their children face.

1. Children constantly watch parents. They do the things parents do, walk and talk like them, and many times eat and drink what their parents eat and drink. Parents who live the Word of Wisdom usually have great influence on their children. Spencer W. Kimball wrote, "We hope our people will eliminate from their lives all kinds of drugs so far as possible. Too many [speaking to parents] depend upon drugs as tranquilizers and sleep helps, which is not always necessary." (*Ensign*, November 1974, p. 6.)

2. Love them. Never let there be a question as to whether children are wanted. Work, play, and share together. Listen to their questions. Some may be very blunt with these questions; others can convey their feelings without a word being spoken.

3. Build and acknowledge individual worth. Help young people to see themselves making a contribution, growing in knowledge and stature, active in school and church activities.

4. Teach youth the harmful effects of drugs while the discussion can still be held on an academic and a spiritual level. Let children express what they have learned outside the home, and then teach them obedience. Gordon B. Hinckley said, "There is not a boy within the sound of my voice who needs to succumb to any of these forces. You hold the Priesthood of God. You are a son of God. You have his power within you to sustain you. Do not let Goliath frighten you. Stand your ground and hold your place, and you will be triumphant." (*Ensign*, May 1983, p. 51.)

WHAT TO DO AFTER DRUG USE IS SUSPECTED OR KNOWN

1. Open up communications. The child must feel that an open discussion is possible and even helpful. Listen to what is said, and what is not said. Try to understand the child's point of view.

2. Express love for the child, not only in silent actions, but verbally as well. Recognize the child as much as possible.

3. Get the youth involved in service to someone or something besides self.

4. Refrain from scare tactics. Inappropriate ones may damage the parent's credibility with the youth.

5. Where necessary, consult local governmental and nongovernmental agencies for help. Their experience can help parents understand that they are neither isolated nor unique.

6. If the situation continues or intensifies, pure, accepting love and continual moral and financial help may no longer be effective. The use of "tough love" may then be appropriate. "Family members need to learn 'tough love,' i.e. doing what has to be done even though it hurts, or not doing something for others that they should do for themselves." (James R. Goodrich, *Ensign*, July 1981, p. 19.)

Such situations may eventually lead to sending a youth out of the home, a very uncomfortable and difficult decision for parents. But lack of effort on the drug user's part can completely disrupt other family members and deplete financial resources. In the face of such danger, "tough love" may be the only possible approach. Above all, basic human fairness must prevail. If it doesn't, the family could lose more than a single member.

7. Pray for the inspiration of the Holy Ghost. Church manuals and professional advice can be a help in strengthening parents. However, answers to specific prayers regarding their child will be infinitely more helpful to faithful, loving, concerned parents than any other source.

(SEE ALSO ALCOHOLISM)

EATING DISORDERS

At first, eating disorders seem strange or foolish to those not affected. Any girl can see when she has lost so much weight that it is hurting her health and appearance, can't she? Why would a girl want to make herself vomit after eating? Couldn't a girl's parents or a physician just explain what it is doing to her, tell her to stop this nonsense, and have her "get control" of herself? Briefly, the answers to these questions are: (1) No, her thinking becomes distorted so that she continues to see herself as overweight; (2) Vomiting after eating too much creates an extremely addictive cycle of building tensions followed by relief and relaxation; and (3) The changes that accompany this condition produce a serious and complex mental disorder that usually requires expert professional help, frequently hospitalization.

Eating disorder problems seem to illustrate the important spiritual need for balance in one's life. While there are many scriptures about the importance of self-control and self-mastery, true self-control asks us to know when to relax instead of continuing to try harder, or how to be gentle with ourselves instead of relentlessly feeling guilt when we have erred. The book of Ecclesiastes describes the importance of balance especially well: "To every thing there is a season, and time to every purpose under the heaven." (Ecclesiastes 3:1; see also verses 2–13.)

Anorexia nervosa refers to voluntary extreme dieting that causes a weight loss of at least 25 percent of normal body weight, or what a person should weigh, given the individual's age and height. Approximately 90 percent of those who are anorexic are adolescent girls or young women between twelve and thirty years old. In addition to physical changes, noticeable psychological factors include an intense fear of becoming obese that doesn't diminish as weight loss progresses; a distortion of the person's body image wherein the person continues to "feel fat" even when she is emaciated; an intense refusal to maintain body weight above a minimal normal weight for age and height.

Bulimia refers to a condition wherein someone, again usually female, eats large quantities of food and then purges the system of the food by vomiting or use of laxatives and diuretics. While the eating and then vomiting may begin as a way for the person to avoid gaining weight, the cycle becomes addicting, a means of responding to pressures and stresses. Over time she is apt to spend more and more of her time and money buying and eating secretively, which builds up tension, and then vomiting to relieve the tension and enjoy a sense of relaxation.

Although people suffering from bulimia are seldom as noticeably thin as those with anorexia, some of the physiological and psychological consequences are the same. Food becomes an obsession. Physical problems range from increased dental problems (due to increased stomach acids in the mouth) to heart problems and kidney failure caused by potassium insufficiency. The chemical imbalances caused by frequent vomiting endanger both the woman's health and that of a developing baby, if she becomes pregnant. Moreover, the risk to unborn children continues for several years after she quits vomiting. Some of the complications can become life threatening. One out of ten people with anorexia die because of the effects of their illness.

Although eating disorders frequently begin with what may look like an innocent diet, the emotional circumstances of the person are usually in turmoil already. She is often a perfectionistic person who has a strong desire for control in her life, and she is usually feeling out of control in many areas. Controlling her diet, either by self-starvation or by the magical solution of purging, becomes a focus for her to feel like she is getting some control again. As the condition deepens, the dietary problems assume more and more importance, distracting her from other life pressures. Finally, the means to establish control becomes the best evidence that she has lost control, as she experiences what has come to be called "dietary chaos."

Following are some danger signs to watch for:

1. Dieting excessively; refusing to eat, to the point of self-starvation.

2. Paying excessive attention to food, calories, and cooking.

3. Refusing to eat but often watching others eat.

4. Excessive exercising.

5. Loss of menstrual periods.

6. Spending much time in the bathroom, perhaps vomiting in secret.

7. Impulsive binge eating, or evidence of large amounts of food disappearing.

8. Depression and inability to concentrate.

9. Withdrawal from friends and social activities.

As mentioned, eating disorders are serious conditions that usually require expert professional help, often including a team approach of a physician, a nutritionist, and a counselor who has specialized training in treating eating disorders. If the problems are deeply entrenched, hospitalization is usually required to provide a "time out" from the current life stresses and get the bizarre eating patterns under control.

WHAT PARENTS CAN DO

It is most important that parents recognize and teach the need for balance spoken of earlier. Parents must be careful to not over-emphasize slimness and attractiveness to their daughters. Even indirectly, a father who demands slimness from his wife, or a mother who is overly concerned with her own weight, will communicate to children: *This is what you must do to feel good about yourself. Being just a little skinny is your best chance for living "happily ever after."* Parents must also remember, of course, that if they find that their daughter is having such difficulties, their example may have had nothing to do with it. From cartoons to billboards to movies, girls are being taught by current fashions that slim equals beautiful. Given the immaturity and intensity of adolescence, many girls are tempted to adopt extreme ways of guaranteeing slimness, with disastrous results.

If parents find that the problem has already begun, it is most important to remember that if the child has been engaging in the behaviors for longer than three months, she will not be capable of thinking accurately with sufficient control to change her life on her own. In fact, she will probably resist her parents' attempts to help her or get help for her. Parents must be willing to seek the appropriate help in spite of her protests. Remonstrations such as, "Don't be ridiculous, you are not fat," or, "You had better eat some more of that food, young lady," will be received in the wrong way, causing more anxiety and determination to not gain weight and, probably, a decision to become more secretive about eating habits. Eating disorders have a powerful effect upon their victims, virtually robbing them of true self-control and clear thinking. More indirect encouragement may be more helpful, such as "You are not eating much today. Are you feeling all right? It is still a struggle for you to eat, huh?" Mild expressions of concern serve better as invitations for the child to talk as well as to recognize that there may be need for change.

Once the child begins appropriate treatment, parents must strive to align themselves on her side in this ordeal. They cannot "tiptoe" around her, fearful of hurting her. Neither can they become obsessed with her eating habits as she has been, worrying and questioning her each day. They must try to make their home a "safe place" for their daughter so that she can express her fears and difficulties, even her strange ideas, without being afraid of them. She must know that her parents will listen in a consistently supportive way. Then they can honestly ask how she is doing as an invitation to share her struggles and receive much-needed love and strength from them.

Of course, the child's absorption in body weight and image usually precludes her awareness of any eternal perspective. She has forgotten that pounds don't matter to God, and that she can be a happier person caring about others than she ever can worrying about her waistline. If the parents can share this perspective with her in scriptural study and earnest prayer, the Spirit of the Lord will whisper the peace and softening of heart that may help her recognize more fundamental priorities. The guidance of the Holy Spirit will be vital in helping her recognize the deceptions of current fashions and short-sighted goals.

Sometimes striving for perfection, on the part of parents or children, leads to looking only for the "bottom line," or end point, as the symbol of achievement. Such a concept is an unnecessarily harsh one by which to judge ourselves or our children. Our direction is more important than our position at any given time.

Finally, remember that parents have needs, too. It can be very frightening to have a daughter behaving so irrationally and dangerously. Parents must seek God's help not just for their child, but for themselves as well, to remain steadfast and loving. They can know through their prayers that he is aware of his daughter, also, and her needs. He, too, will be on her side.

FEARS

(SEE ANXIETY DISORDERS; STRESS)

FINANCIAL RESPONSIBILITY

The Lord has asked that we be wise stewards over his gifts and blessings to us; if we are, he will then bless us with even more. "And whoso is found a faithful, a just, and a wise steward shall enter into the joy of his Lord, and shall inherit eternal life." (D&C 51:19.)

Stewardship and accountability are integral parts of the plan of salvation. Throughout the scriptures we see the Lord's children giving accounting of their stewardships—stewardships that are not only spiritual but also temporal.

MONEY MANAGEMENT

Money management comes easily for some, but for others it can cause frustration, conflict, and unhappiness. Money can be a blessing or a burden. It can provide for life's necessities, helping families "prepare every needful thing," allowing them to be of greater service to others and the Church. Or it can become an odious form of idolatry, where acquisition becomes all-important, either because people do not have enough or because they have too much.

The Lord counsels: "Lay up for yourselves treasures in heaven, where neither moth nor rust doth corrupt, and where thieves do not break through nor steal.

"For where your treasure is, there will your heart be also." (3 Nephi 13:20–21.)

There is no one right way to handle money in a family. Each family's situation differs. The number of children, their ages, the family's income and needs, all make up the base for a financial plan.

Financial problems come to most people, whether they have a lot of money or very little. What makes the difference is *having a plan* that includes individual and family needs and wants, *discussing this plan* together as a family, *budgeting for the necessities* first and using leftover money wisely, *knowing where the money is spent* (keeping a record), *having reasonable expectations* of what the family can and can't afford, and *avoiding debt, wastefulness, and impulse buying.* "For many, enough is not an amount—it is an attitude. And if a family is content to live on what they can earn, and no more, then they will almost always have enough. Enough, at least, to be happy." (Orson Scott Card, *Ensign,* June 1978, p. 17.)

Parents can help prepare their children to be wise stewards

over their finances by teaching them very early how to manage money.

ALLOWANCES

An allowance is a regular amount of money given to each child in a family. There are many ways to give allowances, but two different methodologies seem to underlie most parents' decisions. In the first, money is given as a gift or privilege to a child because each family member shares in the whole aspect of family life and thus shares in the benefits of the family income. Spending money is given to children to help pay for personal items, activities, and other needs. Though their allowance is not tied to doing specific tasks, chores or jobs are still assigned and completed, as that too is part of the whole aspect of family life.

The second method directly relates to the various jobs a child does in the home. The allowance thus becomes an income paid for work performed. With this approach, certain jobs are assigned and an allowance is paid for completion. Most parents do not pay for every job performed, as keeping records for all jobs can become extremely tiresome, and these parents usually feel that certain jobs should be done just because a person belongs to the family. Such family membership at times requires service and cooperation and work without pay.

Many families use a combination of these methods. And some families substitute points, small rewards, or praise for money.

An allowance can help teach children about agency, responsibility, decision making, job standards, work habits, record keeping, saving, dependability, and good judgment. By using it well they can learn to plan for needs, budgeting their means so as to live within them. Most important, it can teach children what it means to pay a full tithe and save for a mission, school, or marriage.

With allowances wise parents also help children with a spending plan. They take them shopping, explaining the cost of various items, showing them the amount in coins and bills, letting them give the money to the cashier, explaining how the expenditure fits into the family budget.

Whatever system of allowances parents decide upon, the following points should be considered:

1. Make the payment system simple, so that both parent and child understand it. For example, the child might receive his regular allowance each Saturday to be his spending money for the week. Or perhaps the child could perform each task on a job list for the week and be paid allowance at the end of that week.

2. Be consistent in the payment.

3. Decide in advance what will be said and done if family expectations are not met or jobs are not completed. For instance, one young mother wanted her children to learn responsibility and the consequence of irresponsibility. The children were required to complete assigned jobs within a certain period of time in the week. If one child did not do an assigned job, she would pay another child to do it and deduct the cost from the first child's allowance.

4. Consider the ages of the children and their money needs in deciding how much allowance to pay. Usually the amount will start out small and increase as the children's financial needs change.

5. Decide if savings accounts, missionary funds, fast offerings, schooling costs, and other such items are to come out of the children's allowance. Make an exact list of items for which the children are responsible.

6. Discuss the allowance amount with your children. Be sure they feel the plan is fair.

7. Balance flexibility with firmness.

8. Periodically assess with your children how the allowance plan is working and what they are learning about financial responsibility.

THE VALUE OF WORK

One mother with young children wanted to start early to teach them the value of work. She assigned each of her three children to do two jobs for her each day. She worked with the children, showing them how to do the jobs correctly. Then she let each child do his or her own jobs alone each day. As they completed the tasks they moved two "helping hands" up a chart. At the end of the week she gave a small reward if they reached the top of the chart. The children did not receive money allowances, but they were given lots of praise and positive reinforcement throughout the week. Small treats, a trip to the library or zoo, or other activities were the rewards at the end of the week.

One wise father taught his son that he could use the family car so long as he paid the costs of operation. The son had also been taught that there were family rules connected with the use of the car. He obeyed these rules and considered the use of the car a privilege. He had also learned the value of hard work as well as the value of money. As he used the car he began to calculate what it was costing him from his earnings. He soon decided to ride his bike to work and other places to save his money. The father was proud of the way his son had exercised his agency and shown responsibility.

Another family developed a Job Book system. Each child in the family has a three-ring binder with several copies of a family form inside. The form lists the assigned job, the date to be accomplished, the job's value, special instructions, and a place to check off when the task is completed. The children also record a running total of cash coming in to their accounts and cash being paid out.

Other families draw up contracts with their children from time to time. A child may want an item that is quite expensive. Parents could have the child work around the home to earn a certain portion of the money needed to buy the item. Then the parents could "match" the child's earnings or pay the remaining cost.

Whatever system of allowance is used in a family (or even if no allowances are given), children can be taught from an early age that basic gospel principles of industry, honesty, agency, responsibility, and stewardship are important. Children can also learn the principle of reward as taught in the scriptures: "Be ye strong therefore, and let not your hands be weak: for your work shall be rewarded." (2 Chronicles 15:7.)

FRIENDS

Joseph Smith said that friendship is one of the grand fundamental principles of Mormonism. It "is like Brother Turley in his blacksmith shop welding iron to iron; it unites the human family with its happy influences." (*Teachings of the Prophet Joseph Smith*, p. 316.) Friends respect each other, care about each other, remain true, and overlook and forgive each other's faults. Our Heavenly Father wants us to be friends to all his children. "This is my commandment, That ye love one another, as I have loved you." (John 15:12.)

A child's first friends are family members. The first school-house is the home, and parents are the first teachers. Their example of friendship, therefore, is all-important.

Parents could do as the wise mother robin. She builds a secure nest for her little ones, feeds and nurtures them. Then when it is time for them to fly she gently and lovingly nudges them out of the nest. They glide to the ground, their wings fluttering—unsure, afraid, not yet knowing how to fly. Then the mother goes down to the ground and teaches them how to find food, and she teaches them to fly. She wants to help them to be on their own.

The following are ways that parents might use to help their children learn to be strong on their own:

1. Refrain from comparing one child with another. "The child who is compared will tend to feel he lives in a world of superiors and inferiors and that his place is only secure as long as he is able to put others down. This is disastrous for constructive social living. . . .

"When mother is noncomparing, trusting, interested in people, and genuinely interested in what the child does, he will tend to be encouraged to relate to people in cooperative, constructive ways." (G. Hugh Allred, *Mission for Mothers: Guiding the Child* [Salt Lake City: Bookcraft, 1968], p. 83.)

2. Introduce children to the outside world in ways that build their self-confidence. Letting a child enjoy the company of other children will help him or her adjust. As children play games with friends, they learn to observe rules, to be considerate of others, and to share.

The Church provides many opportunities for children to play, work, and learn together in the nursery and Primary. As they have experiences together, knowing that parents are close by, they prepare themselves for greater independence.

If children are timid, parents may have to nudge them a little to help them overcome this shyness. Encouraging them to play with others will usually be all that is necessary. Parents might also plan birthday parties or other group outings. Being firm and kind without being harsh gives a child direction.

Meeting grown-ups can be very difficult, and a child may try to avoid unfamiliar people altogether. Saying such things as, "Brad is a friendly person when he gets to know people well," shows consideration for the child's feelings and avoids embarrassing him or the person he is introduced to. Never say such things as "Brad is my shy child," in his presence. If parents practice with the children what to say and do in different situations, they may feel more at ease.

3. Another supportive approach is to have prayer with children, helping them to talk their problems over with Heavenly Father. But be careful not to create problems in the children's minds that they do not see to be problems. Some parents have been known to use prayers in a manipulative manner. Prayer must be sincere and from the children's own hearts. Then they can learn to rely on the Lord's strength.

THE PEER GROUP

During the teenage years, the influence of peers usually becomes increasingly important. While elementary-school-age children hold closer loyalties to parents and teachers, older children tend to listen more to their peers. In their search for acceptance, youth frequently slight parents, rejecting them in ways that are both overt and subtle. Parents who try to hold on too tightly become very unhappy. As children move more and more into the peer realm, they increasingly find that they don't want or need the constant attention of their parents. Parents who do not understand this development often view this rejection as a betrayal.

Parents need to understand that there is in youth an instinct to be part of a group. They organize clubs, group together at play, and want to feel accepted by their peers. They dress and talk alike. They want to be part of the *in* crowd. Wise parents can guide this need toward worthwhile experiences. The Church, for example, offers many social activities where youth can be together with others who have the same standards.

Parents should foster recreational activities that satisfy this urge for social relationship. Dancing, skating, and skiing parties; sleigh-riding, hiking, home music or videos; a dinner with a group at a canyon park or a barbecue in the backyard over the grill are certainly more desirable than many activities from the world that promote idleness and cater to the appetites and passions. Parents need to be involved as much as wisdom dictates in sponsoring the location and activities for such socials.

Parents can also help youth choose appropriate activities for themselves. Instill in them the desire to ask the following questions when they plan socials: "Is this the kind of event that I, in all good conscience, could ask the Lord to bless with his Spirit?" "Would I be willing to have my father, mother, sister, or brother come to this place for their recreation?" "How would I feel if I saw my church leaders here?"

Young men and women are likely to find their life's companion in the social atmospheres they frequent most. If they know this, they will plan more wholesome activities. Group dating is not only safe, it's fun. The same is true about wholesome activities; they're more fun than questionable pursuits.

Teenagers are usually insecure about their place in a group. They sometimes feel awkward. Since peer acceptance is so important to them, they at times become discouraged, feeling that others are more beautiful, more talented, more popular—happier in some way—than they are. Discouragement and feelings of low self-worth can be harmful, especially when youth are taught by movies, television, and advertising that this time of life should be filled with exciting social relationships, yet they find few or no relationships in their own life.

Parents can help their teenagers by showing them that individual worth in the Lord's eyes is not tied to social acceptance. The Lord's approval and friendship should be sought before all others. Elder Marvin J. Ashton said, "If we properly understand our relationship to God and His to us, we will not have moments, days, or lives spent in wondering, 'What have I done to deserve this?' 'What does God have against me?' or, 'Why wasn't I born with the talents of my friends?' " (Ensign, November 1976, p. 85.)

People who spend all their energy wishing they had the talents of someone else often neglect and thus waste their own individual talents. Youth need to compare themselves only with their own potential, and they should take joy in their friends' accomplishments.

Children need to feel accepted by their peers, but they also need one or two very close friends: someone they can confide in and share their dreams, fears, and personal feelings with; someone who will be there all the time and won't laugh at them or put them down. Genuine friendship involves risk. It takes courage to let someone come to know us well. Parents should teach children that to have genuine friends they must also be genuine themselves. They should become the kind of friend they want to have. A true friend looks for the positive, has patience, and is understanding.

The Lord, by his example, clarified the responsibility of friends to one another. He stated: "Henceforth I call you not servants; for the servant knoweth not what his lord doeth; but I have called you friends; for all things that I have heard of my Father I have made known unto you." (John 15:15.)

The Lord taught by word and example that the most important of all things to his friends were the truths of his Father. We have the same assignment to be and teach what the Savior taught. This is what he meant when he said, "As the Father hath loved me, so have I loved you: continue ye in my love. . . . These things have I spoken unto you, that my joy might remain in you, and that your joy might be full. This is my commandment, That ye love one another, as I have loved you. Greater love hath no man than this, that a man lay down his life for his friends." (John 15:9, 11–13.)

No matter how a parent tries, there still may be times when a child will come sobbing, "No one likes me. I don't have any friends." The parent, asking Heavenly Father for guidance, can then work to reestablish the child's self-worth. Parents should avoid such statements as, "That's not true, you have lots of friends." It is better to ask, "What makes you feel like that?" and then listen carefully, reaffirm parental love, point out good qualities in the child's character, and offer support.

One mother taught her daughter that as long as one of the friends never gives up, friendship will never die. A child's true value is what the child feels inside, not the number of friends he or she has.

LEADERS OR FOLLOWERS

Sometimes it may be necessary to stand up against friends. Children then learn what it means to become leaders, rather than followers.

It is painful to see a child forming alliances with others who are poor models of behavior and violate gospel standards. When a child is very young, parents can usually control friendships completely; but, like it or not, the older children get, the less control parents have. This is as it should be, as the opportunity to make choices is an important ingredient in the maturing process. Teenagers are especially apt to resent attempts by parents to choose their friends. It is usually not a good idea to forbid children to see a particular friend, since they are likely to go ahead seeing the friend secretly anyway. This takes all control out of the parents' hands. No longer can they determine place or kind of activity.

A more effective approach is to encourage children to invite their friends home and to be friendly with them. If the friend has characteristics or values that are different from those one's own child has grown up with, these are likely to stand out more clearly against the backdrop of the home environment. In this situation the friend may lose some luster, and a bad relationship is more likely to be weakened. It is also possible that bad friends can be influenced for the good.

As most children mature and develop, unlike the young robin who flies away, they will almost always turn back to their first friendships at home. So parents who are coping with problem friends can take heart; if their child is more influenced by peers than family, they should just be patient. Time is on their side.

GAMBLING

Gambling can occur almost anywhere—from a seemingly inconsequential Bingo game to compulsive wagering leading to financial disaster. We gamble when we offer something of value hoping to gain something of greater value with little or no other effort on our part.

God's plan is not a game of chance. The gospel teaches us that life, from pre-earthly existence through mortality, is to be planned, full, and constant. Luck, or success dependent on chance, is not a factor in our progress. Eternal success depends on following a plan righteously, not on random, uncontrolled occurrences.

People gamble because of pride, conceit, greed (wanting something for nothing), inordinate cravings for adventure or excitement, or a fatalism that makes good luck seem more possible than it is. Whatever the reason, "the church . . . is opposed to any game of chance, occupation, or so-called business which takes money from the person who may be possessed of it without giving value received in return." (Heber J. Grant, *Improvement Era*, September 1926, p. 1100.)

The laws of probability or odds of winning usually can be easily calculated, and inevitably favor whoever is sponsoring the game. A gambling house almost always has a much better chance of winning than does the patron. Slot machines are preset to take in a percentage of money from all that goes in. The only chance the owners of such machines are taking is whether a patron plays or not. It is of little concern to them that someone will win, since most will lose. People, choosing to ignore this reality, somehow feel that the natural laws governing these games do not apply to them. This is folly.

Also, those who gamble for a livelihood are disregarding scriptural admonitions such as: "In the sweat of thy face shalt thou eat bread, till thou return unto the ground." (Genesis 3:19.) This statement emphasizes that we are required to labor honestly for all we receive.

There is also a tremendous temptation for gamblers to enhance their chances of winning by cheating, thereby reducing their integrity and honor.

Potentially the most dangerous aspect of gambling is the craving for excitement. People may feel they have "good luck," or crave the constant exhilaration of unknown outcomes. This craving can become an addiction that causes the person to bet on anything—an athletic event, a horse race, or just the toss of a coin. As this addiction grows, winning or losing becomes secondary to the need to gamble. It can be as potentially harmful as alcoholism, drug abuse, or immorality.

The possible result of such a craving is illustrated by the story of a middle-aged man and his family who lived in a small town on the east coast of the United States. They were the owners of a small but successful business. The father's enjoyment for an occasional bet progressed to a passion, and then to compulsion. As they left to move west, they strapped a mattress on the roof of their car and put their clothing in the trunk. This was all that was left. The family unit eventually disintegrated.

For most who gamble, the time spent betting is the greatest expense. Gambling does not edify, and generally it takes place in unwholesome surroundings not suited to spirituality. When all evidence is assembled, gambling simply has no redeeming value to account for the time spent.

Concerning card playing, Elder Bruce R. McConkie has said: "Members of the Church should not belong to bridge or other type of card clubs, and they should neither play cards nor have them in their homes. By cards is meant, of course, the spotted face cards used by gamblers. To the extent that church members play cards they are out of harmony with their inspired leaders. Innocent non-gambling games played with other types of cards, except for the waste of time in many instances, are not objectionable." (*Mormon Doctrine*, 2nd ed. [Salt Lake City: Bookcraft, 1966], p. 113.)

Concerned parents will make every effort to keep their children free from the problems of gambling. Here are some ideas:

1. Be an example by not participating in gambling. This significantly reduces a child's exposure to gambling. Avoid "pools" on athletic events, card games, involvement with lotteries, or mini-vacations to gambling areas. Usually the children must either remain at home or in restricted areas of a gambling house during such vacations.

2. Explain the odds of losing to youth who are old enough to understand, or who are interested. For example, explain that a person who puts money on a single number while playing roulette has one chance in thirty-five of winning. Explain that to just break even, enough resources should be available to bet at least thirty-five times. Of course this is not a guarantee: There may be two or three groups of thirty-five numbers without a win, only to have a number come up three or four times in the fourth group of thirty-

five. Certainly there is a chance of winning, one in thirty-five, over time.

3. Talk about the environment associated with serious gambling: alcohol, tobacco, varying degrees of dishonesty (or at least deception and advantage taking), immodesty, and usually unwholesome entertainment. Again, this explanation will only be effective if parents themselves have not frequented the places they feel are undesirable for their children.

4. Provide recreational activities for the children. Find activities that are both beneficial and fun for the child and for the family group. Gambling may be fun temporarily, but it is never beneficial or uplifting.

5. Teach children that the reason the media reports lottery and sweepstakes winners is because so few people win that it is newsworthy when someone does.

6. Elder Dallin H. Oaks warns that "gambling's most far-reaching and evil influence" may be that "it dulls the spiritual sensitivities of those who participate in it." Without the companionship of the Lord's Spirit, "we are vulnerable to temptations, prone to criticize, and subject to being tossed to and fro and buffeted by the forces of the world and the works of the evil one." (*Ensign*, March 1986, p. 16.)

The high stakes of losing the Holy Spirit seem reason enough not to gamble.

GOAL SETTING

(SEE PLANNING FOR THE FUTURE)

GRANDPARENTS

Because we believe that families should be and can be eternal, we recognize the importance of close ties with those who have gone before us and those who come after us. Joseph Fielding Smith, speaking of the eternal family, has said: "Neither is it enough that the family unit be preserved. Each generation must be joined to the one that went before. . . . Adam presides, and each patriarch is to preside under him from generation to generation down to the end of time in one grand family." (*The Way to Perfection* [Salt Lake City: Deseret Book, 1975], p. 253.)

A family circle that expands to include grandparents reaps a greater harvest of the benefits and rewards of family relationships: more love, more understanding, more consideration, more respect, and even more security. It is another example of turning the hearts of the children to the fathers. It is not reasonable to think that the hearts of the children should turn only to those who have died and are found only on genealogical records. Alex Haley, who focused the eyes of the world on their "roots," said, "We must turn around especially one inevitably weakening process, which is that fewer and fewer children—black and white alike—are experiencing yesteryear's close exposures to loving grandparents. I think that nobody else can give children, especially toddlers through preteens, quite that irrational love of grandparents. In their own singular way, grandparents somehow sort of sprinkle a sense of stardust over grandchildren." (As quoted in *Exchange*, May 1987, p. 26.)

A warm and loving grandparent can be a pronounced influence in the life of a child, either reinforcing the teachings of the parent or reaching the child when a parent has not been able to. That warmth and love is most often felt and reciprocated by the child. The grandparent-child relationship is special and magic.

Many people tell of having patterned their lives after grandparents who exemplified service, love, generosity, charity, patience, humility, and integrity. A grandparent can be an important example, adding to the child's security and peace.

Some of the things a grandparent can help a child to do are:

1. *Feel wanted.* A grandparent encourages visits by having things available that the children can be interested in, such as toys, books, paper and crayons, and a place to play. The toys at Grandma's house are always novel—different from their own. There may even be a train, a chair, or doll cupboard that the children's own parent used to play with when he or she was a child in Grandma's house. Children with such a grandparent

know they are wanted. They don't visit out of a sense of duty; they want to come.

Also, all children fear losing their parents. Knowing that grandparents are there, who will love them and nurture them, can give grandchildren peace of mind.

2. *Feel important.* What children could doubt their own self-worth when grandparents take time and often travel many miles to attend their programs, talks, graduations, or other important events; or if they live too far away, send cards, letters, or give special attention to the children in weekly family letters? Neither time nor distance must be allowed to crowd out these valuable friendships. Some grandparents send a book and a tape so that small children can hear the grandparent's voice reading to them as they look at the pictures and turn the pages. Telephone calls to the children on special occasions help make them feel important and secure. There is no favoritism or comparisons; each child feels that complete importance. Teenagers and young adults are especially affected by the undaunted confidence and faith in them shown by grandparents.

3. *Feel spiritual.* One woman who has no brothers or sisters active in the Church gives credit for her spiritual growth to her grandmother, with whom she spent considerable time in her childhood. A grandfather checks on all areas of his small grandchildren's spiritual growth while he holds them on his lap and talks about what they learn in Primary, how they love Jesus, how they love their family. Young people are impressed with the importance of the gospel as they see grandparents leave their home and loved ones to go on missions. Grandparents who show by both word and example that the gospel is of vital importance in their own lives often inspire these feelings in others. Those who write journals leaving their testimonies as a legacy may influence generations to come. A grandparent can teach children to be good citizens, love their fellowmen, and obey their Heavenly Father.

4. *Feel pride in family.* As grandparents share events from the past, they can teach children that what they have today is built on what others did before. They can inspire in them a desire to do as well for those who come after them. As grandparents encourage family reunions and outings and show pride and joy in all their extended family, grandchildren can feel that same pride,

knowing that they belong to something special and significant—
a good family.

5. *Feel capable.* Grandparents can encourage talents and interests, remembering that each child is unique in both talents and
needs. Perhaps they can offer incentives for the child to work a
little harder, to be persistent. Frustrations of teen years, fear of
not living up to expectations of parents and teachers, even feelings
of not being able to attract and hold friends can be soothed as
grandparents encourage and express confidence and admiration.

6. *Feel happy.* Through both precept and example, grandparents can teach a child to be happy, to be optimistic, to have faith.
Their capacity to enjoy and love life, their sense of honor, their
ability to have fun with their grandchildren, to stay involved, and
to smile through adversity will have a lasting influence.

HOW GRANDPARENTS CAN BENEFIT PARENTS

The primary responsibility of raising a child lies with the
parents, but there are things that grandparents can do to help
parents with this important role. They can show love, moral support, and encouragement. Listening is vital, and sharing ideas and
wisdom is usually helpful, but grandparents must recognize that
it is the parents' role to make the decisions and the family rules,
and grandparents must respect them. Grandparents, in spite of
the slogan on the popular button, "If Mother says no, ask
Grandma," must never counteract parents' discipline, even if they
believe it to be too strict or too indulgent. And grandparents must
see that children do not play grandparents against parents.

Grandparents can be of physical help in raising a child as
well. Sometimes a mother really needs extra hands, an extra lap,
or even an extra voice to read or tell stories to the little ones as
she encounters emergencies or even a crisis. No one can provide
them better than a grandparent. Even in times of no emergency,
a day or afternoon off from child care once in a while is just what
a mother needs. Single parents, especially, have a real need for
both the moral and physical support that can be lovingly given
by grandparents.

HOW PARENTS CAN BENEFIT GRANDPARENTS

"People everywhere, of all ages, want about the same things from life, something to do that is worthwhile, someone to love, a place to live where they feel comfortable, secure, and healthy. Older people who feel that they are not wanted, needed, or noticed often face more stress that they can stand. Family members can help greatly to lessen this stress by respecting older members' experience, seeking their opinions, and involving them in appropriate activities. Family members should not take offense at disposition and personality changes that occur with the aging process." (*Relief Society Course of Study*, 1975–76, p. 105.)

Most grandparents have few needs, but the ones they do have are often the very ones that are forgotten. Their own children, their most important reason for living, can be paramount in providing for those needs.

A young family can feel free to live its own life. Family members need not feel that they must do all things as their parents did. But a proper respect for custom and tradition is always encouraging to grandparents.

As all people's greatest need is to feel loved and wanted, parents can see that grandparents are included in important family activities. Most of them like to be invited to Sunday dinners, to talks and entertainments the family is involved in. Parents should let grandparents know what is going on in the family. Often they feel forgotten, left out, uninformed. If they live too far away for most of these things, letters and phone calls give them something to look forward to. Don't worry that there is no spectacular news. Just knowing that someone is thinking of them, caring about them, and wanting them included in the family's life gives them joy. Grandparents, too, need feelings of self-worth, and family is the most important provider of them.

Parents can encourage good relationships among children and grandparents. Again, example leads the way. As parents love and care, children love and care. One grateful grandfather, a recipient of care and affection shown by his own children and grandchildren, gives credit to his wife, who showed them the way by tenderly caring for her own mother and stepfather through many years of old age. Her loving example has been duplicated by her own children and grandchildren.

Parents can help children understand the natural process of growing older, remembering that grandparents' activities should be less strenuous. While parents are giving grandparents opportunities to feel needed, they should keep in mind that grandparents should be left options for the use of their time. They need chances and encouragement to pursue interests of their own, developing skills and learning new ones. Parents should not demand grandparents' time for their own selfish reasons. Their energy is not as boundless as it was at a younger age, as parents observed it when they lived at home with them. Nevertheless, using good judgment and observing grandparents' interest and abilities, parents can give them opportunities to help.

Sometimes families have special problems with grandparents. Some may be too independent, while others are too dependent. Some have serious health problems that prove to be a hardship on the family. Some have personality changes that cause discord and heartbreak. Whatever the problem, their own children and grandchildren should help them feel loved and wanted. Nowhere in instructions from our Heavenly Father do we find an excuse to abandon them. Instead, we are told, "Honour thy father and thy mother," and, "Cast me not off in the time of old age; forsake me not when my strength faileth." (Exodus 20:12; Psalm 71:9.)

A family of six daughters were very concerned as their beloved elderly mother lay helpless in her last years. Her patriarchal blessing had promised that her last days would be the happiest days of her life. How could a hard-working, independent woman be happy when she had to be attended night and day by her family? Her prayer had been never to be a burden. But one day, as the daughters were around her bed, she looked up at them and said lovingly, "These are the happiest days of my life, because now I know you love me."

"It is the duty of children to care for their parents. Before placing parents or family members in a nursing home or other extended care facility, family members and priesthood leaders should consult together and prayerfully determine the best course of action. Parents should not be placed in institutions solely as a convenience to their children." (Welfare Services Resource Handbook, p. 45.)

HOW CHILDREN CAN BENEFIT GRANDPARENTS

Children can be a blessing to grandparents by visiting them as often as possible, bringing them up-to-date on their activities and interests. They can show their love by helping grandparents around the house and yard. Phone calls, letters, pictures, and invitations to programs, talks, and special events also help greatly. Children's sharing their talents will bring pride and joy to grandparents' hearts. But the greatest pride and joy a grandparent can have comes from seeing the child be honest, industrious, studious, and faithful to the gospel; in other words, be a credit to the family.

As grandparents and great-grandparents get older, children should be taught to be considerate of their age, to speak slowly and clearly if they are hard of hearing. Sometimes older people are embarrassed to ask a person to repeat, so they miss out on the conversation or have a misconception of what is said. If eyesight is failing, a grandchild can read to them. Let them enjoy the company, but don't stay so long that the grandparents become fatigued. If grandparents are very ill, perhaps all that a child can do is hug them or squeeze a hand, but that will let them feel loved. They will know and care.

If children have no living grandparents, they can look around for other elderly people who have this need, this yearning, and "adopt" them. This has brought joy and meaning to many of both generations.

When it is necessary to have a grandparent living in the home, children should be taught that this can be a blessing. As parents, children, and grandparents accept the arrangement and show pleasure in it, a home is filled with more love, more compassion, and all the attributes of a Christlike life. There will be difficulties; honoring fathers and mothers would not have had to be a commandment if it were easy. We must put forth thought, love, and effort. But the rewards are great, especially in the eternal perspective: Children learn respect, responsibility, compassion, and more of God's plan.

HOW GRANDPARENTS CAN BENEFIT THEMSELVES

Grandparents can help themselves by following good eating habits, exercising, and maintaining a positive attitude about life. These are things they can control. They can't control the death of a spouse or other loved ones, or many of the aches, pains, and infirmities that come with age, but they can control to a great extent what they let these do to their lives. Attitude makes the difference. As one elderly lady said as she took care of her dying ninety-three-year-old husband, "It can't be a burden if I don't let it."

"Those who find themselves alone as old age approaches should remember that the gospel is based on love and service, two things that all of us can give as long as we are allowed to remain on earth." (*Relief Society Courses of Study*, 1975–76, p. 105.) One thing grandparents can do is accept with serenity what is required of them. Grandparents who are too demanding, or too stubbornly independent, or who grumble at their unfortunate lot, are not showing love or service. They make themselves miserable and spread that misery to those whose responsibility it is to serve them. "Enduring to the end" was not meant to be done with "weeping and wailing and gnashing of teeth," but with blessed acceptance and persistent faith in a loving Heavenly Father who knows and understands and loves us still. That, too, is a service. That is love.

HANDICAPPED CHILDREN

(SEE DISABILITIES)

HOMOSEXUALITY

(SEE SEXUAL DEVIANCE)

HONESTY

(SEE CHEATING; LYING; STEALING)

HOUSEHOLD CHORES

From the very beginning, the Lord commanded Adam to till the earth and have dominion over the beasts of the field, to eat his bread by the sweat of his brow. Often the scriptures have admonished us to cease to be idle and to be productive in all of our labors. The commandments given to Adam were spiritual, for the Lord himself said that he never gave to Adam a temporal commandment. (See D&C 29:35.) Work, then, as instituted in the beginning of this earth, is a spiritual principle.

Work is also an essential principle. Parents need to teach their children the value of work, the responsibility of belonging to a family, and the joy of service. Elder L. Tom Perry tells us, "I believe that second only to ensuring that every child receives an understanding of the gospel of our Lord and Savior is teaching them the joy of honest labor." (*Ensign*, November 1986, p. 66.)

The joy of honest labor and the joy of serving others are very similar; in fact, often they are the same. King Benjamin told his people to teach their children "to walk in the ways of truth and soberness . . . [and] to love one another, and to serve one another." (Mosiah 4:15.) As children are taught to work and fulfill their responsibilities, they need to look at it as an opportunity to serve others out of love, not drudgery. Happiness can be obtained by establishing the proper balance between serving and being served. The task of teaching this attitude to children is not a simple one.

Children need the training that comes through having responsibility and learning to work and serve others. An ideal home is like an apprentice shop where children learn skills, habits, responsibility, dependability, self-discipline, and love. It is especially important that children are trained to develop self-discipline. It's not difficult to learn to make a bed; the challenge lies in making it *every* day. And children who gain mastery over little things (such as making beds) will have power over greater things.

There are many other rewards that come from learning to work. Talents and skills are developed. We follow our prophet's guidance to be neat, clean, and well-kept, and to practice proper stewardship of this earth. Good work habits are attained. Working as families helps companionship grow.

How do parents teach children to work? Here are some ideas to consider:

1. Exhibit a proper attitude toward work. Help your child realize that work is a blessing, not a burden. Parents' attitude toward work is reflected in their children. If they have a positive outlook toward their responsibilities and role in life, their children are likely to share the same positive outlook. President Joseph F. Smith gave us this counsel: "We should never be discouraged in those daily tasks which God has ordained to the common lot of man. Each day's labor should be undertaken in a joyous spirit and with the thought and conviction that our happiness and eternal welfare depend upon doing well that which we ought to do, that which God has made it our duty." (Gospel Doctrine [Salt Lake City: Deseret Book, 1939], p. 285.)

Children should be taught early in life the joy that comes from starting and finishing a job that is the workmanship of their own hands. As the old saying goes, "Happy is the man who has work he loves to do; happy is the man who loves the work he has to do."

A group of girls were complaining about the task of doing the dishes in their homes. One girl spoke up to say that she enjoyed washing the dishes. The surprised friends asked her why she felt that way. She explained that when she first was given the responsibility of the dishes she had complained to her mother. The wise mother shared her own attitude that doing dishes was going to be a lifelong job, so she had decided to make it fun. The daughter then purposely made up games, songs, and exciting things to think about while she washed her dishes. This became a habit and made dishwashing fun. All work can become a rewarding experience if approached with the proper attitude.

2. Guide carefully. Don't just tell children to do a job. Show them how. As adults we sometimes forget that some tasks that seem relatively clear-cut and simple to us may be confusing or overwhelming to a child. A mother may say to her daughter, "Please clean up your room," and then assume that if it is not done within a reasonable period of time the girl is disobedient and lazy. But it may be that the girl does not know how to proceed, or she may know through past experience that no matter how hard she tries, her mother will not be satisfied with her efforts.

It is important for parents to provide training and success experiences in order for their children to feel competent. It may be necessary to work side by side with children several times until they can proceed confidently on their own. Building a positive relationship between the parent and child is just as important as getting the work done.

Help young children make their beds every morning for some time. Then by the time they are physically able to handle the task, making their beds has become a habit. Take the time to really train children to clean the bathroom, work in the kitchen, bake cookies, sweep the floor, or care for the yard. Install low shelves and low clothing rods so it is easy to put things away. Performing a task is easy, if one knows how, and children become willing workers when their chances for doing a job successfully are insured.

"Behold, mine house is a house of order, saith the Lord God, and not a house of confusion." (D&C 132:8.) Order is an eternal principle—an important characteristic of the kingdom of God. We are instructed to follow the pattern and set our own houses in order. As God has given us guidance, so should we give it to our children. An orderly home depends upon well-defined and well-understood rules.

Parents should remember that children are always watching. Parents teach what they are and do, more than what they say. Why should children keep things clean if the parent never does? Why should they work with a smile if the parent grumbles and groans?

3. Organize work. "Have you put away your toys?" "Have you fed the dog?" "Have you mowed the lawn?" Constant reminding is not pleasant for a parent or a child. When work is organized and systematic the home runs much more smoothly. Chore lists are one good way to organize work. They eliminate interrupting, nagging, reminding, and forgetting. Lists can be posted on the bulletin board, the wall, the side of the refrigerator, or under each child's breakfast plate. Children also enjoy a "job jar," from which each child draws a given number of slips of paper with chores listed on them.

Deadlines help organize work for children. A family policy could be that no one is served breakfast until he or she is washed and dressed. (It takes a child about two minutes to dress before breakfast and about two hours afterwards.) The policy could further state that no child may leave for school or play until basic morning chores are done, such as making the bed and putting the bathroom in order, dusting the furniture, helping in the kitchen or carrying out the garbage. Evening projects may not be started until the children have done their homework, completed their music practicing, and other responsibilities.

When a child is old enough to work in the kitchen, parents might assign him or her one meal a week to plan, prepare, and clean up. They could work out a menu plan the Saturday before. This gives parents the opportunity to work with the child to teach good nutrition, cooking techniques, and efficient clean up.

Some parents make contracts with their children to do larger tasks. It is agreed upon between the parent and child what is expected and when the task will be completed. Others have used cards that spell out exactly what each job entails. Step-by-step instruction may be included. The ways to organize are limitless, and the need is great.

4. Be consistent. Even though the type of job may vary from day to day, children should be fulfilling some kind of responsibility every day. Parents should decide what they expect and then stick to it. Children will soon accept their responsibilities as a matter of routine. Exceptions could be holidays, birthdays, when a child is ill, or when some special activity or opportunity presents itself. These exceptions are a sign of fairness, not inconsistency.

Being consistent also includes being patient, tender, and persistent. Sometimes the job may not be completed as well or as quickly as you or another family member could do it. Don't take that responsibility away from the child because it wasn't done perfectly, even if you become frustrated. Practice and love will make it improve. Sometimes it is difficult to find suitable jobs for youngsters, but they still need to be learning. Elder L. Tom Perry shared this story: "When my son was about three years old, I took him out to the garden to help me weed. I assumed that he, being low to the ground at the time, would have a real advantage at weeding. Unfortunately for my garden, he had a difficult time distinguishing between the weeds and the young plants.

"I then tried Lee at milking a cow we owned together with a

neighbor. He quickly developed the hand action of a fine milker, but, sadly, his aim was not very good. Whenever I checked on him, he was always surrounded by a white puddle, and the milk bucket was nearly empty. He would look up at me and smile proudly, and my initial inclination to be angry would quickly dissipate—but I was frustrated." (*Ensign*, November 1986, p. 63.)

5. Discipline effectively when necessary. There are times in every home when making work exciting, fun, easy, fair, and organized still doesn't get it done. In fact, conflict over household chores is a common source of disharmony in many families. When disharmony continues, effective discipline is necessary. Wise parents realize that discipline should be a learning experience, not a punishment: "A soft answer turneth away wrath." (Proverbs 15:1.)

There is no discipline in all the world like the discipline of love. The most effective way to discipline a child is through application of the law of cause and effect. Use of natural and logical consequences will eliminate much scolding, punishing, and nagging on the part of the parent.

If the children's dirty clothes are not put in the hamper or clothes chute, then the clothes cannot be washed by the mother. The children either wear dirty clothes or wash them themselves.

When children complain about doing dishes, the consequence is that anyone who is "too tired" or "too busy" to do the dishes is also "too tired" or "too busy" to receive any phone calls or watch television and must spend the evening resting in bed, with lights out and music off.

Being aroused from bed for a trip to the garage may be required for the child who leaves a bike out or forgets to set out the garbage cans.

Because it is difficult to think creatively during a moment of crisis, a wise parent may plan in advance what consequences could be used to fit certain circumstances.

In addition, as with any other problems, the use of good listening and clear message-sending techniques and reconciliation of differences is important when conflict exists over chores.

6. Show appreciation. As parents teach their children to carry a work assignment out to its completion, they should also teach them to take pride in what they accomplish. There is a real sat-

isfaction that comes from finishing a task, especially when it is the best work we know how to do. Children will do almost anything for a parent's smile, a nod of approval, or a sincere word of thanks. Besides expressing appreciation in the usual manner, parents might try some other ways: slipping notes under children's pillows or in lunch boxes, writing a poem, singing a special song. There are many unique ways to show love and appreciation.

No matter how small the task, the child should feel a special feeling of accomplishment. Housework can give children an opportunity to complete something successfully every day.

7. Organize family work projects. Work is not always an individual assignment. Families that work together, pray and study together, and play together reap many blessings. Family gardens are more useful than for just producing food. Who can gauge the value of that special chat between parent and child as they weed or water the garden? How do we evaluate the good that comes from the obvious lessons of planting, cultivating, and the eternal law of the harvest? And how do we measure the family togetherness and cooperating that must accompany successful canning? One man who grew a large vegetable garden was asked what he was growing. His reply was not the usual tomatoes, corn, and carrots, but simply, "Boys."

Family projects are as numerous and varied as the families who have them. Joseph B. Wirthlin, Jr., tells how all the children in his family worked in the family business as they were growing up. In that way his father helped them to learn about the value of work and to earn money. If they ran out of tasks, they knew he would find more for them, and he insisted that work be done well. He also taught them lessons about honor and integrity.

One final point to remember: as parents take the responsibility of teaching their children to work and become useful, happy adults, they always have Heavenly Father as a partner to help, if they will only ask.

HYPERACTIVITY

(SEE ATTENTION DEFICIT DISORDER)

IDENTITY

The need to belong to a group is an active desire for nearly all young people, even as early as three or four years of age. Most parents have seen the tears that come because "Jenny and Rachel don't want to play with me." The need to feel "a part of" seems always to remain.

Yet, for the child's own growth, there are times when he or she must choose to be "apart from," to choose a direction different from the group. How can we distinguish these times? The answer lies in finding an appropriate balance.

Seeking identity is a normal part of the struggle each person goes through. All of us want to know who we are. For the adolescent this search consists of a period of emotional risk taking, and how a parent perceives and responds to this period of development has a significant influence on the degree of conflict that may occur in a parent-child relationship.

Let's consider some of the issues that cloud a child or adolescent's life when searching for identity:

1. *The Follower.* When the desire to be included becomes too strong, children may give up their own identities, becoming, like the chameleon, whatever "color" the group wants them to be. As long as they can remain in the group, pleasing and following the peer leaders, they seem to be happy. Alone, they are often restless and unsure of themselves. Moreover, their sense of self-confidence resides in the hands of others. They have to be very sensitive to what pleases others in order to present themselves favorably, and therefore feel good about themselves. This is a precarious position to be in, because sometimes their peers are not very appreciative. "Follower" children then become confused and discouraged, feeling helpless to know how to behave.

2. *The Misdirected Leader.* Sometimes children who are talented enough, or attractive enough, or even brash enough to become "leaders" in the group, may build a false confidence in their abilities, excluding from their experience humility. Their pride may then lead them to a multitude of problems. They may seek to make their position of power stronger by excluding some and teasing and persecuting others less gifted than themselves.

Leaders, as declared by the Lord in D&C 121:36–38, always run the risk of exercising unrighteous dominion, making unfair demands upon the group, leading them into mischief or very real trouble because such leaders have set themselves above the usual requirements of most people. In order to maintain their position, they may feel forced to abrogate some of their standards, without realizing that they are no longer leading but being pushed.

3. *The Outsider.* Often there are children who have been hurt by rejection or persecution from groups like those we have discussed. Family problems, divorce, poverty, a different cultural background, or physical difficulties may move children to give up, defining themselves as misfits. Having defined themselves as such, they will find validation for these thoughts in the actions of other people, thus creating even greater isolation. Their self-esteem suffers. They begin to believe they won't do well at anything. The brotherhood of priesthood quorums or the warmth of Young Women's activities are avoided. Sometimes relationships with caring adults are even feared. When a child defines hurtful experiences as being "just me," each successive similar event builds a barrier even higher, separating the person from his or her God-given capabilities.

4. *The Rebel.* Rebellious children, like outsiders, may be reacting to get attention. Instead of feeling saddened or hurt by rejection, they choose to act as if they didn't care, "never wanted to be with those creeps, anyway." They may find others with similar feelings and create a new group with a welcome sense of belonging. On the other hand, having decided that they can't have what they want in the "good" group, they may decide to try being bad. The new group may create its identity by being opposed to everything for which the "good" group stands.

WHAT PARENTS CAN DO

Loving parents can begin to create a strong sense of belonging for each child in the home. The family is the first and primary group to which the child belongs, and all that we've said about groups applies to the family. Research suggests that creating a feeling in each child that he or she is precious and wanted is one of the most important elements for successful parenting.

The next step is to allow children to be themselves. As soon as they are capable, they should be allowed to make their own choices in small things such as what to wear, how to wear their hair, how to decorate their rooms, and so on. Children should also be encouraged to voice their own opinions (respectfully, of course).

"Finding one's own, intimate identity can be a great blessing in the life of every human being. Everyone can obtain it if he realizes it comes only through the light of truth or, as explained by the Savior, the light of life. In John 8: 12 we read, 'I am the light of the world: he that followeth me shall not walk in darkness, but shall have the light of life.' " (Victor L. Brown, *Ensign*, May 1983, pp. 60–62.)

Parents can also help their children differentiate between worthwhile criticism of things that can be worked on and the spiteful noise that sometimes comes out of the mouths of other insecure children. The loving strength that comes from the home must outweigh the pressures and criticism of peers.

Each of us has individual gifts and abilities that must be sought by physical and mental effort *and* by spiritual searching. "Seek ye earnestly the best gifts, always remembering for what they are given; For verily I say unto you, they are given for the benefit of those who love me and keep all my commandments. . . . For all have not every gift given unto them; for there are many gifts, and to every man is given a gift by the Spirit of God." (D&C 46:8–9, 11.) Parents can help their children establish their identity by recognizing and developing the children's gifts from God. Thus, when the child asks, "Who am I?" the answer that comes back will be specific, reflecting talents and gifts earned through ennobling effort. It is most important, however, that children continue to remember where those gifts come from. The humility that helps children accept themselves without a false confidence will help them accept others.

God has given us other helps in establishing our identity. Patriarchial blessings and other priesthood blessings are truly God-given definitions of a child's potential. And consistent scripture study is equally vital. "Can you imagine being away from home and receiving a letter from your parents and not bothering to open it or read it? This is what happens when we don't read these precious records. The holy scriptures are like letters from home telling us how we can draw near to our Father in Heaven. He tells us to come as we are. No one will be denied. He loves everyone." (Ardeth G. Kapp, *Ensign*, November 1985, pp. 93–95.) We can sense the love that God, our Heavenly Father, has in inviting us to remember our belonging in his family. This, after all, is where our true identity lies.

INCEST

(SEE SEXUAL ABUSE)

INFANT CARE

(SEE BABIES, NEW)

JEALOUSY

It seems that people experience jealousy at every age. A young child may see other children, even in the same family, with toys that look more attractive than his own. Teenagers may see friends who wear more expensive or stylish clothing than they themselves can afford, or they may see friends who find employment while they themselves can find none. Some may even lose their closest friends to competitive peers, and at times they may make statements like, "Why can our friends do this and we can't?" Even adults are not immune to jealousy. They covet money, positions, and titles. Making derogatory statements about fellow employees; tearing down successes of neighbors or relatives; even criticizing Church authorities, all are usually the result of jealousy.

Generally, jealousy reflects a lack of maturity and confidence in a person's own worth. Sometimes it appears as a misguided effort to satisfy unmet needs. Possibly keen competition has resulted in bitter defeat. Maybe past experiences have caused a history of mistrusting other people's motives and intentions. A misunderstanding or lack of facts may convey false impressions and wrong information.

Consider the following situations:

Bill and Steve have birthdays the same week. Bill got a shirt for his birthday that cost about the same as the presents his brothers and sisters received for their birthdays that year. Steve, however, got a new suit because he was turning twelve and his parents wanted him to look nice when passing the sacrament. Bill thinks it's unfair that Steve got more for his birthday than he did.

Mary and Susan were invited to a friend's party. Mary does well in sports and is always wanted on a team. Susan is on the honor roll at school, but nobody seems to pay much attention to that. At the party, Mary scored the winning point in a game and became an instant hero for being the best. It seemed like Mary was always the popular one and got all the attention whenever they were together. When Susan got home she said she would never go anywhere again with Mary.

Joan was first counselor in her Mutual class for several months. When the class president moved away and the presidency was reorganized, Joan thought she would be the new class president. It made her mad when they called a different girl to be class president after she had worked so hard. She felt like never going to class again.

The following suggestions may be helpful when trying to solve problems like the above:

1. Help children recognize and avoid false pride in physical possessions, worldly titles, or Church positions. These are fleeting and temporary. "Take heed, and beware of covetousness: for a man's life consisteth not in the abundance of the things which he possesseth." (Luke 12:15.)

2. Help children understand that we do not all have the same talents and abilities. The gifts of the Spirit are many and diverse. Explain to children that each person should seek to discover and nurture his or her own God-given strengths and talents. When individual differences are accepted in others, a peace settles on all concerned. Too often we compare our individual selves with the composite total of all the rest of humanity. We mistakenly group the collective strengths of everyone else and make these our own goals. This course will always bring defeat, especially to adolescents.

3. Praise children for their successes and help them minimize their failures. Emphasize what they have, not what they do not have. Point out blessings, joys, special qualities, and strong points. Look for the good in each circumstance. According to his own story, Thomas Edison learned over 100 ways *not* to make an electric light before he found a method that worked. People who feel good about their own lives have no need to be jealous of anyone else. Sometimes writing daily in a journal helps a person see the good in each experience.

4. Teach children to rejoice in the successes of others. Encourage them to give compliments and sincere praise when they see someone else do well. This is Christ's golden rule: "Whatsoever ye would that men should do to you, do ye even so to them." (Matthew 7:12.) It also fulfills Mosiah's request that each should "esteem his neighbor as himself." (Mosiah 27:4.) Some families send a friendly card or make a phone call to offer congratulations to others when they've done well. Handmade notes and awards are great.

5. Encourage patience in children. Help them to slow down and be content. Teach them to bloom where they're planted. Friendships, skills, and accomplishments take time to achieve. Teach children to find success in completing many short-term goals instead of waiting for the one big thing to come about. The mastery of a simple musical scale may be as encouraging as playing a lengthy masterpiece. A single piece of furniture for a newlywed couple can be as cherished as a whole houseful. In a world of immediate rewards, instant successes, and hard competition, it is easy to overlook the small joys—which are the ones that really matter anyway. We all should take time to achieve values that will endure for eternity. Many times young children may appear jealous in moments of stress or tiredness. Often all they need is some love and attention to restore their patience and perspective.

6. Teach children to live the principle of service. Enlarge their circle of concern and help them transfer some of their concern for themselves to concern for others. One father demonstrated this concept by comparing an onion with a rose. The onion is all wrapped up in itself. The rose, however, opens up its petals to reveal the beauties of its heart, and in so doing becomes desirable, fragrant, and a delight to have.

7. Help children to be realistic and to accept life as it is. Help them adjust and compensate when obstacles seem to cause defeat. Much can be learned through trial and error. Children may need to reset some goals or find a different way to accomplish them after they have tried many times and still not felt success. When one boy failed to make the high school basketball team, he was able to be the manager. His association with the team, his friends, and the sport paid lasting dividends. Another girl found that her talent was not being on stage, but rather designing the scenery and making the costumes.

8. Remind children that what a person is, is more important than what a person has. The most important things in life are not things. They are qualities of character and development of potential.

9. Help children to share. Gracious winners always reach out to those who admire them. Sometimes the jealousy of someone else may be avoided through the thoughtful sharing of a friend. When one boy got a new bicycle he immediately took it to a friend so he could also know the thrill of riding a new bike and sharing an event they would both remember. When we help someone else, we also help ourselves.

Overcoming jealousy is a sign of growth. Children are almost always jealous of one another – this is natural and to be expected. It is unnatural, however, for jealousy to continue on into adulthood, and we should seek to help our children control it as soon as possible.

LATE HOURS

What are "late hours"? Any definition is subject to interpretation and personal preference, but late hours are usually considered to begin somewhere between 10:30 P.M. and midnight. The age of the children, the type of activity, the mix of the group, and the desire and inspiration of the parents should all combine to dictate the specific guidelines for a family to follow.

In general, however, staying out late increases the vulnerability of youth. Problems with immorality, physical danger, even simple fatigue are all enhanced by late hours. The tendency to commit crime and the odds of becoming a victim increase with the lateness of the hour.

The darkness that accompanies late hours gives some youth (even some adults) the illusion that their actions may not be seen. Necking, petting, and promiscuous sexual intercourse often take place in darkened areas, where they would never be considered in the light of day.

Our vitality level is closely related to the hour of the day. Since normal family life, school, and employment generally dictate arising early, by 10:30 P.M. the body has been awake approximately fifteen hours. For normal people fatigue has already set in, or will within the next hour or so. Simple fatigue, if continued, begins to manifest itself through reduced mental and physical ability; even basic attractiveness suffers. The Lord's counsel is wise: "Cease to sleep longer than is needful; retire to thy bed early, that ye may not be weary; arise early, that your bodies and your minds may be invigorated." (D&C 88:124.)

As mentioned earlier, crime is more prevalent at night—late night. Citizen groups and crime-prevention agencies of government advise repeatedly to avoid dark places late at night. For all crimes combined, the highest four-hour period of vulnerability is from midnight to 4:00 A.M. It is approximately 40 percent higher than the four-hour period from 8:00 P.M. to 12:00 midnight. Sexually related crime ratios are even higher for the later hours. (From an interview with the Salt Lake City Police Department, January 27, 1987.)

Some family members may try to convince parents that darkness and late hours are not all bad. They may relate spiritual experiences, such as those Joseph Smith had, where an angel visited him most of the night. Gently remind them that where such visions took place, those receiving them were in the proper place and in the proper frame of mind. Usually late hours do not lead anyone to wholesome, uplifting activities.

Parents should consider the following when teaching young people:

1. Train them to arise early. Having some regular chores that require them to arise early, before school or work, will help motivate youth to retire early.

2. Help them avoid late-hour employment. Working at resorts, bars, restaurants, skating rinks, video parlors, movie houses, and other late-open establishments presents a potential for problems. It is necessary for many youth to work. However, in some situations the added income may not be worth the added risks.

3. Speak plainly to youth. The increased dangers of late-night activities are clear, and should be made clear to young people. Motor vehicles combined with alcohol and late hours have a proven record—they are dangerous. Darkness for a couple in the back seat of a car is dangerous. Crime happens late at night.

4. Stress the importance of proper rest. Getting eight hours of sleep each night makes people feel better; they will achieve more and they will enjoy life more. The promise that they "shall run and not be weary, and shall walk and not faint" demands proper rest as much as abstinence from coffee and tobacco. (See D&C 89:20.)

5. Constantly express love and concern for youth. This should be the main method of operation for parents enforcing rule about late hours. This story told by Ardeth G. Kapp, a Young Women general president, may help youth understand: "I remember one evening years ago, while attending a Sunday School party, I looked at the clock, and it was past the time I was told to be home. Just then a knock came on the door. I was horrified—my dad had come after me. I felt humiliated in front of my friends. I thought I wanted to die. I was not pleasant with my dad; disobedience never makes one pleasant.

"A few years later, my friends and I were driving home from a dance across an Indian reservation, ten miles from any shelter. It was 40 degrees below zero, and the windchill continued to lower the temperature. A few miles farther into the blizzard, we discovered that there was no heat in the car. Then the car froze up and would not run. We came to a slow stop. We watched the snow swirling in front of us only until the windows quickly froze over. We were quiet and sober as we contemplated our fate—our lives were in danger. The silence was broken as a friend in the back seat asked, 'How long do you think it will be before your dad will get here?' . . . This time we lived because my dad came through the blizzard to save my life and the lives of my friends." (*Ensign*, November 1984, pp. 96–97.)

6. Acknowledge possible exceptions to the rules you set. As children grow into young adults and begin to live lives of their own, their particular situations may require a change from the established routine. Once in a while a special event may warrant a temporary relaxing of the rules. And those who work nights may have to sleep later and arise later. But the mainstream will continue to arise with the dawn and follow the day to rest.

LYING

The telephone rings; Mary says, "If that's Bob, tell him I'm not home!" "We believe in being honest . . . " (Article of Faith 13.)

Tommy spilled the milk. "Who did that?" asked Mother. "I don't know," said Tommy. "For they were perfectly honest and upright in all things." (Alma 27:27.)

"Robbie flipped me with an elastic!" cried Marsha. "I did not!" said Robbie. "Thou shalt not bear false witness against thy neighbour." (Exodus 20:16.)

Honesty is necessary for our salvation. God is honest and just in all things. (See Alma 7:20.) We too must be honest in all things, if we are to become like him. The brother of Jared testified: "Yea, Lord, I know that thou . . . art a God of truth, and canst not lie." (Ether 3:12.)

In contrast, the devil is a liar. In fact, he is the "father of lies." (2 Nephi 9:9.)

Lying can be defined as intentionally deceiving others. Deception can come through a gesture or a look, by silence, by telling only part of the truth, or by bearing false witness. Whenever we lead people in any way to believe something that is not true, we are not being honest. Satan would have us believe that it is all right to lie. He says: "Yea, lie a little . . . there is no harm in this." (2 Nephi 28:8.) He encourages us to justify our lies to ourselves. An honest person will recognize Satan's temptations and will speak the whole truth, even if it seems to be to the person's disadvantage.

As parents strive to teach their children the ways of the Lord, they will want to teach and exemplify honesty. Understanding some factors associated with lying will help them know better how to teach.

People justify lies in many ways. When we excuse ourselves we cheat ourselves, and the Spirit of God ceases to strive with us. We become more and more unrighteous. Common reasons for lying include:

1. Trying to shift responsibility.
2. Wanting to avoid punishment.
3. Hoping to avoid conflict.
4. Jumping to conclusions.
5. Being envious or jealous.
6. Gossiping.
7. Protecting one's image.

The most important way of preventing lying is to keep a close relationship with the child. The lines of communication should be wide open. Home must be a place where the child feels security and unconditional love.

Each child should be taught what honesty is, why it is right, and that it is expected.

1. Our Father in heaven wants us to be honest. (See Hebrews 13:18.)

2. The Holy Ghost cannot work with us unless we are honest. (See D&C 121:37.)

3. We personally benefit from being honest, in that we have good feelings about ourselves and about others. (See D&C 97:8.)

4. When we are dishonest, we hurt other people. (See Ezekiel 22:12–13.)

5. If we are known to be honest others will trust us. (See Malachi 2:6.)

6. We cannot have an eternal family without honesty. (See D&C 76:60.)

Teach honesty by pointing out examples or stories from the Book of Mormon, Bible, the history of the Church, or the lives of personal friends and relatives.

Regardless of what is said about being honest, parents' behavior and attitudes will teach more than any sermon. Children need to see their parents being scrupulously honest. When parents say: "You are small for your age and can get into the movies for half price," or, "That's all right! This business makes lots of money anyway," or, "What luck, the clerk forgot to charge me for the milk," these parents are showing, through their actions, what they believe. Their children will learn from this model.

WHAT TO DO WHEN CHILDREN LIE

Often a parent's first impulse upon suspecting a lie is to say, "I know you're lying! Now tell me the truth!" The trouble with accusing a child of lying is that it practically invites the child to tell another lie. If children are lying to protect their image of themselves, and parents put on more pressure, the children are going to protect themselves even more—and the lies grow. An atmosphere of love and trust promotes openness much more than one of hostile confrontation.

1. *Love your child.* In Doctrine and Covenants 121:43, the Lord says that when we rebuke someone by the power of the Holy Ghost, we must be sure afterwards to show forth an increase of love. When we find someone lying, it's sometimes a good idea to show forth an increase of love before, during, and after the rebuke. Lies usually come from fear and anxiety. Before children feel safe in letting go of their lies, they have to be sure they will be loved, accepted, and respected no matter what the situation.

2. *Trust your child.* Sometimes parents think their children are lying when in fact they are telling the truth. When accused, these same children are going to conclude—perhaps correctly—that they aren't trusted. More often, however, parents do not know whether their children are lying. If they don't have any evidence—just feelings that something isn't quite right, that something is being hidden—then any accusations they might make will probably do more damage than good. Develop a natural trust in your children, and it will usually be rewarded.

3. *Disapprove of the lie, but don't turn away from the child.* There are times when parents know that their children are lying to them. Usually, when children are lying about something important and they know that telling the truth will result in serious trouble, the truth isn't going to come out quickly or easily.

Once again, the key is love. Show that you don't consider your child an enemy because of a lie. Explain that you are both on the same side. Show that, though you disapprove of the lie, you still love the child. You might say: "Look, sometimes you seem so afraid that I won't accept you, that you think you have to lie. *That makes me feel bad.* I wish you'd tell the truth," or, "I don't know exactly what we are going to do to help you tell the truth, but I think you'd rather not be hiding things, and it would be more pleasant for all of us if you didn't feel you had to lie."

Results probably won't appear instantly, especially if lying has become a habit. You may be rebuffed the first time and the second, and the third, too. But if you keep trying, and if you show your desire to help the child, adding constant and earnest prayers, you will slowly pull the barriers down. The issue is not to condone the lying, but to build a relationship with new understanding that will make lying unnecessary.

Care should be taken when a child confesses having lied. Even though a consequence may follow, the child must associate the negative consequence with his or her behavior, not with the confession.

4. *Don't ask "why?"* Many parents make the mistake of confronting a child with the question, "Why did you lie?" Most children will come up with some kind of rationalization, excuses that will probably sound silly even to them, or they'll answer, "I don't know." They probably really don't know. A more effective question might be, "What did the lie do for you?" Don't dwell on the past; help the child face the future.

5. *Support children as they endure the consequences.* Once children have admitted the truth, the responsibility for what is going to happen next is placed squarely on them. The parents, of course, stand with them as they shoulder the consequences of any lie. Parents can help by saying, "Johnny, do you want to tell Mr. Smith you lied all by yourself, or would you like me to come with you?" or, "Johnny, do you want to tell the teacher about this at school tomorrow, or would you rather telephone him tonight?" Such alternatives and questions should be offered kindly, but firmly.

Children who have lied need to know that, even though facing up to their misdeeds can be painful, they will feel better and cleaner afterward; and they will know that being truthful is right and good.

They also need to know that their parents are supporting them in their repentance.

When the incident is over, the child who has lied and repented needs to know that parents continue to trust him or her. Once a lie has been confessed, it should be forgotten and a new start given. Don't label a child a *liar*, and don't constantly ask, "Is that true? Are you fibbing?"

6. *Don't confuse lying with tall tales.* Parents must realize that little children from ages three to seven possess vivid imaginations. Often their imagination and desire for adventure run away with them, causing them to make statements or tell stories that have no foundation in fact. At such times the parent should listen to the "tall tale" of the youngster, but help the child understand that it is only imagination, make-believe. Children at this age should not be punished for such statements, because they are not yet fully capable of discerning right from wrong or of separating the real from the imaginary. They are merely repeating to parents what is currently impressed upon them. The role of the parent is to gently lead the child to understand the difference between "real" and "pretend" stories, and to know the proper place for each.

Parents can't force their children to be honest. Honesty, like every other virtue, must come from within. It grows inside a child. Gradually, gaining experience, suffering consequences when necessary, children will learn. One lie from a child is not necessarily a sign that thirty more are about to follow. How parents respond to a lie, however, can help the child want to tell the truth in the future.

The Savior said, "The truth shall make you free." (John 8:32.) When parents help their children see that the truth frees them of anxiety, of unneeded guilt, of having to hide things from the people they love, such parents will be well along the road to teaching their children to "walk uprightly before the Lord." (D&C 68:28.)

MARRIAGE

(SEE PLANNING FOR THE FUTURE)

MASTURBATION

Masturbation is not a comfortable subject. In most situations it is taboo to discuss. This increases the mystery, perpetuates ignorance, and arouses curiosity among young people—who will not likely talk it over with the adults in their lives. Instead they may hold onto the misconceptions they have received from peers, and may experiment privately.

In the following pages we will openly discuss what masturbation is, and some things we can do about it. First, we should recognize that there is a difference between masturbation and natural discoveries of one's own body.

"Children will naturally discover and explore their genitals just as they do the rest of their bodies. The male infant's genitals are very sensitive to touch. His penis responds to his diaper and to his parent's touch as they bathe or clothe him. He will often touch and rub his own genitals. A little girl may also explore and handle her genitals. Your reaction to these natural explorations will influence the way a child later feels about his procreative powers. Do not either worry about or encourage the child's explorations. Remain neutral, and the child will accept that these parts of his body are good, just as all the other parts are." (*A Parent's Guide* [Salt Lake City: The Church of Jesus Christ of Latter-day Saints, 1985], p. 21.)

"Throughout childhood, boys and girls have touched their own genitals frequently to wash and to dress. This is a behavior that usually has the same meaning as keeping one's feet warm in the winter, enjoying a swim on a hot day, or scratching an itch. We ought to be friendly to our bodies and appreciate the body's marvelous range of senses. This innocent touching is not the kind of behavior warned against by prophets through the ages." (*A Parent's Guide*, pp. 36–37.)

Young people must know that within young men "millions of sperm grow in the testicles within spermatic fluid. When the fluid and sperm fill the tubules and testes, they are automatically released or ejaculated. This usually happens during sleep and is called nocturnal emissions or 'wet dreams.' Sexual dreams are not always present, but they can trigger a nocturnal emission or ejaculation. In either case this is *not* masturbation." (*A Parents' Guide,* p. 36.)

WHAT MASTURBATION IS

"The sin of masturbation occurs when a person stimulates his or her own sex organs for the purpose of sexual arousal. It is a perversion of the body's passions. When we pervert these passions and intentionally use them for selfish, immoral purposes, we become carnal." (*A Parent's Guide,* p. 37.)

"Masturbation . . . is not approved of the Lord nor of His Church regardless of what may have been said by others whose 'norms' are lower. Latter-day Saints are urged to avoid this practice." (Spencer W. Kimball, as quoted in *A Parent's Guide,* p. 37.)

"Your teenagers will face great pressures to express their sexual feelings in sinful ways . . . masturbation is considered by many in the world to be the harmless expression of an instinctive sex drive. . . . Masturbation is not physically necessary. . . . The so-called sex drive is mostly myth. Sexual intimacy is not an involuntary, strictly biological necessity for survival, like breathing and eating. Sexual intimacy . . . can be . . . suspended for long periods of time with no negative effect." (*A Parent's Guide,* pp. 36–37, 49.)

Masturbation occurs among boys and girls of all ages. The practice is no cause for serious alarm or overreaction. However, the practice can become habitual and progressive, leading to other immoral behaviors. In some cases it is associated with pornography and bizarre sexual fantasies. In view of the counsel from Church leaders, it is important that parents help their children avoid this problem.

TEACHING CHILDREN TO AVOID MASTURBATION

One of our duties as parents is to teach our children that we are created in the image and likeness of our Heavenly Father and his Son, Jesus Christ, and that our bodies along with the sensations and feelings we experience with them are good and wholesome. Children need to learn "that they will find joy in their bodies when they use them virtuously after the manner taught by Christ." (*A Parent's Guide,* p. 37.)

Children must also be educated about the wonderful changes

that take place in their bodies as they grow and develop from childhood through adolescence, into mature adults. These changes are good. They are in the image and likeness of God. Children must be prepared for the emotional and mental influences these physical changes will have upon them.

"At puberty, the girls begins to menstruate, her hips broaden, her breasts develop, body hair grows under her arms and in her pubic area, and she may gain weight. The boy begins to create seminal fluid and sperm cells. His shoulders broaden, his muscles expand, his voice deepens, and he gets taller and heavier. Body hair grows under the arms, on the face, and in the pubic region." (*A Parent's Guide*, p. 36.)

Both young men and young women need to understand how the changes in a young woman's hormone cycle affect her mental and emotional outlook, and how she can develop a wholesome attitude toward herself during the times in her menstrual cycle that may be difficult for her. She may experience physical discomfort such as cramps, as well as some unexpected emotional sensitivity to the opinions and actions of others around her. This may be due to an imbalance of hormones that will usually correct itself as the menstrual cycle continues, but then repeat itself during the next cycle. When this happens she needs special understanding and patience from her family and friends.

Both young men and young women must also understand how young men begin to produce millions of sperm in the testicles within spermatic fluid, and how an excess of this fluid and sperm are occasionally and automatically released or ejaculated during sleep. As explained above, this is called a nocturnal emission or "wet dream." This is the way the Lord intended it to be. When it happens a young man should not feel embarrassed or guilty.

These changes in the female hormone cycle and the development of sperm in young men are wonderful changes that prepare us to become more like God and make it possible to conceive and bear children.

Sexual activity within a healthy, nurturing marital relationship can be virtuous, chaste, respectful, uplifting, and holy, as well as extremely satisfying. A healthy relationship includes a strong commitment to each other, clear communication, tender affection, emotional closeness, mutual respect and trust, and common goals and values. In contrast, sexual activity used solely for the purpose of pleasure, without the attending commitments, is carnal in nature and produces feelings of shame, guilt, and loss of self-esteem.

The most important basis for prevention of masturbation is an understanding of the purpose and plan of life and salvation. Children must know where they come from, why they are here on earth, and what their potential is in the eternities. They must know, without any question, that they are children of our Heavenly Father, that they are created in his image and likeness, that he loves them, and that this earthly experience was designed specifically for them. They must have a personal testimony that Jesus Christ suffered for us all that we might not suffer if we repent of our sins, and that we will be resurrected with a full restoration of our bodies to our spirits in order that we might achieve a fulness of joy. (See D&C 93:33.)

One of the most important and difficult tasks for teenagers is the development of their social skills. Young people need to learn how to interact in wholesome ways with other youths. This is primarily the parent's responsibility, but the Church supports parents by providing Mutual, Scouting, sports, music, drama, and other activities to help youth improve their self-confidence, self-esteem, and their ability to get along with others in a wholesome environment. Social interaction leads to group dating, then to courtship, and on to healthy marital relationships. This in turn makes possible exaltation in the celestial kingdom.

HELPING CHILDREN WHO ARE STRUGGLING WITH MASTURBATION

Some youths, most often young men, are introduced to masturbation by their friends. Others discover it for themselves or have overheard conversations about it at school. The pleasure they enjoy in masturbation encourages them to continue, while at the same time they feel ashamed and unworthy. These mixed feelings of pleasure and shame lead to confusion and stress.

It seems that Satan whispers in our children's ears that masturbation is just a small thing—until they have indulged. Then he tells them it is such an overwhelmingly horrible sin that they can never overcome it. Satan wants them to be discouraged and feel hopeless.

Young people need to understand that the Savior himself went "forth, suffering pains and afflictions and temptations of every kind. . . . and he [took] upon him their infirmities, that his bowels may be filled with mercy, according to the flesh, that he may know according to the flesh how to succor his people according to their infirmities." (Alma 7:11–12.) Therefore, the Savior is the one person who understands all feelings, good or bad. He understands all temptations and weaknesses. He knows how to have empathy, and how to give us comfort in time of need.

It is important that parents do not overreact if they discover that their child has experimented with masturbation. A few occurrences do not necessarily constitute a habit, particularly with younger teens. The tendency can usually be stopped before it becomes a severe problem. With love and willingness to understand their child's newfound feelings, parents can help cultivate that which is "praiseworthy and of good report" within their child, and the child in turn will gladly and willingly avoid this unworthy practice.

Parents can help their children maintain a realistic perspective and know that sexual feelings are good, and from God, and can bring great joy when held within proper bounds. Then encourage your children to look at the good things in their lives instead of their weaknesses. Most young people who masturbate are honest, conscientious, and sensitive. They have great value in the world and even greater potential in the eternal worlds. The habit of masturbation can become progressive and lead to other problems, but the more a person looks at the gloomy side of things, the more likely that person is to continue the self-defeating behavior.

Parents will find it most helpful to be specific in pointing out young people's value. Help them focus on their strengths and the good they have done for others. Continually be supportive and encouraging, not condemning.

A seven-year-old girl was found alone on her bed masturbating. She complained that she experienced irritation and itching. This led her to masturbate. Her mother helped her find a soap that cleansed her without causing irritation, and this cleared the way to help her overcome her problem. Each time her parents found her masturbating they would lovingly and kindly say, "Sweetheart, please don't rub your body in that way. That is not a good habit to develop. It's time to come help me bake cookies/ go to the store/practice your piano." With their efforts to keep her busy doing constructive things, the masturbation gradually disappeared.

A five-year-old girl was seen masturbating during sharing time in Primary. Her teacher quietly moved over next to her, kindly put her arm around her, smiled, and helped her sing the songs with the others. This distraction replaced the masturbation with a rewarding, wholesome activity.

A father walked into the bathroom and discovered his thirteen-year-old son masturbating. Both were shocked and speechless. It took a while before either could say anything. The son, embarrassed, quickly escaped to his room. The father thoughtfully followed, trying to calm himself. He knocked, was invited in, and said, "I apologize for walking in on you. I felt embarrassed and I'm sure you did. But I am happy, in a way. I guess I have neglected talking to you about some of the changes you are experiencing in your body. As a young man you are developing a special power to become a father. When you are married and with your wife that power will bring you great joy and happiness in your marriage relationship, and will make it possible for you and you wife to have children. It is a sacred power that you must learn how to control. I am concerned that you may be developing a habit that is not good, and will be very difficult to overcome in the future. I love you and I want to help you be happy and have good self-esteem. May we talk about this for a while?"

A discussion followed in which questions were answered, love was expressed, and values were taught. The father became a friend and partner with his son to help him master himself. The father did not punish his son, scold him, or scorn him for discovering one of his godlike traits.

When working with a child to overcome masturbation, you must work hard at being understanding and gaining your child's trust so he or she will honestly report to you. Satan would have all of us maintain the facade that "All is well." If a child who is struggling with masturbation gives you a good report you may be well pleased and reward the child. Unknowingly you may have rewarded the child for deceiving you.

In such sensitive and important matters it is essential that we help our children tell us the truth without fear. Conversations with our children should not occur only when they are having trouble. This will pay undue attention to their unacceptable behaviors, and we may unknowingly reinforce these. However, it can be very helpful to focus attention on the struggles a child is going through as he or she tries to avoid masturbation. Encourage the child to share feelings and thoughts with you.

It seems that there is often a chain of events leading a young person to masturbation. The chain contains many links, each one leading to the next. One of the early links is a resolve not to repeat the masturbation. This resolve is usually self-defeating because it keeps the subject clearly in the mind of the individual until he or she eventually obtains relief through masturbation. This is like promising oneself, "I will not think about a purple tree!" The more we resolve not to think of the forbidden item, the more clearly it is embedded in our mind. We cannot force ourselves *not* to think of something. We choose what we *do* think about, rather than choosing what we *don't* think about. It is much easier to replace a thought than to erase a thought.

Other links in the chain of events include self-debate and feelings of weakness, hopelessness, and despair. Often one or more of these links are tied to necessary daily routines, such as bathing, or going to bed. Children succeed better when they stop fighting against the evil thoughts that come into their minds and instead find other things more rewarding and useful to focus their attention on. This will forge a different set of chain links. These new links can lead to wholesome behaviors instead of masturbation.

Sexual feelings, social frustration, loneliness, and rejection do not have to be sexually expressed. There are other alternatives. Some anxious youths tend to fight against their feelings, denying them and thus increasing their own anxiety and motivation to masturbate. Several other alternatives exist. Planning in advance what the chosen response will be improves the chances for success. The youth may confide in a trusted person, pray, write down thoughts and feelings, or consciously repeat positive statements. Some useful self-talk phrases are:

"Troublesome feelings and desires will not last forever—they will cease. I can hang on for a few more minutes."

"Even though I may be feeling this way, I choose not to act on it."

"I have the strength to allow this feeling to come and go without it dictating how I will behave."

"I will be meeting with my father (or bishop) this Sunday and I want to give him a good report with a success story that I achieved greater self-mastery."

"I am just preparing to meet with someone I admire very much, and I cannot do this in that person's presence."

"Suppose the Savior were here with me now. How would I feel and how would I behave?"

These statements are useful in many instances. However, they may not help the child who seems addicted to masturbation as a mood-altering activity, or as an escape from stress or pain in life. Some young people have participated in masturbation frequently and long enough that it has become a type of addiction. Much like alcoholism or other drug addictions, this addiction is mainly psychological, rather than physical. Addicts have come to depend upon their addiction for escape from pain, relief from stress, and moments of pleasure in an otherwise painful life. Indulgence in their addiction temporarily alters their mood from normal to a false feeling of well-being or euphoria. As the effects wear off, the individual sinks below normal, to feelings of pain. The addict repeats the addictive behavior, this time seeking relief from the pain that resulted from the previous indulgence. Using a drug or behavior to relieve the pain caused by the drug or behavior is futility itself.

Frequently a cycle develops in which a young person may feel lonely, inadequate, or rejected by friends. Initially the person will suppress or deny these unpleasant feelings, but anxieties and tensions build inside until he or she "acts out" or escapes with masturbation. There is an immediate sense of pleasure and relief of anxiety, which is rewarding for a brief moment. This is followed by guilt, remorse, self-reproach, and feelings of unworthiness. These feelings are added to the original ones of loneliness, inadequacy, and rejection. Then the cycle is repeated.

To help young people break this cycle, we must not heap on

them further guilt for their masturbation. They have sufficient to motivate them. Too many negative feelings immobilize and create feelings of hopelessness.

Strong, powerful confrontation and intervention combined with tough love are essential to break this cycle. The same intervention process that is frequently used with alcoholics can be very helpful. Information and literature concerning homosexuality may also be helpful, though one should not assume that masturbation is an offense equal in seriousness to homosexuality. Nevertheless, some of the ideas and concepts used to help homosexuals overcome unnatural sexual preferences can be very helpful with one who chronically masturbates. (See "A Letter to A Friend" by Spencer W. Kimball, brochure available at LDS Church distribution centers.) Parents may also profit from seeking help from professionals who share the gospel values of self-control, chastity, virtue, and avoidance of masturbation.

Efforts must be made to help young people see the adults in their lives as a resource. We must join forces to jointly attack a problem, not attack each other. Until parents and children are on the same side of the issue, no progress will be made, and much harm can be done. Parents who hope to help must have a relationship of trust with their son or daughter. They must be able to have a very open, frank talk *with* (not *to*) their child, expressing their love and desire to help.

In the case of young women who masturbate, a talk with a loving, appropriately affectionate father can be helpful, but he should not invade the young woman's feelings of modesty or privacy. Parents should not pry into the details of the process except as needed to be of help. A young woman may feel more comfortable talking with her mother, who could consult with her father as needed.

A young man could benefit from a talk with whichever parent is easiest for him to approach, but fathers can be a significant role model and may have some empathy based on personal experience. For those without fathers, the bishop is usually an excellent source of help.

For both young men and young women, a priesthood blessing from their father or their bishop can be very helpful.

Knowing where, when, and how masturbation takes place may

be of great help so long as parents don't ask for embarrassing details. Parents can use this information to help the young person structure his or her life to avoid temptation.

One young woman, age ten, who had been molested by her father earlier in life, resumed a habit she had formed in childhood. She took unusually long showers, raising the suspicions of her mother. When confronted by her mother she denied any problem. Later, ashamed, she admitted to the problem, which usually occurred in the shower. They agreed on time-limited showers with a progress chart that focused on time management, not on masturbation. Points earned toward special treats and privileges helped motivate the girl to shower faster, eliminating a major source of temptation to her. Soon she was so busy with many rewarding things that her interest in masturbation faded away.

A young man who lacked confidence and was shy and withdrawn was introduced to masturbation by another boy while working on a farm. The practice increased secretly until it became a daily ritual either in bed or in the bathtub. His divorced mother discovered semen deposits on his pajamas and bedding more frequently than normal for wet dreams. She talked with the bishop, who interviewed the young man carefully and with great love. Though he prodded the youth gently and finally even asked outright, the young man refused to admit there was a problem. The bishop did not know what to do next, so he said, "Okay, fine, I want you to know I am your friend. I am here to help you. If you ever want to talk about anything, I'm available." They talked about other things briefly and parted with expressions of warmth and friendship.

The bishop then called LDS Social Services and consulted with a professional therapist in preparation for the next opportunity. Later, the young man asked to talk with the bishop. Cautiously and awkwardly he brought up the subject. The bishop was patient, kind, and accepting. He did not condemn, preach, or scold the boy. He did not tell him to use more will-power. He offered support, encouragement, love, acceptance, fellowship, and asked if they could meet together weekly. Each time they met, the bishop asked the boy how his struggles with masturbation were coming along. The bishop explored the boy's efforts to overcome rather than his failures. These meetings continued for many months and a close relationship developed.

This young man had many setbacks. He used many techniques to help himself, including physical activity, busy schedules, priesthood blessings, fasting and prayer, and weekly interviews. But *the most important help he received was a testimony that he was loved by his Heavenly Father* and that he must keep struggling, be humble before God, and be patient with himself.

He later served a mission and, though he masturbated occasionally on his mission, he never lost sight of his eternal potential and his goals. He was helped to keep things in perspective. He knew that he was a conscientious, honest person with real intent to do good. He also knew that masturbation, though not approved, was not an unpardonable sin, nor an overwhelming, incurable addiction. With patience, love, support from others, and continual effort he knew he could overcome it, and he did.

With masturbation, as with any other weakness, we should always remember the hope we receive from the Lord: "And if men come unto me I will show unto them their weakness. I give unto men weakness that they may be humble; and my grace is sufficient for all men that humble themselves before me; for if they humble themselves before me, and have faith in me, then will I make weak things become strong unto them." (Ether 12:27.)

MEDIA INFLUENCES

We are living in a media age, an age when mass communications are widely available and highly influential. News programs can scare us, nature programs can inform us, obscene and pornographic programs can degrade us, and Church programs can inspire us, all over the same media form.

Parents who would never allow their children to open and tamper with poisons may allow these same children to freely expose themselves to "poisonous" movies, videotapes, records, magazines, songs, and television programs. Then the parents wonder what happened when their children get sick—spiritually, if not physically. It is vital that we expose some of these harmful programs for what they really are—Satan's tools to destroy us.

Some of the negative influences of the media creep into our lives subtly, and they can become addictive if left uncontrolled. Parents should try listening to some of the songs their children listen to, reading the books and magazines they read, and watching the television and movies they see. Undoubtedly parents will be a bit shocked. But what can we do?

President Ezra Taft Benson has said, "The leisure time of children must be constructively directed to wholesome, positive pursuits. Too much time viewing television can be destructive, and pornography in this medium should not be tolerated." (En-sign, March 1977, p. 19.) We can begin by limiting the time children spend with the entertainment media. But it is important to replace what is taken away. Parents should subscribe to good publications and have material available to take the place of "poisonous" media.

Also, parents must set the example themselves. If a story is considered harmful to children, it is equally harmful for adults. Though a book or a movie may receive secular awards and honors, it still may not be appropriate for a Latter-day Saint home. Parents need to consider the appropriateness of each program individually.

One mother explained, "It was the same every day. My children sat mesmerized in front of the television set. Their rooms were a mess, their homework wasn't done, and they wouldn't do their chores. And it seemed that the longer they watched the more irritable they became. I felt like throwing out the television. I finally told them that the TV had to be turned off. And so off it went for a week.

"Amazing things happened! Rooms were cleaned, homework was completed, and good books were opened and were read by everyone. And the most surprising thing was that family members actually started talking to each other."

Not all media influences are bad, however. To achieve a balance, guidelines should be discussed and agreed upon by the family. It is important to talk things over together as a family—that way, no one resents the decisions that are made. Decide together what you will watch.

The following guidelines have worked well for some:

1. Unless something is really worth watching, keep the television off.

2. Try not to use television as a baby-sitter.

3. Remember that immorality, vulgarity, and violence are "poisonous" and should be avoided.

4. Review in detail what children see.

5. Calendar and enjoy special programs or movies together as a family.

6. If television is to be viewed on Sunday, align the material with the purpose of the sabbath day.

7. Allow children to be part of the selection process as much as possible.

8. See that homework and chores are done before the television is turned on.

9. One family worked out a plan where each of their children was given eight 30-minute coupons per week. After schoolwork and chores were finished, they could "cash" their coupons in on programs approved by the family. If they chose to watch a two-hour sports program, for example, that used up four of their coupons.

Parents can become experts in understanding the needs and concerns of their children. They have the right and responsibility to set limits. Children need guidelines. Together, working with the Lord, family members can learn to escape the barrage of media specials and spectaculars that poison. As families do this, they will find that they are talking more to each other, listening more to each other, and discovering more things about each other than they ever have before. In addition, children will read more and find other forms of recreation that can be much more fulfilling.

MILITARY SERVICE

(SEE PLANNING FOR THE FUTURE)

MISSIONS

(SEE PLANNING FOR THE FUTURE)

MOVING

When a move or transfer is necessary, parents should be aware of family members' feelings. Ruth gave us an example to follow when she told Naomi, "Whither thou goest, I will go; and where thou lodgest, I will lodge: thy people shall be my people, and thy God my God." (Ruth 1:16.)

However, moving may be harder for some members of the family than for others. Younger children may see it as a new adventure, and will usually move easily as long as they have the security of their family. Older, teenage children, who live in a more peer-oriented society, may not want to leave their friends, their school, and their future plans. They may feel that their activities are more important than their parents' needs. To move away where they become "unknown" will certainly threaten their security.

Prior to a move, a family planning and discussion time is very important. Through the parents' influence, an attitude of excitement and adventure rather than fear can be developed. New opportunities and possibilities for growth can be brought out. Parents need to learn and understand their children's fears and concerns. They can minimize the children's difficulty of separating from friends and familiar surroundings by doing the following:

1. Let the children know about the move as soon as possible. This allows them to prepare emotionally for upcoming changes.

2. Let each child freely express feelings about what moving means to him or her. These can range from great excitement to extreme anger. An upset child needs to be listened to. Express your understanding and appreciation of how a move will affect the child's life.

3. Try to pinpoint the child's greatest concern. Ask about leaving friends, school, ward, favorite places, about the challenges of living in a new community.

Such discussions can help reconcile the children to moving. If children persist in being angry and negative about a move, let them know that they have a right to their feelings as long as these are appropriately expressed, but that the needs of the entire family must be considered first. By sacrificing present desires, family members can achieve long-range goals and strengthen family unity.

Although moving may be more difficult for some than others, children are resilient and will usually adapt to their new surroundings and eventually come to see the wisdom of moving. The adjustments will be greater when moving from a long-term residence. Children may accept the move more easily if arrangements and promises are made for return visits and the writing of letters to maintain friendships. These promises made to children must be honestly kept.

Family members need to work together in the actual process of moving. Some personal possessions may have to be left behind; it is often impossible to move everything that has been acquired. Some families who move frequently encourage each family member to select one significant possession to be displayed in a place of honor in the new home.

When a young woman who had moved ten or eleven times during her school years was asked what the best part of moving was, she replied, "It was so exciting finding out about the new country or city, then having a say in choosing the house, selecting colors to decorate the different rooms, and being assigned a corner of the lot in which to plant a garden or do whatever I wanted."

A NEW HOME

President Benson has said, "One great thing the Lord requires of each of us is to provide a home where a happy, positive influence for good exists." (Ensign, May 1981, p. 34.) Whether a move is made into a wood, brick, or thatch house, apartment, or trailer, the lodging should become a place where something of heaven is built into the foundation. Our challenge is to make our earthly home like our heavenly home.

A new home, regardless of how long- or short-lived it may be, should be prepared as if it were permanent. A woman who was required to move frequently because of her husband's employment was questioned by her neighbor as to why she was planting tulip bulbs when she would not be there in the spring to see them bloom. She replied, "I may not be here, but someone else will. I always try to leave my homes, temporary as they may be, a little more beautiful because I was there."

Parents should guide their children in finding value, becoming loyal to, and accepting the new place as "home." Avoid constant comparing of past residences. The attitude you bring to your new location will determine your happiness there. An old story tells of a family moving to a new town who stopped just on the outskirts. Seeing an old man walking on the side of the road, they stopped to ask, "What is this town like?"

The man replied with a question: "What was it like where you came from?"

"Oh, it was wonderful!" they answered. "The people were so friendly."

"It's a lot like that here," the man replied.

Soon after, another family came by. "What's this town like?" they asked.

"What was it like where you came from?" the old man asked in return.

"Oh, it was a hateful place; everyone was so nosy and quarrelsome."

"It's a lot like that here," the man replied.

When you move to a new home you usually move into a new ward. Developing new church friends as quickly as possible is important. (This responsibility falls upon the ward members as well as the new family.) If from the beginning you expect the new ward to be different from previous wards, you will be able to cope with the differences. The gospel is universal, but wards can vary widely throughout the world.

You should not wait for someone to reach out to you just because you are new. You may need to make the initial move. Introduce yourself to others; meet the bishop, the Relief Society president, and the new teachers your children may have. Volunteer your own talents and time. Be dependable and responsible. Invite others to your home. Look for families with children the ages of your own, and help them become acquainted.

Think positively. Look at strangers as friends you now have the chance to meet. Don't confine your new associations only to Church members.

As wards receive new members, the ward itself also carries the responsibility of becoming acquainted with new people. One ward has its activities committee prepared to organize an open house for newcomers. This is held at a member's home and is open to anyone who would like to meet and visit with new neighbors. This informal and relaxed situation is greatly appreciated by both old and new neighbors.

One way to gain an appreciation for your new location is to learn about it. Make yourself familiar with necessary places: church, schools, stores, libraries, recreation areas, doctors, and so on. Teach this to the whole family. For very young children, take some walking explorations to help them get to know their neighborhood and to dispel their fear of getting lost. Accompanying older children to school activities, on shopping excursions, and to amusement areas will help. Along with learning where places are located, you might spend some time studying and appreciating the local history.

Moving isn't a trauma to everyone. Having the right attitude can make a change very exciting. This may be a chance for a new start, a chance to be a different and better person—the person you really want to be.

As people make frequent moves they learn to understand differences and become more tolerant. They realize that all people have something to love. When they care, that caring usually returns. From their new experiences, they develop a wider background and knowledge.

When making a move to a place where members of the Church are few or none, living the Church standards becomes very important. Those youth who do very often become the leaders and are greatly respected by their peers. What a growing experience! Always be a source of encouragement to your children in a family move. Let them feel your understanding of their challenges and radiate a positive attitude.

Regardless of how far or how often you move, the Lord will always be willing to accompany and support you in righteousness. "Therefore, continue your journey and let your hearts rejoice; for behold, and lo, I am with you even unto the end." (D&C 100:12.)

MUSIC

(SEE MEDIA INFLUENCES)

OBESITY

One of the instinctive desires of children and adolescents is to resist being different. They feel alone if their differences are too apparent. Childhood obesity brings painful isolation. The child may be taunted, causing physical, emotional, and social trouble, creating scars that last into adulthood.

Research shows that childhood obesity has many causes. A leading factor is increased television viewing by children. One researcher suggests that there is a two percent increase over normal body fat for each hour a child averages in front of a television per week.

Second, many children have high-calorie snacks easily available throughout the day. And third, children generally perform fewer physically demanding chores around the house because of modern conveniences.

If obesity occurs in the preschool child, there is a 25 percent chance of that child being obese as an adult. (Garn and Levey, "When Your Child is Overweight," *Parade Magazine*, May 3, 1987, p. 12.) Chances of adult obesity increase to 80 percent for the obese adolescent. ("Staying Healthy; Welfare Services Suggests How," *Ensign*, January 1981, p. 15.)

Don't be overly anxious with the very young child. Contact a doctor to determine whether a child really is overweight. A doctor should be the one to decide if weight loss is necessary; he or she should supervise any diet programs.

Dr. Rudolph Leibel, a noted weight expert, says, "Pushing the fat child too zealously . . . in a very low calorie diet could stunt growth, decrease muscle mass and, in a very young child, adversely affect the brain development. The safest way to manage overweight children is to let a child grow into his weight." (*Parade Magazine*, May 3, 1987, p. 12.)

Some children, by virtue of heredity, grow larger than their peers. Sometimes they even eat far less food and yet remain bigger. These children should be taught to accept themselves with dignity. The physical problems will probably be less than they imagine.

There are many things parents can do to help with weight problems:

1. Don't add to a child's stress by nagging or belittling. Offer love and support regardless of physical appearances. Often food becomes a comfort in times of distress. A child who is criticized, ignored, or feels low self-worth may pick up eating to soothe wounded pride. It is a habit that often deepens the wound. If this is the case, talk to the child; see if he or she feels that this is a problem. Allow the child to suggest alternatives to overeating.

Some possible ideas to consider with the child: eat slowly, learn to enjoy and savor the food, use a smaller plate, put the fork down between bites, wait before having seconds.

2. Set dietary goals. It is difficult for a child to be the only family member on a diet. A modest program of reachable, defined dietary objectives will usually bring the weight down in a natural fashion, and will increase the health of all family members.

Eliminate as many fats and refined sugars from the diet as possible. Use lean meats, fish, skinless poultry, low-fat dairy products, whole-grain breads and cereals, beans and peas, and other fruits and vegetables. The Word of Wisdom suggests using all wholesome herbs and fruits in their season and the flesh of beasts "sparingly." (See D&C 89:10–12.)Many good books containing suitable menus are on the market.

Offer fresh fruits, plain popcorn, a single, moderate serving of ice cream, or a small bag of chips for treats. The important things to watch here are frequency and quantity. A limited number of snacks may make dieting easier and thus more effective.

Avoid forcing children to "clean up" their plates. A better solution is to have the child take small portions at first, eating them before taking more.

Teach by example; whether dining at home or away, parents should choose their own food wisely.

3. Promote moderate physical exercise for the entire family or by joining your child in activities such as ball playing, bicycling, and swimming. Working physically is also important and healthful. Mowing lawns, gardening, vacuuming, and scrubbing are examples of healthy exercise. Exercise can be more exciting if done with others—family, neighborhood, church, and civic groups.

Physical self-mastery is advised by Paul:

"And every man that striveth for the mastery is temperate in all things. . . . But I keep under my body, and bring it into subjection." (1 Corinthians 9:25, 27.) Children may need help doing this, but the effect is worth the effort.

PATRIARCHAL BLESSINGS

(SEE PLANNING FOR THE FUTURE)

PEERS

(SEE FRIENDS)

PLANNING FOR THE FUTURE

Life did not start at birth. We came into this world with talents, gifts, and blessings obtained in the premortal life. As we continue to progress through mortality, the Lord will guide all who seek to know his will. Therefore, each of us should stay close to the Spirit to find out how we fit into the Lord's plan—how we might do the Lord's will. We will then fulfill the purpose of our creation and return to the Lord's presence properly prepared for celestial glory.

Although each of us is unique, there are common elements in the future that most of us will face, and for which we all must plan. Some of the most important include patriarchal blessings, missions, temple marriage, career preparation, and the establishment of eternal families.

PATRIARCHAL BLESSINGS

A patriarchal blessing is a personal, written revelation given to faithful members of the Church who request it. It contains promises of blessings available through faithfulness and diligence in serving the Lord. It also declares a person's lineage. It can give spiritual strength and serve as a guide for faithful members prayerfully planning for the future.

A member of the Church may request a patriarchal blessing

any time after baptism. The teenage years are often a time when youth desire a greater knowledge of the Lord's plan and their place in it. Missionaries are instructed to receive a blessing prior to entering the mission field. Older individuals who have not yet received a patriarchal blessing may also find great comfort and encouragement in such a blessing.

To receive a patriarchal blessing, a person must obtain a recommend from the bishop. He then makes an appointment with the patriarch of the stake or area.

Proper preparation for the blessing can include fasting, prayer, and study. One should go to the appointment with a desire to know and obey the will of the Lord. Following the blessing, a written copy will be sent to the person to whom the blessing was given, and a copy will be kept on file in the Church archives.

Each candidate receiving a patriarchal blessing should be spiritually mature enough to understand the blessing, and should desire it for himself or herself. Classes or groups should not be encouraged to receive blessings together. Only one patriarchal blessing should ever be requested from the patriarch.

A father, as the patriarch of the family, may give blessings to his children as often as his children desire them. These blessings may be recorded in personal journals, but are not kept in the Church archives. If a person loses the written copy of his or her patriarchal blessing, additional copies may be obtained from the Church. Since the blessing is a sacred personal revelation, it should be kept private and not discussed with others who would treat it lightly, nor should it be compared with the blessings of others. It may be reviewed often by the person and used as a guide in interviews with understanding parents or bishops.

MISSIONS

Preparation for missionary service is the responsibility of every priesthood holder in the Church. Many single sisters and adult couples have the opportunity to serve as well. "It becometh every man who hath been warned to warn his neighbor." (D&C 88:81.)

Whether the plans are immediate or long-range, all families in the Church should plan missionary service into their future. Parents can help their children prepare for missions in many ways. They can help them live worthy lives; give them experiences in

Christian service; prepare them financially; help them to be mentally ready; and help them develop socially. Even when children are young, parents can help them to "understand the doctrine of repentance, faith in Christ . . . to pray, and to walk uprightly before the Lord." (D&C 68:25,28.) Participating in family home evening, regularly attending church services, filling priesthood assignments, and being regularly interviewed by a father or other priesthood holder can do much to help prospective missionaries stay worthy.

Financial preparation for missionary service should also be a part of every family's plan for the future. Young people can start a missionary savings plan, making regular contributions, even when they are very small. Income from employment, gifts, or other resources could be carefully preserved. When an immediate family member is not serving full-time, it may be possible for some families to assist their extended family. Local priesthood quorums and the Church's general missionary fund all have need for contributions to support members on missions who cannot afford to support themselves.

Mental preparation for a mission might include study of a foreign language, development of good study skills, scripture memorization, and gospel scholarship. Enrollment in seminary and institute programs can be very helpful with these skills.

A balanced personality with good mental health adjustment is important for a missionary. Good work habits should also be a goal of each youth. These can be established through teaching self-discipline, participating in extracurricular activities or athletics at school, or learning a skill, such as a musical instrument, voice, dance. Part-time employment or work on a farm also helps teach the discipline of work.

Social skills and graces should be taught in the home by the parents. Good manners, conversational experience, and an attitude of service and cooperation with others are important to prepare a proper people. Cooking skills, principles of nutrition, personal hygiene, grooming, and clean dress are necessary. Spirituality, testimony, prayer, scripture study, faith, and repentance should all be part of the preparation for missionary service. In addition, association with returned missionaries can be a strong influence for those who may have concerns or reservations about serving a mission.

MILITARY SERVICE

Many countries require their citizens to serve in the military forces. All Church members have a sacred obligation to be loyal and patriotic to their government. "We believe in being subject to kings, presidents, rulers, and magistrates, in obeying, honoring, and sustaining the law." (Article of Faith 12.) "Let no man break the laws of the land, for he that keepeth the laws of God hath no need to break the laws of the land. Wherefore, be subject to the powers that be, until he reigns whose right it is to reign." (D&C 58:21–22.)

Parents can help their children to know the correct information and options available or required in the military. In some cases, full-time missions may have to be carefully coordinated with military obligations. For others, many opportunities may be available in the military, such as on-the-job training, college scholarships, part-time employment, financial assistance, career exploration and training, and even church and missionary service opportunities.

Prior to entering the military, a person should have an interview with the bishop. Materials are available from the Church Military Relations committee. The location of the nearest church services and names of chaplains can be determined. Church publications and magazines can also be ordered, as well as a small set of scriptures and church books. These are usually provided free of charge. The bishop will also make available to those who have received their endowments special instructions regarding the temple garments. Family members can offer support through their faith, prayer, correspondence, and love. Those living near military installations may assist by providing Church programs and wholesome community activities to personnel stationed there.

TEMPLE MARRIAGE

The single most important decision a person makes in mortality is to marry the right person in the right place at the right time. The most careful plans need to be made to make temple marriage (or sealing after civil marriage) a part of the future of every member. Parents can assist children by keeping open the lines of communication, teaching correct gospel principles, assisting youth with the development of wholesome associations with positive friendships, and by providing appropriate opportunities for social growth and experiences in the home and community. Perhaps the best teaching parents can do to prepare children for temple marriage is to be an example and be married in the temple themselves.

Even though individual maturity and readiness for courtship and marriage vary among individuals, the Lord has outlined the proper sequence for events to occur that lead to temple marriage. President Spencer W. Kimball said: "Now is the time for you to plan good strong marriages and organize your programs and set your standards and solidify your determination to prepare for that married period of your lives which will be beautiful and rewarding. Accordingly, my beloved young people, you should be serious-minded. Life is not wholly for fun and frolic. It is a most serious business. You will do well to grow up as children, associating with both girls and boys for those first years. When you get in the teenage years, your social associations should still be general acquaintance with both boys and girls. Any dating or pairing off in social contacts should be postponed until at least age 16 or older, and even then much judgment used in selections and in the seriousness.

"Young people should still limit the close contacts for several years, since the boy will be going on his mission when he is 19 years old. There should be limited contacts and certainly no approach to the intimate relationships involving sex. There must never be any sex of any kind prior to marriage.

"Every boy should have been saving money for his mission and be free from any and all entanglements so he will be worthy. When he is returned from his mission at 21, he should feel free to begin to get acquainted and to date. When he has found the right young woman, there should be a proper temple marriage. One can have all the blessings if he is in control and takes the experiences in proper turn: first some limited social get-acquainted contacts, then his mission, then his courting, then his temple marriage and his schooling and his family, then his life's work.

In any other sequence he could run into difficulty." (*Ensign*, February 1975, p. 2.)

To be married in the temple, a couple should usually be Church members for at least one year. The husband must hold the Melchizedek Priesthood. A temple recommend must be obtained from the bishop and countersigned by a member of the stake presidency or other authorized person. Instructions will be given at that time regarding the temple garment. The temple personnel where the marriage is to be performed should be notified in advance so adequate accommodations can be provided. After the temple ceremony a couple should return to the temple as often as possible. They should devote the rest of their life to making the temple marriage a celestial marriage. Many helps on parenting and family relations are provided in Church magazines, lesson manuals, family resource materials, and in classes taught by each organization of the Church.

CAREER PREPARATION

It is the responsibility of every person and each family to provide for their own needs, as far as possible within their own ability. Adam was instructed to work by the sweat of his brow all the days of his life. One purpose of the welfare program of the Church is to teach the dignity of work. In order to have the time necessary for successful family relationships, and to have time to build up the kingdom of God on the earth through service to the Church and community, it is important that children carefully plan and prepare themselves for careers that provide sufficient financial support for their needs and the needs of family members.

The most noble of all careers is parenting. Young brethren need training and experience working with infants and young children. Priesthood lessons and family activities teach important lessons in being successful and loving fathers. Young women should learn skills of homemaking and working with children, as well as develop careers suitable for employment outside the home in case the need for them to work outside the home ever arises.

Parents have many opportunities to teach their children how to prepare for the world of work. Small children can learn to take care of toys and be responsible for small household tasks. The care of a pet can teach responsibility. Communication skills of reading, writing, listening, and speaking can be practiced in family settings. Parents can be actively involved in the child's school classes by serving as volunteers and teacher assistants. A pleasant environment for homework can be provided, along with appropriate encouragement and assistance. Successful personal relationships and getting along with others can be modeled.

Most schools, libraries, and government agencies provide resources to assist with career selection. The Church has ward, stake, and regional employment centers that may be of assistance. Post-high-school training should be part of the plan for each youth. Professional, vocational, technical, or apprenticeship training programs should be carefully evaluated. Constant on-the-job training, in-service, and professional development programs, and the upgrading of skills and abilities, should be taken advantage of throughout one's life.

PORNOGRAPHY

To members of the Church and moral people throughout the world, pornography is abhorrent. Their spirits and their consciences are repelled by the filthy smudge pornography places upon every contact it makes in the community.

The thirteenth Article of Faith says: "If there is anything virtuous, lovely, or of good report or praiseworthy, we seek after these things." Conversely, if there is anything repugnant and filthy we should detest and resist it, recognizing it as an enemy and antagonistic to the Lord's plan.

Pornography degrades, dehumanizes, and exploits those who participate in its promotion, those who view it, and those who are inadvertently and unwillingly subjected to it.

Elder David B. Haight, of the Quorum of the Twelve Apostles, has said: "Over the past twenty years a plague of pornography has swept across most countries of the world with increasing momentum and devastating impact. What began a few years ago as a few crude picture magazines that startled sensitive people has grown to hundreds of publications, each seeking to outdo the others with increasingly shocking content. . . .

"New technologies that can bless our lives in so many positive ways are also being used to spread pornographic corruption. . . . Cable television and satellite transmissions . . . are also being abused. Video recorders now can bring to homes lurid portrayals that contaminate those who view them." (*Ensign*, November 1984, pp. 70–73.)

President Spencer W. Kimball said, "So long as men are corrupt and revel in sewer filth, entertainers will sell them what they want. Laws may be passed, arrests may be made, lawyers may argue, courts may sentence . . . men of corrupt minds, but pornography and . . . insults to decency will never cease until men have cleansed their minds. . . . When the customer is sick and tired of being drowned in filth . . . he will not pay for that filth and its source will dry up."

Continuing, President Kimball said, "Hence it is obvious that to remain clean and worthy, one must stay positively and conclusively away from the devil's territory, avoiding the least approach toward evil. Satan leaves his fingerprints." (*The Miracle of Forgiveness* [Salt Lake City: Bookcraft, 1969], pp. 229, 232.)

Elder Haight continues: "Only when men and women concerned for their families and communities let their voices and their influence be felt in thoughtful, rational ways will we alter the destructive course on which we are traveling. Silent indignation may be misinterpreted as approval. Irrational action may be ineffective because it is regarded as prudish rather than thoughtful." He further suggests several steps for parents to use when trying to halt pornography:

1. "Discuss with your children of appropriate age, and in sensitive ways, the harmful effects and addictive nature of such material. Rigidly monitor the selection of television programs, movies, videocassettes, music, and other forms of entertainment for your family. . . .

2. "Foster in your homes a love of knowledge through uplifting literature; wholesome books; selective movies and television; classical and exemplary popular music; entertainment that uplifts and edifies the spirit and mind. . . .

3. "Let our voices be heard in our communities—members and nonmembers alike. If something offends standards of decency, our voices should be heard. We would encourage members to

persevere in their efforts to work with local groups and to establish a visible relationship with other like-minded citizens, and seek to preserve our quality of life by encouraging steps against such material. . . .

4. "Actively approach the management of some stores, movie theaters, bookstore, television and radio stations, with a request to withdraw indecent materials from public display or use or patronage. Of course, such efforts should be consistent with the constitutional process, exercising gentle persuasion. . . .

5. "Make our own elected officials and law enforcement people aware that we support the fair enforcement of laws prohibiting obscenity and regulating indecency, thank them for their past service and present efforts, and encourage them to continue the difficult and sometimes thankless task of strictly enforcing the existing laws in a consistent and fair manner. . . .

6. "Where legislation is needed to meet new technological advances in cable and satellite transmission, let us support the enactment of reasonable laws and regulations that would help reduce the number of those whose lives will otherwise become marred by addiction. . . .

7. "Let us exercise our faith and prayerfully seek help from God our Father in this vital task. There are some who believe that the pornography industry is out of control, already too powerful to curb. . . . We know that people of good will, united in such a worthy cause, where the moral fiber of our nations may be at stake, and aided by divine power, can overcome any obstacle and meet any challenge to help our Lord and Savior to bring to pass the immortality and eternal life of man." (*Ensign*, November 1984, pp. 70–73.)

It is all righteous parents' desire that their children be spared exposure to, and influence of, pornography. However, there may be times when this cannot be avoided. The following suggestions may help when dealing with such situations.

It is a tragic reality that even children of younger years have fallen prey to the evil influence of pornography. It is not always possible to monitor what children are exposed to outside the home. In one instance, an eight-year-old child viewed an X-rated video while visiting a friend. Upon discovering what had happened, the wise parents of this child turned what could have been a destructive experience into an opportunity to teach their child righteous principles.

They began by deciding not to act alarmed or punitive toward the child. Rather, they gently encouraged him to talk about what he had seen and how he felt about it. Although they had wanted to wait for a more opportune time, the parents chose to take this moment to explain the importance, beauty, and sacredness of sexual relationships between a husband and wife. After teaching their son about the proper and only acceptable use of the procreative powers, they then said that evil people wanted to take this special gift of our Heavenly Father and turn it into something that was degrading and filthy. That is what he had seen on the video. They lovingly insisted that it was wrong to watch such things, and that they should be avoided at all times. When any of his friends made such wrong choices, he should leave and tell his mother or father. The boy was then given a father's blessing.

Parents should understand that how a child reacts and is affected by such an exposure to pornography will depend largely on how they react to the child. Little if any harm can come from such an occurrence if the parents treat the child with love and patience, teaching instead of punishing.

The problem of pornography changes somewhat as children approach their teens. How often have the sensibilities of a tender, loving mother been shocked when she discovers a pornographic magazine not-so-discreetly tucked away between the pages of an algebra text while cleaning underneath the bed of her teenage son? The normal reaction of many parents would be to think that their child has become a "porno-junkie" and that they have failed in raising him to be righteous. While the gravity of such moments should not be minimized, parents should understand that many young people will be tempted by pornography, and that with firm and loving concern, such problems can usually be corrected with little long-lasting negative effect.

If you should discover that your child has possession of a pornographic magazine or has watched a pornographic film or video, take the time to thoroughly discuss it with the child. A hasty whirlwind of punishing language will do little if anything in helping to resolve the problem. Let the child know that you are genuinely concerned by giving the necessary attention to the situation.

As you talk with your child, asking questions that will allow the child to evaluate his or her own behavior can be helpful. You may want to ask:

As you look at such material, how do you feel? Do you feel uplifted or edified?

What do you suppose the people who create pornography want to appeal to inside of you? Is it something that you really want to be a part of?

How does watching pornography fit in with your beliefs as a member of the family? As a member of the Church?

Parents should remember that adolescence is a time when children must learn to understand their sexuality and its proper role in their lives. The temptation to resort to pornography will diminish if parents encourage their children to talk about their feelings as their bodies change and they make the transition from child to adult.

If it is apparent that a child's obsession with pornography has become an uncontrolled habit, this may indicate a graver problem. Professional help should be sought.

President Ezra Taft Benson has emphatically stated, "There has never been more expected of the faithful in such a short period of time than there is of us. Never before on the face of the earth have the forces of evil and the forces of good been so well organized. . . . The final outcome is certain—the forces of righteousness will finally win. But what remains to be seen is *where* each of us personally, now and in the future, will stand in this battle—and how tall will we stand?" (*Ensign*, April 1987, p. 73.)

Individuals must first purify their own lives and then strengthen their homes and beware of the insidious forces that desire to thwart eternal progress. Jesus Christ's hope is all-encompassing, and will offer peace and protection to those who humbly follow him.

(SEE ALSO MEDIA INFLUENCES)

PROFANITY AND VULGAR LANGUAGE

Words have great power. They can uplift and encourage or hurt and degrade. A single word can instantly create a mental picture or produce a strong emotion. Our Father in heaven knew the power and influence of language and he blessed his children, above all his creations, with the ability to communicate through speaking and writing. He has taught the importance of using this great privilege for pure and uplifting purposes. And he has spoken of his displeasure when men abuse this privilege. "Thou shalt not take the name of the Lord thy God in vain; for the Lord will not hold him guiltless that taketh his name in vain." (Exodus 20:7.)

"But I say unto you, Swear not at all . . . " (Matthew 5:34.)

"Let no corrupt communication proceed out of your mouth, but that which is good to the use of edifying, that it may minister grace unto the hearers." (Ephesians 4:29.)

"Wherefore, let all men beware how they take my name in their lips—for behold, verily I say, that many there be who are under this condemnation, who use the name of the Lord, and use it in vain, having not authority." (D&C 63:61–62.)

"There are several kinds of profanity. First, there are those expressions in which the names of Deity are used. This includes such expressions that are derivatives of the names of Deity, such as *jeez, gol,* and so forth. We find offense in both the title of Deity being used in a profane manner and the shortened or adulterated versions.

"Another kind of profanity is a group of four-letter words that are commonly used in anger, frustration—and even, sad to say, everyday speech. They are a cheap substitute for an inadequate vocabulary, and there is no excuse for their use by people who know better and who are adult enough to think before using them." (Robert E. Wells, *New Era,* September 1987, p. 6.)

Even though some words may seem to be harmless substitutes for swear words, such as *darn, heck,* and so forth, these words do not clearly describe to ourselves or express to others our true sentiments. Good mental health requires that we become able to identify and share our thoughts, beliefs, expectations, and feelings in clear language. When you hit your thumb with a hammer, the pain is intense. Clearly describing how it hurts will be more healing than just sending out raw anger. When something you have been working on falls apart or doesn't turn out right, describing your frustration and feelings of inadequacy followed by a silent prayer will obviously help more than cursing yourself, your materials, your equipment, and your associates.

Vulgar language is disrespectful or hostile in nature. Constant expressions of hostility and anger are vague and of little value. Just about all they do is produce more anger more easily. In contrast, precise words that identify our true feelings can be very therapeutic.A grandmother, after tending three sick grandchildren for a week, was criticized by her daughter for not having taken the children to the doctor. The grandmother became resentful and angry and swore as she told her daughter to find someone else to care for her children next time. With the help of a friend the grandmother learned that her true feelings were better expressed with words such as: unfairly criticized, misjudged, misunderstood, unappreciated, used, and taken advantage of.

She went back to her daughter and said, "I apologize for being angry with you when you picked up your children last week. My true feelings were that I felt misjudged by you and unappreciated for the many sleepless nights I spent taking care of your sick baby. I raised you and your five brothers and sisters with help of our family doctor and I don't think you give me credit for knowing what the doctor would recommend we do. I did the best I could. I made some sacrifices to care for your children so you could have a vacation. I was willing to do that until you criticized how I handled things. Then I felt used by you. Now I am not interested in caring for your children because I don't think I can please you. I don't like to be criticized. I want to have a better relationship and to reconcile our differences. I would like to discuss it further when you are ready."

The daughter then cried and confessed that when she had taken the children to the doctor he had confirmed that the grandmother had talked with him by phone and had done all that was needed, and that he told her to continue the same routine with the other children until they were well. The daughter asked for her mother's forgiveness. They embraced and completely cleared up their ill feelings. Then they had a heart-to-heart talk, sharing

other feelings and needs with each other. This was made possible
by the clear, descriptive language used by the grandmother.

By our language we can show we are a reverent and wholesome
people who understand the sacredness of the names of the Father
and the Son and our eternal relationship to them. There are also
many ways we can help children learn to choose uplifting language. Here are some ideas:

1. Set a proper example in the home. Show your children how
to express their feelings, whether good or bad, with descriptive
words.

Sometimes parents do not realize that they are teaching their
children to express anger and frustration with the four-letter words
that they themselves use. Later they are shocked to hear their
children repeat these words.

A father and son sat milking the cows together early one
morning. As the tail of the boy's cow hit him in the face, the boy
let out a stream of profane words that went on until he had fully
vented his hurt and anger on the cow. The boy gave no thought
to his language because he had grown up hearing his father constantly express himself in like manner. Upon hearing his son's
profanity, the father was deeply dismayed and sat in silence for
some time, realizing what had taken place. Slowly he drew his
stool over to his son's side, put his arm around him, and said,
"If you will never speak like that again, neither will I."

2. Teach family members that when we use obscene, vulgar,
profane, or slang words they offend the Holy Ghost and cause
him to withdraw from us. Parents who hear children using unacceptable words should tell them firmly, "We do not talk that
way in our family."

3. Teach children the sacredness of the Lord's name and the
appropriate times we use the names of Deity. President Kimball
impressed upon Church members the reverence we should have
for these sacred names. "In the hospital one day I was wheeled
out of the operating room by an attendant who stumbled, and
there issued from his angry lips vicious cursing with a combination
of the names of the Savior. Even half-conscious, I recoiled and
implored: 'Please! Please! That is my Lord whose names you
revile.' There was a deathly silence, and a subdued voice whispered, 'I'm sorry.' " (Ensign, February 1981, p. 3.)

4. Teach children to have love and respect for other races and ethnic groups, and to refrain from telling insensitive jokes and stories about them. Encourage them to develop a healthy sense of humor and learn some appropriate jokes to tell and share with others.

5. Use family home evenings and family discussions to teach about the importance of refraining from using vulgar and profane words. Ask children to tell how they feel when they hear people swear or tell a dirty joke. Explain that the embarrassment and discomfort come from the Holy Ghost, who tells us that these things are not good.

6. Teach children how to be an influence for good by encouraging others to avoid unclean or profane speech or gestures. Elder Rex D. Pinegar of the First Quorum of the Seventy tells the following experience:

"One day my older brother, Lynn, came hurrying home from high school basketball practice, bringing a teammate with him. Upon entering the house, both made a dash for the kitchen to satisfy their hungry appetites. My brother's friend loudly described his feeling of hunger by using a few vulgar and profane words to accent his anxious mood. Lynn quickly, quietly, but firmly said, 'Hey, don't talk like that. My little brothers might hear you. I don't want them to learn words like that. Besides, they might think less of you than they ought to.'

"Unknown to my brother, my friend and I did hear that conversation, but the profane words were quickly erased from my mind by the thoughtful concern and courage shown by my older brother. That experience made a positive, lasting impression on my young mind. At the risk of sacrificing a friendship, his kindly chastisement of his friend taught me a lesson of love and concern for others and of courage to uphold the right." (Ensign, May 1974, pp. 68–69.)

7. Build children's vocabulary with uplifting and beautiful words so they feel confident in expressing themselves and using the gift of speech to help them progress in all walks of life. Fill their lives with the teachings of the gospel so that they know when they have the Spirit and when they do not.

The damage done by using vulgar language or listening to off-color stories may not be immediately apparent. But the Spirit leaves us when we choose these ugly things of the world, and it is difficult to entice it to return. As the Savior warned: "Every idle word that men shall speak, they shall give account thereof in the day of judgment. For by thy words thou shalt be justified, and by thy words thou shalt be condemned." (Matthew 12:36–37.)

8. Teach children to have good manners, to show respect, and to be polite and reverent. Teach them these skills beginning at infancy. Thank them and praise them when they are polite and respectful.

9. Encourage children to evaluate the books, television, and movies they see that use vulgar language. Caution them to fill their minds with pictures and words in harmony with gospel teachings.

When parents hear their child swear, they should say firmly and clearly, "We do not use that kind of language in our home." If this does not work, isolate the child in the bathroom or another area of the home with instructions to think about what he or she has said, then come talk it over. Then help the child put into clear, appropriate language how he or she felt and what was really meant.

You may also wish to hold a family council meeting to discuss the use of language. As a family, make a list of words that describe feelings, and decide how to help each other avoid vulgar or any other words that do not clearly describe what you think or feel. Finally, pay attention to and give immediate credit for any progress a child makes in clearly expressing feelings in acceptable language.

If children have developed a bad habit of using profane words, help them develop new speech patterns and encourage them to ask in their prayers for the Lord's strengthening influence.

One person tells of his struggle to overcome a lifetime habit of vile language:

"Giving up the actual obscenities was easy. In fact, one of the first signs of success was that vulgarity began to offend me. Within two weeks, however, I was talking the same way as before, except that the expletives were words like 'shoot,' 'darn,' and 'gads.' But since I viewed the words as harmless, I used them without restraint; I depended on expletives more than ever.

"Then one day it occurred to me that over the years I had developed speech patterns that relied heavily on swear words. By retaining those speech patterns, I was still offending many listeners, who were reminded of vulgar words by the substitutes. I realized I'd probably never fully escape the use of vulgarity if I continued using the substitute words.

"I solved the problem by changing the way I talked. After a sentence with a swear word or a substitute word slipped out, I mentally reconstructed the sentence without the expletive and repeated the new sentence aloud. Eventually, I developed non-vulgar speech habits." (Kent H. Roberts, *Ensign*, January 1982, p. 35.)

Often when we hear the profanities and obscenities around us we can relate to what Lot felt as he was "vexed with the filthy conversation of the wicked." (2 Peter 2:7.) Latter-day Saints can use the gift of speech to bless others and themselves. Through this power the Lord can use us to cheer, praise, encourage, and console. If we love the Lord we will not offend him with profane or impure language.

QUARRELING

(SEE TEASING AND QUARRELING)

REBELLION

Latter-day Saint parents can be especially susceptible to rebellion from their children. The standards that are precious to such parents are extremely obvious. And children who have the inclination to rebel or wish to hurt their parents can focus on these standards as an easy target. Outside the Church, where values may not be as clearly defined, there is usually a greater tendency for children to select other targets as a focal point for their disobedience. They often turn against school or government officials—wherever there is restraint there will often be rebellion. Knowing this may comfort Latter-day Saint parents, and it should increase their understanding. When they ask themselves, "Why me?" or, "What could I have done more?" at least they will understand that rebellion affects many parents in the Church.

Rebellion is described and forcefully treated in the scriptures. Most often it is found among those going against or rejecting our Father in heaven. He is merciful, however, and ever receptive to repentant souls who see that they have erred and are sorry. This gentleness and love is illustrated in the Gospel of Matthew: "Bless them that curse you . . . pray for them which despitefully use you. . . . That ye may be the children of your Father which is in heaven: for he maketh his sun to rise on the evil and on the good, and sendeth rain on the just and on the unjust." (Matthew 5:44–45.)

We do not swat insects with a large stick when they threaten a meal displayed on fine china. The reason is self-evident. Damaging the insect may result in far greater damage to something more valuable. Seldom does the disobedient act of a child merit a "big stick" approach: the value of the soul is too great to be placed at risk by some small temporal infraction.

Rebellion or disobedience covers a spectrum, ranging from very small to major offenses against authority. The more serious the offense, the more careful parents must be in the actions they take. A successful reconciliation will result most often if parents gain an understanding of the cause. Rebellion may be manifesting a child's sadness or hurt feelings. It may be to cover despair. If it is from some perceived hurt caused by parents, children may try to return that hurt. Their attacks can be most effective, even devastating. Rebellion may also be an indicator of other problems, particularly if it is out of character for the child concerned. It can even be a means of reaching out. The child may know no other way.

What can parents do to prevent or deal with rebellion?

1. Build a relationship of mutual trust and respect. Elder H. Burke Peterson tells of a taxi driver he once met who made sure he was home every evening to be with his son. When asked why, the man replied, "I know he will only be obedient if he knows of my love and respect for him and also feels love and respect for me." (*Teach Them Correct Principles*, p. 56.)

Perhaps no point made in this writing is more important than the one above. Parents should start very early to build personal relationships with their children. Hours spent wrestling, horseback riding, playing basketball, bicycling, or just talking when children are six or seven years old will repay parents many times over when those children reach their teens. The quality of the relationship a parent has is the foundation for successfully dealing with rebellion. This relationship must start young. And even if a parent doesn't now have such a relationship, it is *never* too late to start. It always pays for the time invested.

2. Do not rescue children from the consequences of their behavior. Consequences differ from punishment. Consequences are the direct results of a child's behavior. Punishment is a form of retribution imposed by one in authority. Though it can be fair, punishment often incites counterreactions from those punished. Allowing the natural or logical consequences to follow unacceptable behavior can be a more effective tool.

Rebellious children tend to believe that they are somehow able to avoid the consequences of their acts, that they need not fear the law, harm, or accident. Transgression of a spiritual law seldom results immediately in a severe punishment. Consequently, the rebellious often tempt officers who are charged with enforcement of spiritual laws because these rebellious ones feel invincible, or they may just be caught up in the moment of excitement. Even though these feelings are incorrect, parents would do well to remember their own youth, and say as one prophet: "For we ourselves also were sometimes foolish, disobedient, deceived." (Titus 3:3.)

This is not to say that parents should justify the rebellious acts of their children because of their own, which may have "turned out all right." But remembering their own youth may add insight and wisdom in handling a rebellious child. Wise parents can allow consequences to follow without using punishment for revenge.

3. Do not treat children as possessions. This truth should remain uppermost in parents' minds: Children are not possessions. They are part of parental stewardship. The Lord forgives whom he will forgive, but parents must strive to forgive all people (especially their children).

4. Avoid preaching and commanding. Sin intensifies the distinction between right and wrong in the mind of a transgressor.

Those who have acted contrary to what they know to be right are keenly aware at first that the act is out of harmony with their principles. Belaboring and overstressing what is "right" is usually unprofitable. Calmly and quietly pointing out alternatives and consequences is usually more effective.

A parent may say, "You *will* take a seminary class!" The chances of the child actually taking the seminary class, however, may well be diminished with this approach. And even if the child obeys, the chances of his or her actually learning something in seminary are very slim. However, even this approach may be successful, if proper training and respect for parents have been attained very early in a child's life.

5. Recognize the causes of your child's rebellion. Sin is not the only cause for rebellion. Often it is merely a stage the child is going through. One father noticed that each of his daughters at about age fourteen began to violently dislike the household chores assigned to them. Each one in turn seemed to show the same reaction. Though he continued to insist that the chores be done, he also noticed that at about age sixteen these same daughters seemed to settle in, perhaps resigned to the inevitability of the tasks. At least what appeared to be rebellion gradually subsided.

Children usually rebel as they seek for their own identity. They want to be their own unique selves, apart from their parents and family but, paradoxically, identified and one with their peers. Helping children to be themselves begins early in their childhood. This will tend to reduce their need to rebel later.

Children who are given many personal choices early in life learn at an early age who they are and what they like. They also gain confidence in making decisions. Choosing to wear poor color combinations, skipping their homework, oversleeping and missing the school bus, or overspending may all provide valuable opportunities for children to learn, provided they experience the consequences of their behavior and are not bailed out by rescuing parents. Typically, conscientious parents tend to pressure or force their children to do what is right, then rescue them when they make unwise choices or act irresponsibly. This sets up the conditions for rebellion later in life. Children quickly learn that it is important to mother that they wear color-coordinated clothing, comb their hair, shine their shoes, and so forth. Mothers frequently say, "What kind of mother would I be if I let my child go to school looking like that?" This just gives the rebellious child more ammunition to use against the mother. Some things are less important than others. When a child begins to feel the difference between wearing shoes on the right feet versus having them on the wrong feet, that child will be willing to learn the difference between the right and left shoes.

6. Keep your sense of humor. Rebellion may take on many faces, and each face may require a different approach. Humor (not sarcasm) is often a very good distraction from a rebellious attitude. Helpful humor is gentle and reflects the simple, obvious truth of an incident. Humor may be based on the actions of the parent, but should not be sarcastic, downgrading, or critical of the child. The laughter that follows must never be at the child's expense.

One father became tired of hearing his children say "This is boring!" when they were asked to practice the piano. He developed a standard phrase as a comeback: "Boring can be fun, you know." It wasn't long before the children knew that any gripe about piano would be met with the same response. The apparent irony of the statement always intrigued them, and it wasn't long before they would say themselves, "I know, I know, boring can be fun!" And off they would go to practice the tedious notes, knowing that the eventual reward was indeed probably worth the "boredom" of practice now.

7. Reflect gospel values without imposing your standards on your children. Raising children in conformity with Church recommendations is extremely important. Regular scripture study, family home evening, personal and family prayers, and regular attendance at meetings with the proper Spirit all help to build a foundation for a joyful future. But, they do not guarantee a child's respect for parents or obedience to their teachings. They do provide a foundation upon which a child may build, and to which he or she may return. (See Proverbs 22:6.)

8. Ask for the Lord's help. A parent may use fasting and family and personal prayer to find the solution to a problem. Parents may also wish to share with their children spiritual experiences they have had that helped them determine their own course.

9. Become a consultant more than a supervisor to your chil-

dren. Be a teacher or a consultant for as long as you have a listening audience. When you see barriers or defensiveness, stop teaching. Observe and listen until you regain the child's attention. Consultants are invited to share in their knowledge so that the client may make a more informed decision. The client (in this case, the child) remains free to make the choice (and responsible for the consequences of that choice). Supervisors often give directions that are resented and followed only when someone with authority and control is watching. As soon as the supervisor or parent is out of sight, the children will do as they please without considering the wisdom of their parents.

As rebellious children become more set in their ways, they may become less and less aware of the distinction between right and wrong. Help them to understand that the decisions being made are theirs, that the consequences, joyful or distasteful, will be the result of their own decisions. Refrain, where possible, from demanding that they do what you (the parent) want. In the child's mind, this can shift blame for the actions from the child to the parent. Learning obedience may be a long, uncomfortable process. The Lord says, "My people must needs be chastened until they learn obedience, if it must needs be, by the things which they suffer." (D&C 105:6.)

10. Observe your child's behavior. Watch carefully to determine how the child values himself or herself. If genuine achievements or accolades received as a result of honest accomplishment do not buoy a child up, at least temporarily, it may be an indication of growing rebellion. When usual forms of recognition do not motivate, a child may look for other, less desirable ways to find fulfillment.

11. Separate your own identity from that of your child. Separating yourself from your child will lessen the pain and embarrassment you feel when your child does things that displease you. It will also give your child more credit when he or she achieves important things in life. This will also take away the child's control over you.

Understandably, you will feel embarrassed and hurt when your children do things that violate your lifestyle, standards, and values. You may fear being rejected and misjudged by your own friends. You may also feel blamed or may blame others for your child's behavior. Children quickly learn the things that are important to parents, and will often use those to establish their own individuality. Imagine that your child belonged to your neighbor. How would you treat the child then?

When you feel separate from your children you can agree when others share with you their criticism or their praise. One father of an outstanding son was approached by several people after his son's missionary farewell and told how fine and impressive his son was to them. Instead of accepting the compliment for himself by saying, "Thank you," the father said, "I agree. He really is a fine person. I respect him greatly and I enjoy being his father." This father had another son, a so-called "black sheep." He had the experience of having people complain to him about the wayward son's behavior. He would reply with, "Yes, it is very frustrating. He is not choosing to do what is best for himself and I find my role as his parent to be very challenging. I would appreciate your help and your suggestions."

12. Continue the normal family routine. Family life should not be centered around a rebellious child. Parents should consider and discuss the feelings of the other children. Since all individuals are different, reaction to undesirable behavior within a home may range from support to extreme anger at the rebellious one. Rebellion is not a reason for changing family rules, but it may be an occasion to review them objectively.

A family faced with a child who stubbornly refused to obey family rules (even though all other members had agreed that the rules were necessary) eventually consigned the rebellious one to his fate. He had to leave the home. They expressed a desire for him to change and join their family again, but held firm that family rules would have to be obeyed. The young man packed his bags and boarded a bus. After a ride of 150 miles and a night sleeping beside the roadside, the boy returned, acknowledging the justice of the rules.

Parents who live their lives for their children, trying hard to provide them with a haven away from the world, sometimes seem to find only partial success. If this seems so, parents should look closely and deeply at their own setting. If some children seem to hear and understand clearly what is said, but one does not, perhaps the sounds the rebellious child hears are not from the parents at all. Parents should persist in their efforts, continue in their hope, recognize the limitations of their influence, and acknowledge the freedom of the soul. If none of the children seem to hearken, professional counseling may assist parents in their efforts to perfect the family setting.

Always remember that parents are important, too. Their wellbeing and healthy survival are enhanced if they realize that they are the same people they were before this problem, and their selfworth should not be diminished by it. Dispel any guilt feelings that are inappropriate. Most important, improve the quantity and quality of your communication with others. Include your friends when you feel comfortable doing so. Discussion helps to clarify perspective.

13. Never give up. You don't fail as a parent until you give up on your children.

(SEE ALSO RUNAWAYS)

REMARRIAGE

Marriage is part of God's plan for eternal progress and joy. But some parents find themselves in situations where either the marriage fails or one spouse passes away. As a result, parents and children often come to experience some difficult changes. One of these is the possibility of remarriage. After a certain healing period, there is usually that inner desire to again have a mate. This generally brings with it new, sometimes wonderful experiences, and it always bring new problems.

Before stepping into a new marriage, carefully consider and discuss how the arrangement will affect all concerned. How will discipline of the children be handled? How will finances be merged? What role will the gospel play? Of course, it is impossible to solve all these issues before marriage, but talking as much as possible before remarriage will help. Take time to imagine things that could go wrong and anticipate solutions.

If finances can be worked out, building or buying a different home is probably the most sensible decision. This way there are no memories to challenge the new family. Children in the same bedroom will have *our* room, not *my* room that now must be shared. If this is not possible, and the family moves into *his* or *her* home, there should be a freedom to change things, maybe even redecorate. Involve all family members, thereby making it *our* home.

New family members should take every opportunity to become acquainted. Learn to be as comfortable as possible with each other. Arrange for as much interaction as possible—with such activities as picnics, sports, visits to the zoo, and meals. Soon these activities should become times of enjoyment together.

Names may cause problems. Asking a child to call a new father "Dad," for instance, may cause the child to feel disloyal to the natural father. An arrangement between child and new parent should be reached together as soon as possible. Allow the child to help decide what to call the stepparent.

An oldest child may feel very displaced by a remarriage, being bumped out of the leadership role, and may need special attention. Some children try to force their remarried parents to make a choice between them and the new spouse. Extra time and understanding will probably be necessary.

The ages of the children often determine the amount of adjustment necessary. Younger children usually accept a new parent more readily. Be aware that bonding to another person does not automatically occur just because a marriage has taken place. If it happens at all, it will take time and honest effort on the part of all involved. Full acceptance has no timetable. In time, though, a oneness will usually develop.

As new mothers, new fathers, new brothers and sisters, new grandparents, aunts, and uncles are mixed together with new likes and dislikes, the new family starts to develop a flavor. Have faith—faith in yourself, your family, and the gospel.

Where possible, strive for temple marriage. If a wife has been previously sealed to a worthy partner and the partner has died, such a sealing would not be possible. However, when it can be done, being sealed in the temple adds commitment to the partnership. In any case, if the partners are worthy, the marriage can take place in the temple (perhaps for time only). Having the same goals and beliefs is important. "Be ye not unequally yoked together with unbelievers: for what fellowship hath righteousness with unrighteousness? and what communion hath light with darkness?" (2 Corinthians 6:14.)

GOSPEL GUIDELINES FOR THE NEW FAMILY

Plan and want to succeed. "Without faith it is impossible to please" God. (Hebrews 11:6.)

Love each other. "This is my commandment, That ye love one another, as I have loved you." (John 15:12.)

Serve each other. "Ought not ye to labor to serve one another?" (Mosiah 2:18.)

Keep the commandments. "If thou lovest me thou shalt serve me and keep all my commandments." (D&C 42:29.)

Pray. "Ask, and it shall be given you; seek, and ye shall find; knock, and it shall be opened unto you." (Matthew 7:7.)

Family prayer, family home evening, church meetings, scripture study, and paying tithes all bond a family together. This does not happen overnight or without any trials, however.

DISCIPLINING THE CHILDREN

Putting two sets of children together will require patience. Disciple can be a very difficult task.

Some couples find it helpful to agree that the natural parent will primarily discipline his or her children, and the stepparent will be the only one who dispenses rewards—money, allowances, and so forth. This helps break up common manipulation patterns that children develop.

Parents with children in a remarriage must agree early what method of discipline will be used and what rules of behavior the children will follow. Strict discipline may have to wait a little until there is a bonded relationship with all the children. One young man tells of his experience with his stepparents: "When I met my new stepmother I told her, 'You're not my mother. You don't love me. I don't have to do anything you say.' She surprised me by saying 'That's right, I'm not your mother. We will just have to learn to love each other.' From that time on I tried to do everything possible to get her love. She treated me very fairly. When I broke a rule I experienced the consequence. When I did what was expected I received those rewards. One of the happiest days in my life came when I was twenty-five years old and went to the temple to be sealed to my father and stepmother."

All couples who successfully put together two families must learn the necessity and value of clear and healthy communication, wherein they always come to understand each other, even though they may not always agree. Then they must creatively find ways to cooperate, even in the absence of agreement.

They also must learn that some children refuse to cooperate and be helpful. Parents cannot be as successful without the full cooperation of children, but this cannot be forced or controlled in all cases. They must find sufficient meaning and value for themselves in the marriage relationship and in their joint relationship with most of the children to endure the problems created by a few, without feeling as if they have personally failed.

If a child suddenly has to compete with several new brothers and sisters for attention that he or she has previously enjoyed undivided, the transition can be difficult. One teenage stepson said, "It was hard to think that Dad was spending all of his time with my new brother or that he was much easier on him." Another said, "We get along great. It's easier than with natural brothers. We are good friends."

One stepfather gave this advice: "When you put two families together you get a package deal, an instant family. You have to love all the same and treat each the same. It's easier to discipline your own. Sometimes I have to bite my tongue when my wife is disciplining my children. We have to support each other. As we all came to love each other we showed it by actions, and in words and feelings."

Another father expressed his concern for his son who lived with the mother and was able to visit only for short vacations. "I always wondered if my son was achieving in school and growing in the ways of the Lord."

The noncustodial parent should be involved whenever it is possible and beneficial to the child. This can happen when all the parents cooperate with each other, setting aside their own differences.

Two things that are sure to spoil a remarriage are favoritism and unjust criticism. If these can be checked early, chances of success are greater.

KEEP THE COURTSHIP IN YOUR MARRIAGE

Parents in a new marriage are under tremendous strain with their newly formed family. In all of this, they have great emotional needs themselves. They must be certain to cultivate their relationship with each other. Each has probably been used to making final decisions alone. Now they must share that responsibility. They will certainly learn new customs and habits from each other. Time must be set aside for parents to talk, laugh, and love. Constant courtship is necessary. Not only will it strengthen love, it will also help the children to better accept and trust the new parent. Couples who are truly committed to their marriage, who are determined to make it work, usually can.

As President and Sister Ezra Taft Benson marked their sixtieth wedding anniversary, it was said of their success: "Through it all they remained a team, equally yoked, he growing step by step into worldwide responsibilities, she keeping the continuity and building the strength of the family while becoming a gracious hostess; both constantly supporting each other." (*Church News*, September 7, 1987, p. 16.)

Second marriages can work. No marriage becomes perfect overnight. Children can adjust to new parental arrangements if the groundwork is properly laid and built upon.

RESPONSIBILITY

It has been said that it is more important to be trusted than to be loved. A responsible person is one who accepts and keeps commitments, who can be depended upon. This person can be trusted. The Lord expects us to use our time and talents and intelligence to think, to act, to make commitments, to keep commandments, and to accept real responsibility.

It is important to teach our children that to be responsible is a foundational principle of the gospel. Children need to obey, to honor, and to live righteously.

Each person is responsible for his or her own life. It is easy to try to pass blame for our mistakes to others: to parents, to government, or to some social situation. But no excuse or alibi, no shirking can eliminate the fact that each person is responsible for his or her own success or failure.

Adults should teach their children that few character qualities are more important than dependability, and that genuine satisfaction comes with facing our problems and solving them, by facing facts, by being a person who can be relied upon.

In teaching responsibility, we as parents should first look to the Lord for an example of the perfect teacher. From him we can get our guidelines. In the same way that the Lord teaches us, we can teach our children.

The Lord said, "This is my work and my glory—to bring to pass the immortality and eternal life of man." (Moses 1:39.) Our own work and our glory is to help him bring to pass our own immortality and eternal life as well as that of our children. He achieved his own exaltation and showed us how to work out ours. As we work to achieve our own salvation, we can show our children how to work out theirs. That is the ultimate responsibility for us and for them.

When Adam was forbidden to partake of the fruit of the tree of knowledge of good and evil, the Lord added, "nevertheless, thou mayest choose for thyself, for it is given unto thee." (See Moses 3:17.) We see from this that the Lord gives rules or commandments, then allows his children to have their agency, knowing what the results or consequences will be if the rule is not obeyed. "But, remember that I forbid it, for in the day thou eatest thereof thou shalt surely die."

Joseph Smith used the same method of teaching, saying, "I teach them correct principles and they govern themselves." (John Taylor, *Millennial Star* 13:339.)

We usually rejoice over the great gift of agency, but we often ignore the accountability that comes with it. Our blessings or our sufferings depend on our choices. There is no better method of teaching our children than to help them be accountable.

How can parents get their families to take responsibility? Parents must first love unconditionally. Then they must set guidelines, and follow through on seeing that the guidelines are met. With this as a pattern, parents can plan duties for their children, helping them acknowledge these duties as their own responsibilities.

Stephen L. Covey helps define the duty of parents: "Children first need examples or models to follow. They need understanding and respect; they need clear limits, well-established rules, and consistently applied discipline. They need explicit teaching and testifying; they need order, system and regularity; they need work and responsibility, and to give an accounting; they need time for fun, free expression, and good humor." (*Spiritual Roots of Human Relations* [Salt Lake City: Deseret Book, 1976], p. 210.) Making sure that the children have these needs taken care of is the duty of parents.

Children need to see examples of parents living up to their commitments and showing that they value work and take pleasure in it. Those children who see parents honor their promises and commitments, including punctuality, are much more likely to be responsible persons.

Because governing one's self takes years of practice, parents should help their children start early by allowing them to make choices. Begin by making choices simple and rewarding. If you ask a small child, "What do you want for lunch?" the answer might be anything or everything, good or bad. This kind of decision usually frustrates children because they can't think of anything. But if they are given a choice between, say, chicken soup or macaroni and cheese, the choice is simple and they feel satisfied in their choice.

As children grow in years and understanding, choices can be expanded. Parents often hesitate to let children make decisions because of the chance of mistakes. But we learn by doing; people grow by making mistakes. Wise fathers and mothers let children make their own decisions. They are thereby developing men and women who can stand on their own feet. Parents can provide children with a rich variety of opportunities for decision making, based on age and their ability to profit by experience.

Remember that too much of getting their own way can create self-willed, self-centered, or just plain spoiled children. There are certain decisions that are for the parents, not the child, to make. Rules of safety, bedtime, and mealtime can all be decisions that children can help make, but toddlers don't choose whether or not they play on the banks of a canal. Teens may not decide whether to go to a party or movie that parents know is soul-destructive. These choices are the responsibility of the parents.

Daily chores are another vital element in teaching responsibility. Family members should understand that there are certain things that must be done around the home to keep it running smoothly, and that they all have responsibility. Parents can guide the family as they plan daily and weekly jobs, making each person feel like a needed part in the sharing and sacrifice required in running an orderly home. A weekly family council is a good time to list such tasks. Parents' responsibilities should be included, such as earning the living, bathing the baby, and so on. Each person should have chores that he or she alone is expected to do regularly and well. Even a three-year-old can dust the bottoms of the dining room chairs.

A young mother explained to her afternoon guest: "Excuse the unpaired socks on the family room sofa. We had a household accident this morning which upset our schedule. Jason didn't have time to finish his chores before he left for school. It it still his responsibility and he'll do them as soon as he gets home." Most mothers would have preferred to fold the socks up and get them out of the way, but consistently teaching her children was more important to this wise mother.

If children fail to do their chores, determine the reason. Did they not understand? Are they lazy? Are the chores beyond their ability? Do they need some training or an apprenticeship with the parent working with them for a time? Whatever the reason, the parent shouldn't do the chore for the children. Remember the Lord's example: He never does for us what we can and should do for ourselves. (See D&C 9:7–8.) The chore is the child's stewardship. Insist that it be completed. Lovingly encourage, teach, show the way as necessary, but it is the child's responsibility. Be strict and be consistent in following through.

Children need clear limits, well-established rules. Help them to understand that every organization has rules or laws. Rules give us order and security in our homes as well. One rule that many families have is that the child must finish homework and chores before playing or watching television. Others might rule that children can specify a particular time when they will do homework. Whatever the rule is, parents must be firm and see that the children know that they are responsible to follow it. Children must learn that they are accountable for their share of the work. They must keep their promises and commitments. There is no such thing as being half-responsible. A person is either responsible or irresponsible. How dependable is a watch that tells time part of the time, but is off part of the time? How good is a fire alarm that might work and might not? It would be better not to have one at all. False security is a dangerous thing.

The Lord has told us what he thinks of neglected responsibilities. To the servant in the parable who had gained with his talents he said, "Well done, thou good and faithful servant. . . . I will make thee ruler over many things: enter thou into the joy of thy lord." But to him who had been slothful, he called him a wicked servant and took away his talent and gave it to the one who had many. (See Luke 19:11–28.)

Just as the servant in the parable was asked what he had done with his talents, the child might be asked by the parent, "Have you finished your assignment?" "Tell me what you did." "How do you feel about it?" Let the child take the responsibility of making the evaluation. An unfulfilled assignment calls for an appropriate punishment, just as a broken family rule calls for "natural consequences" or punishment. The punishment, however, must be clearly understood by the child.

All discipline must be done with a spirit that radiates love, however firm the parents might be. Children must be given a chance to repent. As Alma said to his son Corianton, "But there is a law given, and a punishment affixed, and a repentance granted; which repentance, mercy claimeth." (Alma 42:22.)

There will be times when children are angry and rebellious. There may be times in their anger when they think they hate their parents. This will pass. Just be sure that there is never a time when the children think their parents hate them. Studies have shown that in reality children feel more secure when parents care enough about them to make rules and insist they follow them. Discipline combined with love will help a child prepare for life.

REVERENCE AND RESPECT

"Children have no respect for their elders. Buildings are being defaced. Writing appears on public monuments. Profanity is heard on every side. The nation has lost its memory of those who established it. Even our temples have been desecrated."

Such a statement may have been front-page news yesterday, or during the times of the early Greeks and Romans. Disrespect and irreverence have been concerns of mankind as long as society and civilization have existed. One of the most pronounced outbursts of Jesus' indignation was directed toward the moneychangers who desecrated the Lord's temple. The outrage and shock of sacred things being laughed at, ridiculed, and defiled continues today. What are parents to do? How can they teach their children to be reverent?

President David O. McKay spoke of the importance of being reverent, calling it profound respect mingled with love, a "complex emotion made up of mingled feelings of the soul." Reverence embraces regard, deference, honor, and esteem. Without some degree of it, therefore, there would be no courtesy, no gentility, no consideration of others' feelings or of others' rights. It is the fundamental virtue in religion. (See David O. McKay, *Pathways to Happiness*, p. 258.)

As with other virtues, reverence has its foundations in the home. Families should practice being reverent at home. Prayers at mealtime, personal prayers, and family home evening are all times to teach a spirit of gratitude and demonstrate quiet respect and love for each other and for Heavenly Father. It is hard to teach children to be quiet in church if that is the only time they are ever taught to sit still. It is during personal and family prayer that little ones learn to bow their heads, fold their arms, and close their eyes while Heavenly Father is being addressed.

Children should be taught early to show respect to one another, parents, grandparents, visitors, and people in authority. The example of the parents will be the best teaching available, as children listen to the things that are said and watch what their parents do in sacred places. It is important that children see their parents kneel in prayer, speak with respect of other people, and worship in reverence. One boy learned about reverence from his father: Even though no words were spoken, the boy always noticed his father take off his hat when the flag was presented, and when he entered a building. The son also noticed how his dad closed his eyes and lowered his head when a prayer was said.

REVERENCE AT CHURCH

Reverent worship gives sacred meaning to holy things. Churches are dedicated and set apart as houses of worship. People who go to the Lord's house do it to get nearer to the Lord and commune with him in spirit. To know he is there is reason to behave with respect, manners, and reverence. Talking is subdued, confusion and disorder have no place, and the feeling is worshipful. Adults can help improve reverence through their example. Children can learn that it is disrespectful to talk during a sermon, to misbehave in class, or to leave before being dismissed. They learn that love of the Savior, self-control, and self-discipline become the guiding forces to revere the Lord. Then reverence is more than just being quiet. It is a reflection of the inward feelings that come from the heart and the mind, based on personal experience and a witness of the Spirit. Sometimes people attend meetings with selfish motives. They may be asking, "What will I get out of this meeting?" rather than, "How can I give something that will help others?" Such an attitude rarely fosters reverence.

It is important to build proper habits that invite reverence. Being on time, dressing nicely, being clean, getting drinks of water and going to the rest room before the meeting starts, all add to a reverent attitude.

In teaching reverence, consider the normal stages of growth for a young child. Babies are learning about their new muscles and voices. As they grow older they love to climb, turn pages, and use their new vocabulary. A parent can take advantage of these normal patterns in life by providing quiet activities appropriate to the child's experiences. An infant can be made comfortable with blankets, bottles, and cuddling. Sometimes a restless child may need to be taken out of the meeting to the foyer or mother's room. Toddlers can learn to whisper, and need a lot of interaction like hugs, winks, smiles, and praise. Quiet books, cloth toys, and sponge blocks can be useful for keeping them entertained.

The instant a child does anything that disturbs others nearby, that child should be taken out of the chapel by a parent or older sibling. One effective approach is to leave all toys and possessions behind, find a cold, hard, metal chair and sit the child down, saying, "When you are ready to behave in a way that will allow others to enjoy the meeting, tell me, and we will return to the chapel." When the child is ready, smile and return to the warmth of the chapel, where the child may have a few quiet toys. Do not reward misbehavior by releasing the child from the confinement of the chapel to run freely in the halls, play with the drinking fountain, and draw on the chalkboard.

As children grow older, they can learn to be actively involved in Church meetings. This may be the only time all week when a family sits together; they should treasure those experiences. Learning the hymns can help children be more interested in the music. Discussing talks or lessons after meetings helps reinforce the principles taught. Taking notes on the talks and lessons and reviewing them at home later can help keep any meeting interesting. Sitting on the front row where children can see and hear has helped some families. How much more reverent is the family that prepares ahead of time for meetings, arrives before the meeting begins, and places themselves in a position to enjoy the Spirit and put worldly concerns out of their minds.

The scriptures teach the importance of reverence in worshipping the Lord. Moses was told: "Put off thy shoes from off thy feet, for the place whereon thou standest is holy ground." (Exodus 3:5.) Jesus cleansed the temple because of merchandise. (John 2:13–16.) Temples are a special place of reverence not to be defiled, "for I will not come into unholy temples." (D&C 97:15–17.) Paul taught the early saints to have respect and reverence for themselves. (1 Corinthians 3:16–17.) Many other references are made to reverence for priesthood authority and Church leaders.

President Spencer W. Kimball made an important statement about our state of mind and reverence. He said: "As with the other principles of the gospel, reverence leads to increased joy. We must remember that reverence is not a somber, temporary behavior that we adopt on Sunday. True reverence involves happiness, as well as love, respect, gratitude, and godly fear. It is a virtue that should be part of our way of life. In fact, Latter-day Saints should be the most reverent people in all the earth." (*Church News*, September 18, 1976.)

If we love the Lord, we will have reverence for him, for his house, for his servants, for his priesthood, and for ourselves.

RUNAWAYS

The "oneness" between the Father and Son mentioned in John 10:30 should be a basic goal for parents. Great strength emanates from such companionship, and parental support warms and strengthens the offspring. Most children who run away fail to sense this "oneness" in their homes. Our Father in heaven and his Son created the whole earth with a single set of truths to govern that creation, and these truths apply to everyone. If parents teach their children God's principles, discipline the children with consistence, express love to them in word and in deed, listen carefully and counsel forthrightly, children have a greater chance of realizing that running away is not a solution to their problems.

Runaways come in all ages, sizes, races, and prosperity levels. However, the majority of them are between fourteen and sixteen years old. Those younger than fourteen almost always return quickly (overnight).

Specific reasons for running away may include parental disharmony, problems in school, parental abuse of alcohol or drugs, a new stepparent, or child abuse in one of its many forms. Some children, especially older ones, leave because they feel it is time, and they want a new adventure. Sadly, many run away because they are asked or told to do so.

Again, younger runaways generally stay close to home, within a few miles. The older ones tend to gravitate toward larger cities that have a reputation for excitement, glamor, or fun. They seek places where their anonymity will be more easily maintained. Girls are more likely to run away than boys. Few carry any financial reserves or have the ability to earn a living. If they remain away from home for any length of time, they will probably participate in some form of crime to survive.

Parents must look deep into their own hearts. They must be

fair and gentle with themselves as they decide if any of their actions could have influenced a child to run away. Parents should participate only in activities that encourage righteous desires, making the children want to live at home until it is proper for them to leave. Parents should refrain from anything that does not enhance beauty and harmony between family members. All family members should engage in thoughts and actions that will build a reservoir of uplifting, joyous memories. Both parents and children should commit to change what is not right.

Having a child run away is a traumatic experience that may dull parents' sense temporarily to any calm, logical action. The following items, however, are steps you can take immediately to begin the process of finding the child; they should precede longer-range planning.

1. You may choose to call the police right away when you believe your child has run away. Give them a good description. However, realize that in most areas running away is not an offense. The police will not actively pursue children or pick them up unless they commit a chargeable offense.

2. Pray to Heavenly Father for wisdom and inspiration in finding the child, and for the child's safety. You may also pray for divine intervention.

3. Contact the parents of your child's friends and let them know you are looking for your child. Often those parents unknowingly let a runaway stay in their home.

4. Be calm if the child contacts you by telephone. Thank him or her for calling. Avoid becoming emotional, either angry or overly joyful.

Find out where the child is quickly before second thoughts cause him or her to break off the contact. Make this contact rewarding for the child. Don't punish the child for reaching out to you.

MAINTAIN YOUR NORMAL ROUTINE

While the child is gone, parents must continue on and cope with a difficult, ever-present awareness that the family is incomplete. They need not feel guilty or excessively depressed, or withdraw from those about them, because a child has made the decision to run away. However, these feelings are natural reactions. The following suggestions may help:

1. Disrupt the relationship with the other children as little as possible. Parental responsibilities to the other children have not changed.

2. Parents, or a single parent, may find solace in writing letters to the runaway child. Letters written two or three times a week might be therapeutic, even if they cannot be mailed. Express love, concern, and desire for the child's safe return, seal the letter, and give them to the child when he or she comes back.

3. Parents will feel better if their friends, neighbors, and Church leaders are told of the situation. The constant inquiries about the status of the child will be a reminder of how many people really care.

4. Local police agencies can help make up posters that can be placed in prominent local places. Whenever a letter or phone call gives a clue to the child's whereabouts, forward posters to the local government authorities in that area.

5. After prayerful consideration, parents may decide to visit professional counselors to help them through this particularly stressful time.

Children may leave unexpectedly, causing uncertainty and worry, then anxiety, perhaps fervent prayers, even certain promises to the Lord for a child's safe return. The child returns. Joy floods the parent. But, if an almost instantaneous analysis reveals that the child is well, resentment for the concern he or she caused may quickly replace joy. Then anger is manifest, especially to older children. Children returning home usually see only this anger. They need to see the relief from worry, love, rejoicing at their return, knowledge that part of the parent went with them and returned with them. They ought not to suffer for returning home.

The Savior reminds us in the parable of the lost sheep that the man called in his neighbors and asked them to rejoice with him when he found the sheep that had strayed. (Luke 15:3–6.) Rejoicing at a runaway's return is natural and right. In the classic scriptural story of a runaway, the repentant prodigal son returned home to a royal welcome and a feast sponsored by his father.

But what happens after the "feast"? Runaways of different

ages return home for different reasons, and with different attitudes. Some return only to run again. With the prodigal son, the attitude was one of repentance, of a willingness to change and to stay home. Runaways need to observe that in their absence there has been sustained well-being of the family, that the same principles that may have caused their temporary absence have continued as a bulwark for this successful home, that the government and the rules within the home are still intact, and will continue to apply to all inhabitants of the home, and, that the love for him, and his status in the family, is unchanged, neither greater nor less than his siblings. Brothers and sisters of the runaway may resent all the pain caused to themselves or to their parents, or may be jealous of his or her newfound attention. Parents should reassure them individually and privately of their great love and appreciation for them.

These words may be only as "sounding brass" to parents whose runaway has been gone for weeks, or months, or years. Each parent's trial is different, each can be heartrending, and all require patience and long-suffering. All parents are waging a war with the adversary to save their children and themselves. Winston Churchill perhaps best expressed a tenacious philosophy that parents of runaways would do well to remember: "Never, never, never, never give up."

We as parents should love all our children, those who run away and those who do not. Some children (and some parents) earnestly listen to counsel, while others heed it little. Regardless of all the parental efforts, all the love, and even extended, near-frantic prayers, certain spirits respond only in their own chosen way. After parents do all they can, the greatest gift, that of agency, cannot be superseded. The ability to choose our own way through our mortal existence is most sacred, and even God in his desire to save his children would not let Satan imperil this gift. (See Helaman 14:30–31.) We must follow his example in faith.

(SEE ALSO REBELLION)

SATAN WORSHIP

To most members of the Church, thinking about and discussing Satan is disquieting, even frightening. To think that some
people would worship him or even consider him an object of
veneration is incomprehensible, even grievous.

In this discussion, Satanic ritual will not be specifically cov-
ered; the secret oaths of Satanism are heinous and should be
shunned. The prophet Alma and others have specifically warned
the Saints against them. (See Alma 37:27.) The purpose here will
be only to inform the Saints that such exist; they have existed
from the very beginning. Knowing this, the Saints will be prepared
through righteousness – the only effectual counter during any age
to Satan's devices.

Sinning or doing wrong in the sight of God, due either to
weaknesses of the flesh or lack of commitment, is not Satan worship. Loving Satan more than God and participating in his rituals,
however, is Satan worship.

Satan worship is not new, nor is it a passing fad like long hair
or loud music. Prior to our mortal existence, Satan, one of God's
children, rebelled, desiring to take away our agency. He coveted
the glory of the Father, and "a third part" of the hosts of heaven
turned their allegiance (worship) from the Father to him. (See
Moses 4:3 and D&C 29:36–38.)

After being cast out of heaven, Satan came among our first
parents, Adam and Eve, and their children, saying that he, like
Christ, was a son of God. Some believed his claims "and they
loved Satan more than God." (Moses 5:13.) Cain was one of
these. (See Moses 5:18.)

"And Cain was wroth, and listened not any more to the voice
of the Lord. . . . Wherefore Cain was called Master Mahan, and
he gloried in his wickedness." (Moses 5:26, 31.)

Lamech, the fifth generation from Cain, like Cain entered into
a covenant with Satan. When Irad, his great-grandfather, exposed
him to the sons of Adam, Lamech slew him "for the oath's sake."
(Moses 5:50.)

Later, Satan tried to convince Moses to worship him, but he
was unsuccessful. On the American continent shortly before

Christ's birth, Satan was somewhat successful. (See Alma 37:22–23.) This success continues in our day. Says President Ezra Taft Benson: "Never in our memory have the forces of evil been arrayed in such deadly formation. The devil is well organized." (*Ensign*, December 1971, p. 53.)

When Satan and his angels were cast down to earth they retained their knowledge of the spirit world. This can be seen in the repeated instances in the New Testament where evil spirits recognized Jesus as the Son of God. (See Acts 19:15.) This knowledge increases their cunning. Satan himself was known as Lucifer before the fall. It means lightbearer, or shining one. Another name, the devil, means adversary.

Satan is also known as the father of lies. He is without honor, scruples, or sense of fairness; he will use cunning, deceit, half-truth; he will use music, the arts, procreative powers, money, or whatever else is available to capture the souls of men. Part of his success is based on his ability to convince young people that he does not exist at all, that they are acting out their freedom when they do his bidding. "And behold, others he flattereth away, and telleth them there is no hell; and he saith unto them: I am no devil, for there is none—and thus he whispereth in their ears, until he grasps them with his awful chains, from whence there is no deliverance." (2 Nephi 28:22.)

Thwarting Satan's plans starts with understanding who he is. Here are some things parents should watch for:

1. *Drugs.* Marijuana, cocaine, alcohol, and so on—all of which lower the physical and spiritual defenses—at first seem to provide youth with a new courage. Ironically, if use of these substances continues and addiction occurs, a person is not free, but tightly chained.

2. *Excessive or unrealistic pressures.* Such pressures, especially when created in the home by parents, may cause youth to rebel. Parents would do well to work gently with their children, accepting what they are able to do.

3. *The idea of Satan as a Savior.* The true evil in Satan may not be seen at first because good and bad become intertwined in some minds. Half-truths, such as "God created both good and evil," appeal to some.

4. *Hard rock music.* With its rhythm, loudness, repetition,

gyrations, darkness, strobe lights, and psychedelic design, hard rock music is a swinging door to drugs, sex, rebellion, and godlessness. (See Ezra Taft Benson, *Ensign*, December 1971, p. 53.)

5. *Games.* Face cards, Ouija boards, and Dungeons and Dragons are games that sometimes lead to experimentation with Satan. They should be avoided.

6. *Searching for identity.* The future may not seem clear to many youth. In their search for identity, some will explore Satan as a possible role model. Youth should be carefully guided so that Satan's true goals, which are evil, become clear to them.

7. *Power in exchange for souls.* Satan does not honor his commitments. (See Alma 30:60.) The example of Korihor could be vividly taught to youth. Through it and others like it (Cain, for example; see Moses 5:29–41), young people can know that it is unwise to deal with the father of lies.

SATAN HAS LIMITATIONS

Satan does not know all the purposes of our Father in heaven. (See Moses 4:6.) He cannot deceive and mislead those who are sincerely seeking truth by answering their prayers. (See Joseph Fielding Smith, *Answers to Gospel Questions*, 5 vols. [Salt Lake City: Deseret Book, 1979], 3:85.)

Joseph Smith had much to say about good and evil spirits and their influence upon man: "He then observed that Satan was generally blamed for the evils which we did, but if he was the cause of all our wickedness, men could not be condemned. The devil could not compel mankind to do evil; all was voluntary. . . . God would not exert any compulsory means, and the devil could not; and such ideas as were entertained [on these subjects] by many were absurd." (*Teachings of the Prophet Joseph Smith*, p. 187.)

"All beings who have bodies have power over those who have not. The devil has no power over us only as we permit him." (*Teachings of the Prophet Joseph Smith*, p. 181.)

"In knowledge there is power. God has more power than all other beings, because he has great knowledge; and hence he knows how to subject all other beings to Him. He has power over all." (*Teachings of the Prophet Joseph Smith*, p. 288.)

"Salvation is . . . to triumph over all our enemies. . . . And when we have power . . . and a knowledge to triumph over all evil spirits in the world to come, then we are saved." (*Teachings of the Prophet Joseph Smith*, p. 297.)

"The greatness of his [Satan's] punishment is that he shall not have a tabernacle." (*Teachings of the Prophet Joseph Smith*, p. 297.)

"So the devil . . . seeking whom he may destroy—any person . . . that will yield to him, he will bind him and take possession of the body and reign there, glorying in it mightily, not caring that he had got merely a stolen body; and by and by some one having authority will come along and cast him out and restore the tabernacle to its rightful owner." (*Teachings of the Prophet Joseph Smith*, pp. 297–98.)

He cannot imitate the sign of the dove, signifying the Holy Ghost. (See *Answers to Gospel Questions*, 2:77.)

He is without intelligence, or the glory of God, which is light and truth. (See D&C 93:36–37; Bruce R. McConkie, *Mormon Doctrine*, p. 195.) Therefore he can be detected.

If a young person feels that he or she is possessed, lovingly assure the youth that Satan has no power unless we ourselves give him that power.

What can be done to help one who has become involved with satanism?

1. Parents can help the most. As they talk to their troubled youth, they must refrain from any inclination to expel the child from home. Parents need to say "I love you," and mean it. Love, not force, is the best motivator here. Often young people who embrace satanism are merely acting upon their own rejection or alienation. They seem to be society's outcasts, and they will seek companionship where they can find it. They aren't so much worshipping Satan as merely seeking to belong.

2. Call in others—priesthood leaders, home teachers, scoutmasters—who have the youth's confidence. Help young people to tie God as well as accomplishment into Church activities. Bishops who are humble, receptive, and open with people may also be of great help. These youth need people who can love them, regardless of the deeds they personally have performed.

3. Convince youth that agency is a magnificent gift from God, and that they should not give it away by making a commitment to the adversary. Strenuously try to persuade them that repentance

is possible. Some of those who break away from Satan worship still believe that Satan owns their souls, that no matter what they do they cannot get out of it. This is not true. Repentance is available to all. Heavenly Father offered forgiveness to Cain even after he had begun to love Satan more than God. (See Moses 5:23.)

It is important that youth understand that true repentance does not necessarily mean they will forget totally what they have done. It is to be hoped that children will remember their misdeeds and the lessons they have learned from them. But they will have no need to dwell upon these experiences as they focus their attention on the good in their lives.

4. Teach youth to pray to their Father in heaven always, with sincerity. By prayer they may come to know their Father in heaven, know the true source of good, obtain the light of Christ, be uplifted and have their souls filled, and know the mysteries of God. They can even cry unto him against the devil. (See 2 Nephi 32:9; Alma 26:22; 34:17–27; Moroni 7.) A father's blessing may also provide comfort and counsel.

The Savior said, "Get thee hence, Satan." (Matthew 4:10.) Moses did the same. (See Moses 1:18.) Joseph Smith also overcame Satan. (See Joseph Smith–History 1:16.) A Latter-day Saint child is on the winning team. We must not let Satan and his followers convince our youth otherwise.

SCHOOL PROBLEMS

Problems at school are also problems for the home. When a child comes home with a failing mark, a black eye, a stolen pocketbook, a reprimand from the teacher, or a thousand other possible problems, the home also has a problem. Beleaguered parents often do not know where to turn or what to do. The following fundamentals may help:

First, diligently try to understand what has happened before doing anything. All too often parents lash out at the first available target when they get notice of a problem. This target is usually the child. Instead, when problems arise, ask your children to sit beside you and calmly explain their side of the situation. They will probably be in an even greater turmoil than you are, knowing they will most likely have to bear the brunt of any coming consequences. If other parties are involved, try as much as possible to get a clear look at the problem from their point of view. Make no early or rash judgments.

Second, evaluate the relative seriousness of the problem. Poor performance academically is not good, but with effort it can be resolved. More serious are problems where injury occurs. School property may have been damaged, bodily injury to others may have happened, and, most serious, hard-to-repair psychological damage may have occurred. Where problems are *serious*, seek help immediately—a doctor, lawyer, bishop, school official, or sometimes a schoolteacher may have to be consulted.

Finally, where possible, bring closure to the problem as quickly as possible. If damages must be paid, pay them; if teachers' feelings are to be soothed, soothe them; if the child has been harmed, try to correct it. The sooner a problem is solved, the less lasting and damaging its effects. Involve the child in any of the above actions that may be appropriate.

SOME COMMON PROBLEMS

1. *Bullying.* Younger children often come home crying because a bully has hurt them, taken their lunch, or called them a name. Parents may have to teach their children some assertive skills. One father boxed with his fifteen-year-old son for a week to prepare him for a coming confrontation with a bully. When the bully realized that his victim had prepared for him, the confrontation never materialized.

Parents need to take care, however, not to encourage their own children to the point that they become the bullies. Also, if children are obviously being tormented by bullies of much greater size or skill, proper help or authority needs to become involved. Where possible, let children work out problems themselves. If your child is the bully, lovingly but firmly show that such action will certainly have its consequences.

2. *Stealing.* Children at times do steal—shoplifting, stealing from lockers or satchels, and taking books, for example. In spite of parents' best efforts, these things do happen. Closely monitor your child's possessions. If the child unexplainably comes up with

a new sweater, for instance, find out where it came from. If your child's locker is broken into, go to school officials so that they can be aware. It is, however, not their primary responsibility to teach honesty. They, like police, should enforce law, but parents should teach honesty as a prerequisite to academic study.

3. *Cheating.* Cheating is a form of stealing, and should be dealt with just as severely. However, it is much more common than stealing, and this commonality lends a psychological overtone to the act that can be difficult to deal with. Many young people do not recognize the seriousness of cheating. This may be because they do not see education as a valuable commodity. At any rate, we need to teach that stealing another's efforts is just as serious as stealing that person's pocketbook. Ask children how they would feel if someone stole an idea from them and profited from it. Teach, also, that a day of reckoning inevitably comes. Embarrassment, shame, and discomfort are the only ends to the cheater's road.

4. *Disrespect.* In most countries education is valued so highly that rudeness and disrespect are simply not tolerated. Where they occur, however, parents need to take action. A teacher's time is far too valuable to be wasted by having to spend much of it on the rude and the abusive. Teachers and parents cure rudeness first by preparing quality instruction. This usually stops the problem. Where it fails, and it sometimes does, the rude one needs to be quickly isolated and deprived of educational benefits until he or she can behave. This usually has the desired effect. When even this fails, however, parents and teachers should look together for deeper, underlying causes.

Discipline problems usually occur because the child is not getting enough attention either at home or in the classroom. Redirecting attention toward a student's positive contributions to a class setting may help solve a problem before it becomes too serious.

Most important, parents should be involved in any decision affecting their child. The long-term benefits of helping the teacher far outweigh any temporary salving of the ego they might get from putting blame on the teacher's shoulders for a child's disrespect.

5. *Truancy.* Education cannot take place if a child is not in school. Insist that children attend and be on time. Where a child

simply refuses to comply, it may be well to take that child out of school for a period of time and enroll him or her in an apprentice program of some type. This usually has one of two effects: the child quickly sees the value of a formal education with all its accompanying activities; or the child actually finds a niche outside the traditional education system. Not all people are suited for academic achievement, and skilled handwork will always be in demand. Care should be taken, however, to fulfill the lawful requirements of any local government.

There are many things parents can do to prevent these types of school problems before they start. Here are some suggestions:

1. Keep a spiritual atmosphere in the home.

2. Read to the children.

3. Praise successes and minimize failures.

4. Visit places to excite curiosity about the world: forests, zoos, museums, the library.

5. Teach your children good work habits.

6. Foster independence at all levels.

7. Work with goal setting.

8. Encourage children to expect good things of themselves.

9. Monitor television watching so that it is educational and not destructive. Television is a great educational tool, but a child also needs the creativity of play, meditation, and work.

10. Be aware of and strive to correct any physical or emotional problems. Check vision and hearing. Any problems such as hyperactivity, slow learning, or dyslexia should be dealt with early. Then the child can have positive experiences rather than negative ones.

WHEN PROBLEMS DO ARISE

When parents begin to suspect that problems are occurring, they need to keep the communication channels open. Children need to know they have a friend at home, one who wants them to be happy. Then, as parents deal with the problems, they need to keep in mind the needs of the individual child. Following are some things parents can do to help their children overcome school difficulties:

1. Provide a regular schedule for study. A well-lighted, secluded

study area with access to a dictionary or other learning tools is very helpful.

2. Be certain that the child gets proper rest. Elementary-school-age children generally need eight to ten hours of sleep a night.

3. Maintain communication with the school. Again, deal early with any symptoms of learning difficulty. Be aware of the services that the school offers: counseling sessions, progress reports, parent-teacher conferences, timing of midterm reports and report cards, special needs for the handicapped, special opportunities to excite interest (such as vocational classes, special interest classes, or honors classes). Balance the academics with electives and extracurricular activities.

4. Use tutors if appropriate. Qualified members of the ward can be called on through the bishop to give time and additional instruction. Family members, too—older brothers and sisters—can use new techniques they have learned. An uncle, aunt, or grandparent may also serve as a valuable resource.

5. Inform the teacher of the child's special interests, giving that teacher added insight on how to capture the spirit of that child.

6. Use the Spirit to lift feelings of low self-worth. That restoration of personal value and self-worth will usually be rewarded by a better attack on school studies.

7. Maintain patience. Keep working at the problem. A mountain can be moved in parts and pieces. Do something every day, however small, to help remedy harmful situations.

8. Make use of the special qualities of seminary teachers, enlisting their help and insight from the dual perspective of school and Church. Also, use father's blessings or priesthood blessings in times of stress.

Often school problems are symptoms of other problems. Feelings of inadequacy, rebellion, social rejection, and boredom can be taken out on any symbol of authority. At these times, parents themselves may become despondent, feeling that such activities as bizarre dress, disinterest, nonattendance, and low achievement are the result of parental failures. However, parents should never give up. In truth, continued love and diligent patience usually solve most school-related problems.

SELF-CONFIDENCE

The scriptures are replete with examples of individuals who lacked confidence, but who, through faith in the Lord, found they could serve him. Enoch, for example, when the Lord called him to prophesy, said, "Why is it that I have found favor in thy sight, and am but a lad, and all the people hate me; for I am slow of speech; wherefore am I thy servant?" (Moses 6:31.)

Some of our weaknesses are God-given. They are given to us for the purpose of bringing us to a state of humility so we can discover *him*. "And if men come unto me I will show unto them their weakness. I give unto men weakness that they may be humble; and my grace is sufficient for all men that humble themselves before me; for if they humble themselves before me, and have faith in me, then will I make weak things become strong unto them." (Ether 12:27.)

Although God seeks to bring us to a sense of our own weakness, he does not intend that we be paralyzed by a sense of inadequacy. Rather, he intends that we come to a powerful sense of our adequacy *through him*. Consider this counsel: "Let thy bowels also be full of charity towards all men, and to the household of faith, and let virtue garnish thy thoughts unceasingly; *then shall thy confidence wax strong in the presence of God.*" (D&C 121:45; italics added.)

How, then, can we help children wax strong in confidence and fulfill their own measure of creation?

1. Teach children who they are. *Be* what you want them to become. Love them as the Savior loves you.

2. Express your feelings to your children and encourage them to express how they feel about things. Take time to listen and value what they say. Bear testimony of the Lord's hand in your own life as you daily live to fulfill your own errand from the Lord. Point out how the Lord is aware of your children's lives, and cares what happens to them.

3. Be patient. Let children experience anything worthwhile that they are capable of handling. Teach them to pray over all aspects of their lives—for their family and friends, over their worries and concerns, over their school assignments and their lost puppy and everything that teaches them to depend on God.

4. Provide opportunities for your children to do things at which they will succeed and feel confidence in their abilities as a result.

5. Let children make mistakes. Encourage them to try again. Explain that everyone makes mistakes. The Lord wants us to stretch our abilities and to learn from our mistakes. Then we will be compassionate toward others who make mistakes.

6. Look for the positive in children. Frequent and sincere credit, recognition, and encouragement build self-confidence.

7. Never compare one child to another. Children are different and should be respected for and encouraged in their own interests, abilities, and desires. Do not try to turn your children into what you always wanted to be or an extension of yourself. They came here with their own assignment; help them to appreciate their uniqueness and discover what that assignment is.

8. Express approval when your children display initiative or courage in doing something. If they have a positive experience, they will have the confidence to try it again.

9. Parenting without the guidance of the Holy Spirit is too difficult. The Holy Ghost will prompt and soften, pace and encourage. As you seek for the guidance of the Spirit, help your children seek for it, too. The Spirit will lead and ratify their lives and will take them exactly where the Lord wants them to go.

10. Help children to anticipate the wonderful ordinances that they will be privileged to experience.

11. Teach children that the world is a good place. God planned it to help us grow.

12. Prepare children to receive their patriarchal blessings. Let them know that such a blessing is the Lord's message to them. It will help them to understand their earthly measure and their eternal potential.

13. In order for the Savior to be "the way, the truth, and the life," children must know of him. They must know of his life, his words, and his mission in their behalf. They must know of repentance and what it means to partake of the Savior's atonement. It is impossible for them to understand their worth without learning to know Him. Because of each person's infinite worth, our Savior paid an infinite price to ransom us and make it possible that all someday may be as he is. This is the greatest available key to self-confidence: confidence in the Lord.

SELFISHNESS

President David O. McKay once said, "Selfishness is the root from which spring most human ills and sufferings. Selfishness promises satisfaction, but its fruit is disappointing and produces only ill will and unhappiness." (*True to the Faith*, compiled by Llewelyn R. McKay [Salt Lake City: Bookcraft, 1966], p. 193.)

On the other hand, losing ourselves in service to others and to Christ gives us the happiness most people search for through their selfish acts. All of us are somewhere along this line of getting and giving, including our children. What can parents do?

First, parents can become more aware of their own selfish acts and begin the process of change in their own lives.

Parents should also begin early to distract little children from acts of selfishness. The age of two seems often to be the "me" stage. This is natural, and almost the only thing parents can do is to gently guide children into more mature sharing. A parent can't always explain why sharing will make a child's life happier. Understanding will come as the child matures. Force never works in the long run; children only learn this principle with patience, redirection, and firm, consistent guidance. Some little ones may be especially stubborn, so be patient.

Finally, teach the pain that comes from selfishness. "That which a man serves himself upon the platter of selfishness and greed may appease his mortal appetite, but it will leave him spiritually starved and malnourished. . . . Greed, envy, covetousness, lust, rebellion, thievery, idleness, lying, hypocrisy, backsliding, immorality, infidelity, pride, arrogance, gluttony, and most other evils are the products of a selfish life." (William R. Bradford, *Ensign*, April 1983, p. 50.) When we are selfish we block the Spirit of God out of our lives and invite in only loneliness.

Family home evening is a good place to study situations like the following, asking the children for help toward solutions. Do not use the evening to point out specific, personal faults, but teach the general principles of unselfishness.

Jerry, age three, has a toy that he values very much. He has a friend who comes over and wishes to play with the new toy for a while. Jerry objects strenuously, causing quite a scene. How might this be handled?

1. Determine cause: Jerry honestly loves his toy. He may think sharing means to give it away permanently.

2. Redirect action: Reassure him he will get the toy back. Mention that his friend may have some toys he might like to play with when he goes over to his house.

3. Mention pain involved: Point out how hard it is to keep our friends when we don't share.

4. Give positive feedback: Praise Jerry for how grown up he is when he shares. Let him be aware that Mommy, Daddy, and Jesus are happy with him when he shares.

Stanley has an extensive Christmas list, far more than the family can afford and more than is good for him. He pouts when given the information that the list is above the family's means. What can the parents do?

1. Determine cause: One reason for Stanley's greed may be that his friends are given far more than is good for them. Stanley may compare himself with them.

2. Mention pain involved: Discuss the lack of spiritual feeling or anger that the family may be experiencing.

3. Use family home evening discussion: The family might use this time to discuss real meaning of Christmas. Perhaps they could undertake a project to share with a needy family.

4. Give positive feedback: Offer a genuine response of love for the children's recognition that someone is happier because their family shared.

Chris has a forceful personality. He crowds in the cafeteria line at school, steps ahead when in line at the movies, talks for long stretches on the telephone and refuses to admit that anyone else's call is as important as his.

1. Determine cause: Chris may feel low self-worth; he may feel a need for attention, even undesirable attention. Spend some one-on-one time working this problem out. Be firm in teaching that this kind of behavior is unacceptable—people who use it find they are left alone.

2. Use family council: Discuss love for one another. Set some time limits mutually agreed upon. Stress the golden rule.

3. Mention pain involved: Talk about feelings of inadequacy and the need for real listening to each other's ideas.

4. Give positive feedback: Praise successes.

Alisha wants a new dress for the prom. The one she wants is fashionable but very expensive. When she is told that the dress is out of range for the family budget, she responds with, "But, mother, you just ordered new drapes for the living room. If you can have nice things, why can't I?" How might the mother respond?

1. Determine cause: Alisha may find teenage competition very stressful. She may see herself as less than successful in obtaining dates.

2. Mention pain involved: Point out family bickering or lack of cooperation between family members.

3. Use one-on-one conversation: Indicate that the drapes are a project to benefit the whole family. Alisha herself will probably be happier if her date comes to pick her up in a nice house. Set up a compromise. If the girl has a job, she may furnish the material; if not, she could do odd jobs to earn money to buy it. The mother then may use this opportunity as a teaching moment in helping the girl sew the dress, or she may offer to sew the dress herself while the girl is earning the money to purchase the fabric and helping around the house.

4. Give positive feedback: Compliment the girl on her appearance in the dress, and on her sewing ability if she makes it herself.

After some theoretical discussions, move to practical actions by inviting your children to share the joys of acts of selflessness.

1. Invite your children to work with you on a Church Welfare project or help a neighbor move in or out.

2. Set up a project for family giving. One family wanted to help their children find suitable activities for the Sabbath. Instead of watching TV, they allowed their children to bake some cookies, which they took to a family who needed some special attention. They spent some time in conversation and an extension of family-to-family love.

3. Have a family home evening project of writing letters to ward missionaries, making these letters especially newsy and cheerful.

4. Set up a thank-you note experiment. Some teachers use a writing assignment where they have students write a heartfelt thank-you note to someone in their past who has touched them

in a special way. The results are surprising in that many of the recipients have never known how much good they have done.

5. Participate in a secret kind acts program. Encourage the children into a family unity project to do three acts of kindness to a sibling. Sometime during the day there would be an informal reporting to the mother or father of helpful or kind actions and the responses that follow.

6. Read the *Ensign* article on selflessness by Elder H. Burke Peterson (May 1985, p. 67) to your children.

You might use a family council to set up projects to develop habits of cooperation early in life. Engage the children's agreement with those projects. One family set up a kind acts experiment for their smaller children. They emphasized sharing, general acts of kindness, speaking kindly to one another, obeying parents, and doing assigned jobs. A set of treasure symbols (smiling-face stickers) was displayed. Each evening or at noon, the mother would discuss with the children their kind acts and remove the stickers from the display, and allowing the child who had participated to put them in his or her own envelope. The children then planned the activities they might do when the symbols were all earned: a picnic in the park with Grandpa and Grandma, a trip to a local fast-food restaurant, a visit to local places of interest. Older children need a different approach, but mutual agreement should always be emphasized.

Some children will take advantage. Watch for symptoms of selfishness occurring in a pattern leading to a habit. Parents should take many opportunities to allow children to serve them. We love those we serve.

Satan is a cheat. Our Father in heaven gives us wonderful opportunities for growth, and Satan presents in their place attractive counterfeits. "Men are, that they might have joy" (2 Nephi 2:25), our Heavenly Father counsels us, but Satan tries to make us feel that joy comes from putting worldly desires ahead of spiritual ones. As a result, we grow in selfishness, and thus in loneliness and unhappiness. As the time swiftly approaches for the second coming of the Savior, Satan intensifies his attack on sacred things. "This know also, that in the last days perilous times shall come. For men shall be lovers of their own selves, covetous, boasters, proud, blasphemers, disobedient to parents, unthankful, unholy, without natural affection." (2 Timothy 3:1–3.)

Even with proper training, some children still exhibit stubborn characteristics. Parental consistence and use of earnest prayer and fasting for individual help in such cases is essential.

SEX EDUCATION

Just as we would not expect schools or neighbors to teach the doctrine of the priesthood or the plan of salvation to our children, neither should we delegate the teaching of such subjects as reproduction, sexual processes, and sexual purity to others. The nature of these subjects is holy; therefore, none but those who have true understanding of these principles should be entrusted to teach our children.

The world's perspective is not ours, and neither is the world's manner of teaching. The adversary quickly exploits the most sacred subjects on earth, perverting and abusing our understanding. He places the family under attack by encouraging sexual promiscuity. We must be on guard against him. To do this we should assume the responsibility for our own children, informing them on sexual subjects.

We should also understand that if we do not teach our children about sex, someone else will. Such outside teachings usually have the wrong emphasis, or may include total misinformation.

"It is important that you teach your children about sexuality. The Lord has given the responsibility for the teaching of children to parents, and this is one area where children need accurate and morally correct information. The subject of sexuality is discussed so openly in today's world that your children cannot avoid hearing about it. But most of what they hear will teach them the world's abuse of the power of procreation. The home must be the place where they can learn the Lord's plan for the use of this power and gain the strength to withstand the falsehoods taught by the world." (A Parent's Guide, p. 29.)

Sex is a difficult subject for many parents to discuss with their children. They avoid it because it is awkward for them and they feel embarrassment. Usually this is because of their own lack of preparation, or perhaps they were not taught correctly by their own parents. In spite of this, parents need to do this teaching themselves. The whole subject begins with an attitude, not with one ceremonious conversation fifteen minutes before a child enters puberty. It begins with the parents' attitude toward their own male and female sexuality and their own wholesome acceptance of each of their children.

"We believe in being honest, true, chaste, benevolent, virtuous, and in doing good to all men. . . . If there is anything virtuous, lovely, or of good report or praiseworthy, we seek after these things." Let this standard guide the selection of information and the manner in which it is presented.

"Choose books about human intimacy carefully when you teach your children. . . . The tendency of much current literature is to focus on the processes of sexual behavior and to neglect the social and spiritual consequences of improper behavior. Unless information on human relationships strictly accords with the revealed word of the Lord, it will be at best incomplete and at worst sensual and devilish in content and purpose." (A Parent's Guide, p. 9.)

The relationships that parents build with their children during each child's early years will have a lasting influence on the way the children feel later about developing their own intimate relationships. Even while children are very young they can be taught the value of loving and being loved.

The period of life from birth to approximately three years of age is the time when a child becomes aware of gender—of being a boy or girl. As sons and daughters of God, they are "privileged to be males or females by divine creation. . . . Whichever gender they are, they are of great worth." And both are wonderful. As they get older, "teach them that their gender influences their goals and that, depending upon their gender, their goals are to become effective fathers or mothers. Such early gender identity removes uncertainty about the worth of the child and builds security regarding his future." (A Parent's Guide, p. 19.)

During the early years, parents should be careful to react properly to young children's discoveries of their own bodies. "Male and female children will naturally discover and explore their genitals just as they do the rest of their bodies. The male infant's genitals are very sensitive to touch. His penis responds to his diaper and to his parents' touch as they bathe or clothe him. He will often touch and rub his own genitals. A little girl may also explore and handle her genitals." A parent's "reaction to these natural exploration will influence the way a child later feels about his procreative powers. Do not either worry about or encourage the child's explorations. Remain neutral, and the child will accept that these parts of his body are good, just as all the other parts are." (*A Parent's Guide*, p. 21.)

It is important for parents to feel comfortable using correct biological terms when describing the body. Families may have familiar little terms that are easier for the young child, but as children grow up they should be taught the correct terms for body parts and functions.

Timing is very important in teaching sexual subjects. Most parents want to know, "When do we teach and how much do we say?" In any case, parents should be very careful not to say too little too late, or too much too soon. Every child's maturity rate is different. Some children have more curiosity, or they may have older siblings who introduce sexual processes to them earlier than other children. Also, the media is responsible for children's exposure to many explicit subjects that often take premature explanations. Therefore, parents need to be sensitive to the individual needs of each child. Prayerful consideration and listening to the promptings of the Spirit for your own children will assist in the pacing of this information.

"In matters of human sexuality, honesty and accuracy are important. Your children will hear of this subject in various ways. They may bring home offensive language, questionable stories, and blunt questions about sex. If they are to maintain gospel values, you need to answer their questions. Rationally answer, question, or seek sources of information together with the child. If ever there is a crucial time for open parent-child communication, it is during such conversation. This does not mean that you should force the child to confront details. The child's own pace is usually the best indicator of how and when to proceed." (*A Parent's Guide*, p. 29.)

A simple guide to follow is to *tell children what they need to*

*know in order to cope with their age, their development, and
their social situation.*

For instance, children three to six years of age do not need to
know about adult sexuality; they don't need to know about the
pleasure associated with the sexual experience. But they do need
to know where babies come from and the names of body parts.
They need a little bit of information, but not the complete story
about the reproductive process. Too much explicit information
can be stimulating to their curiosity, and then it becomes too
confusing. Give children what they need and can understand; then
sexuality becomes a sequential process as they mature.

School brings many new experiences, and sometimes more
information is imparted to youngsters than parents desire to hear.
There will often be considerable sexual talk. For this reason, emphasize to your children that there are subjects we save to talk
about in our family. These subjects are not to be talked about
with friends or people outside the home. Tell them that sex is a
sacred and special subject that moms and dads like to discuss
with their children. Tell them, "Anytime you have a question
come and talk to us, but let your friends' moms and dads talk to
them when they choose to."

Some children do not ask questions, but they also need to be
prepared. If a child is between the ages of eight and nineteen and
has seemed unconcerned, the parent should look for the right
opportunity to introduce the subject of sex. A new baby arriving
in the family or a pet about to have babies can be a natural
introduction to the subject. Set up a quiet time, a time of confidence, perhaps bedtime or a ride together in the car or on a bicycle.
Simply state: "I have noticed you have never wanted to know
about sexual issues. You are at a point in your life when you need
to know about some of these things." Then tell some of the
simple, honest facts, such as the following: "Heavenly Father
made men and women's bodies different for a wonderful purpose.
One of these purposes is so babies could come to the earth. Babies
come in a special way and it takes both a mother and a father to
accomplish this. You may have noticed or wondered about the
differences in the bodies of little girls and boys. Boys are stronger
and are to be fathers. Mothers are made by our Father in heaven

so they can have little infants grow inside them until they are ready to be born."

Proceed with information appropriate to the child's situation and then leave the door open for him or her to come back to you. If that doesn't happen, continue going back, giving a little bit at a time until that child has been given all that he or she needs to know.

MODESTY IN THE FAMILY

Family and personal modesty should be encouraged among family members. Parents should set the example and gently set standards for the family to follow. Little children can be overwhelmed with the differences in an adult body compared to their own. However, parents shouldn't overreact if a child happens to come upon them unclothed. Don't act embarrassed or "dive for cover" and make them think there is something unusual to hide. Just ask the child to hand you your robe, or put a towel around yourself, so it seems very natural. Privacy, modesty, and dignity are wonderful attributes to display. The *Parent's Guide* advises: "Be cautious to keep your own bodies and intimate sexual relations private. Children do not need to see or hear details of your private sexual life. They see and hear enough in the normal course of family life. They may feel threatened if a parent becomes too descriptive. Children usually learn subtly and cumulatively from ordinary daily contacts." (Page 30.)

SEX EDUCATION IN THE SCHOOLS

Many educational systems throughout the world have felt it necessary to introduce sex education in their school curricula. Though they may have good intentions, it is nevertheless the privilege of the parents to teach sexuality to their children. There are several reasons why this type of information should be taught in the home rather than the school:

1. Maturity in children varies greatly. Teaching sexuality may plunge children into a world they are not ready for.

2. Seldom is moral leadership taught along with the anatomy and physiology of sex. The ramifications of this policy are that "information only" is dispersed. There is seldom any counsel

given on how to deal with sexual feelings, and God's moral laws are almost never taught.

3. Coeducational instruction—viewing pictures and diagrams side by side on sensitive sexual subjects—breaks down a natural barrier between girls and boys and erases the inhibitions that should be present before marriage.

4. Schools do not permit the injection of religious information and gospel truths in the subject of sexuality, yet to Latter-day Saints it is vital and one should never be taught without the other.

Members of the Church should work closely with school officials and the PTA in a mood of patience and love. Carefully persuade others to see the ramifications of improper sex education programs. Always keep in mind that we are members of the Church of Jesus Christ, and extend friendship and tolerance for all people.

SEXUAL ABUSE

It is remarkable that when the people of the American continent pleaded silently for the Savior to tarry with them longer, he first healed the sick and the infirm and then called for their children. Following his marvelous prayer in their midst, "he wept, and the multitude bare record of it, and he took their little children, one by one, and blessed them, and prayed unto the Father for them. . . . And he spake unto the multitude, and said unto them: Behold your little ones." (3 Nephi 17:21-23.) We can share in both the Savior's joy and the joy of these children's parents as they witnessed the ministering of angels to their little ones.

Sometimes, of course, it may seem as if we must wait until our own little ones are asleep before we can glimpse their great value to us. The press of school or work responsibilities, childish disobedience, insecurities, or the fact that some of our little ones are now bigger than we are requires those moments of repose in order for us to find again how important they are to us.

It is tragic that some people whose lives have been twisted by their own pain and evil choices would violate the innocence of children by abuse, especially sexual abuse. Yet abuse does happen, and we must call upon the great love of the Savior as well as the best professional skills available to heal the wounds of both victims and perpetrators. While the focus of this discussion must be upon the recognition and treatment for children sexually abused, it must not be forgotten that sincere repentance before God will ultimately cleanse and free the offender from his or her sin, and that complete forgiveness on the part of the victim will prevent the growth of bitterness.

"Fathers, you cannot abuse your little ones without offending God. Any man involved in an incestuous relationship is unworthy to hold the priesthood. He is unworthy to hold membership in the Church and should be dealt with accordingly. Any man who beats or in other ways abuses his children will be held accountable before the great judge of us all. If there be any within the sound of my voice who are guilty of such practices, let them repent forthwith, make amends where possible, develop within themselves that discipline which can curb such evil practices, plead with the Lord for forgiveness, and resolve within their hearts henceforth to walk with clean hands." (Gordon B. Hinckley, *Ensign*, May 1985, pp. 48–51.)

Sexual abuse has been defined as "any contacts or interactions between a child and an adult in which the child is used as an object of sexual excitement or gratification for the adult. (Sexual abuse may also be committed by a person under 18.)" (National Center on Child Abuse and Neglect, *Special Report Child Sexual Abuse: Incest, Assault, and Sexual Exploitation*. USDHHS Pub. No. [OHDS] 79–30166, Washington, D.C., 1978.) Sexual abuse can occur both inside and outside the family. It can be divided into several categories: *incest*, where physical sexual activity takes place between members of a family; *exhibitionism*, involving the exposure of genitals of an adult male to girls, boys, and women; *molestation*, which includes touching or fondling the child in sexual areas or encouraging the child to fondle or masturbate the adult; and *sexual intercourse* and *rape*.

PREVENTION OF SEXUAL ABUSE

Unfortunately, it is not possible to prevent all sexual abuse. However, some facts about the nature of such events and their offenders can help parents protect their children.

First, parents must choose carefully the "thin line" they must walk between alerting their children appropriately to possible dangers, and, on the other hand, frightening them so severely that these warnings create emotional difficulties. Certainly, children—boys as well as girls, because boys are victimized more than is usually recognized—must be instructed to avoid being alone at night in isolated situations, such as parks or streets. Most parents have given their children instruction about not accepting rides or favors from strangers. The Boy Scout concept of safety in using a "buddy system" is most worthwhile. Children should understand that if someone shows them his genitals, they should run away and get help from an adult. Children should be given some frank instruction about their body parts (with appropriate names for those parts). They need to understand that their genitals are private, but not "dirty," and that no one has a right to touch them, unless it is a trusted person helping them keep clean or a doctor or nurse who is concerned about their health. They can be promised that they will know with the help of their Heavenly Father if someone is doing something to them or asking them to do something that is not right. Children must understand their right to refuse, and they must know how to get out of a bad situation as soon as possible. They should be taught to come and tell a trusted parent or other adult immediately, no matter what the offending person said. They must be assured that even if the other person tries to make them feel guilty or threatens them, there are adults who will understand and protect them. This is especially crucial (and difficult) when the offender is one of the child's parents. Early detection and treatment for a sexually abused child is crucial to his or her emotional, physical, and spiritual health.

Most abuse occurs between a child and someone he or she trusts to some degree. Without becoming overly cautious or anxiously protective, parents can observe and monitor the relationships their children have with adults and other children. Many good questions can be asked of children when they have been tended or have been away from home. The following are some examples.

"What games did you play?"

"What did you enjoy doing the most while I was gone?"

"Were you treated well?"

"Did you have any trouble?"

"Do you want to do that or go there again?"

"Which baby-sitter do you like the most?"

"What do you like so much about that sitter?"

"What is it you don't like about that sitter?"

The answers to these questions can give you peace of mind or cause for concern. Children generally want to tell the truth, but often they don't have the opportunity. Just being attentive, quiet, and pausing long enough after a good question will give some children the opening they have been hoping for.

Children have vivid imaginations, and they tend to remember best the version of an experience they told last. Each time an experience is retold it tends to become embellished and distorted. Rather than remembering what really happened, children (and adults) tend to remember what was talked about last. What is verbalized is often reinforced in a child's memory.

When you suspect abuse, do not ask leading questions to get the child to tell you what you fear has happened. Use a tape recorder, another trusted adult, or take careful notes, and simply ask the child to tell you about what happened. If you have reason to believe that child abuse has occurred, obtain the services of a professional investigator or therapist who can record the facts on videotape.

As a general rule, children minimize rather than exaggerate the truth when they have been abused. They fear retaliation or revenge from the offender, anger from the other parent, embarrassment, shame, punishment, and so forth. Children are emotionally distraught when they disclose that they have been sexually molested or abused. Adults must assume that what is said is all true, but not the whole truth.

An excessive interest on the part of an adult toward a child may signal a need for care and supervision, especially when the plan is for the child to spend considerable time alone with the adult, for instance, camping or "sleeping over."

Parents should work to insure that a bonding takes place between infants and fathers. This helps to build within the fathers a taboo against incest. Also, incest between brother and sister is a more repulsive idea to children who are bonded. Parents should also work to keep their own marital and family relationships loving and harmonious. Children suffering low self-esteem and loneliness in rigid, unaffectionate, or chaotic families are more vulnerable to approaches from outsiders. Tragically, a large percentage of the incidence of sexual abuse occurs in the home between fathers and daughters. Fathers must be aware of the temptation toward unreasonable control that could warp and destroy appropriate feelings for their wives and children.

Mothers can create an atmosphere of affection and warmth with their husbands and children. Sometimes, because of various circumstances, the mother cannot or does not fulfill the traditional role of homemaker. The preparation of meals, the care of the home, and finally the confiding of marital relationships may be left to the oldest daughter—with disastrous consequences, leading to an incestuous relationship. Sometimes mothers have unintentionally allowed this to happen. It is essential for them, when this occurs, to take courage and seek out those who can and will help.

SYMPTOMS AND WARNING SIGNALS

Children are sometimes coerced, threatened, or too ashamed to tell their parents or other caring adults about the experience of being sexually abused. Thus, parents should be aware of behaviors on the part of the child that may indicate need for loving inquiry.

Any sudden, unexplained onset of emotional problems should be reason for concern—phobias (strong fears), depression, acting out (defiance and rebellion), decline in school performance, or a variety of physical complaints like headaches or stomachaches. Sometimes children become abnormally apprehensive about being alone, or being alone with a particular adult with whom they previously enjoyed activities. They may evidence a preoccupation with sex in behavior and language or become promiscuous. Runaway behavior on the part of adolescent girls is frequently associated with physical and/or sexual abuse. (Care must also be taken to not develop a paranoia about sexual abuse. Some fathers have suffered unjustly from the accusations of others when they were totally innocent.)

Concerned parents, Church advisors, or priesthood leaders can be of vital help to children and adolescents by creating a relationship and atmosphere that invite the child to talk about his or her feelings. Although it may take more than one such conversation, the invitation and patient willingness to "be there for them" are essential ingredients. At some point, if children obviously have something they want to talk about, but can't bring themselves to say it, the adult may have to help by gently asking the questions directly.

WHAT TO DO WHEN SEXUAL ABUSE IS REVEALED

The revelation by a child of sexual abuse usually creates a crisis in the family, especially in the case of incest. These feelings are often followed immediately by great anger toward the offender. Yet, in the midst of these feelings, the overriding concern must be for the welfare of the child. First, and most important, children must know that they are believed, or at least taken very seriously. They must be invited to tell as much of the story as they are willing at this time to talk about, without the adult responding too quickly to insufficient information. The adults need to help the children understand that they are not to blame for the events, in spite of their probable feelings of guilt and confusion. The children also need to hear that though this is a difficult time, they did the right thing by reporting, and that the situation is going to improve over time. Children will need to be told that others, including legal authorities, may need to be informed, and that this is part of what it takes to deal with the problem.

Next, sexual abuse is a matter which requires the help of professional authorities. It is not a problem, particularly in the case of incest, that can be handled privately in the family or with the priesthood leader. Usually the child will need to be protected from further abuse or threat of abuse from the offender. Again, in the case of incest, the offender should be required to move to some alternative living arrangement while treatment and legal and Church procedures are undertaken. Apart from the authorities mentioned, it is important to provide the child and family with as much confidentiality as possible. Knowledge of a child's victimization in the school or neighborhood can sometimes add to the shame and confusion of the child, who may believe that somehow this must be his or her fault.

It must be emphasized, however, that desire to protect the family from shame *should not extend to keeping the situation from the awareness of both Church and legal authorities.* In the eyes of the Lord, a person cannot truly repent of sexual abuse without confessing the offense before proper spiritual authority. Moreover, in many states it is a law that abuse must be reported; that is, someone who knows of abuse and does not report it is guilty of criminal offense.

Professional counseling for problems of sexual abuse is, as mentioned, extremely important for the child, although he or she may act as if everything is all right. Research has shown that many victims, as children, denied their problems and tried to make them go away by pretending they weren't there. Instead, they experienced more serious and long-lasting difficulties later on, especially when faced with the challenge of intimacy in relationships and marriage.

Counseling is never an easy process. Throughout the experience, the child will need consistent encouragement and support from loving family and the small circle of others who need to know. The impact of abuse from strangers or nonintimate acquaintances can be overcome within a reasonably short period of time. However, the closer the offender is to the nuclear family circle, the more devastating the emotional damage will be.

In the case of incest, because separation or divorce in the family may ensue, or the family member may be imprisoned, children will feel great confusion and guilt over the turmoil, feeling that, somehow, it is their fault. They must be reassured again and again that what they did was right to do. Though it may be very painful, what is happening may be the greatest possible blessing in the life of the offender, helping the person face the problem and overcome it.

Finally, the calming presence of the Spirit of the Lord must be sought for all those involved. Priesthood blessings, loving counsel from priesthood leaders, earnest prayer, and striving to live the commandments will help create a sanctuary of protection from the buffetings of such a personal and family crisis. As an old saying goes, "When you find yourself in a terrible storm, pray. He will either calm the storm or calm you in the storm."

SEXUAL DEVIANCE

In one Sunday evening talk with his father, a seventeen-year-old youth commented, "Dad, how come God gave us these feelings about sex? We are supposed to have them, but they cause so much trouble. Wouldn't it be a lot easier to live the commandments if they just weren't there to worry about?" The father thought wryly to himself as he considered his answer, "Yes, and it would be much easier if we didn't have to explain them to our children, too."

Bruce C. Hafen, president of Ricks College, spoke directly to the boy's question: "The idea of romantic love, so commonplace that it is touched upon in virtually every popular book or movie or magazine, is also at the very center of the gospel of Jesus Christ. It is one of the greatest of God's laws that 'a man [shall] leave his father and his mother, and shall cleave unto his wife: and they shall be one flesh.' (Gen. 2:24.) And, 'neither is the man without the woman, neither the woman without the man, in the Lord.' (1 Cor. 11:11.)" (*Ensign*, October 1982, pp. 64–69.) Like all of God's commandments, proper use of sexual powers holds great promise, and violation of God's law has potential for great harm.

Proper sexual understanding is vital for parents. Misunderstanding or misdirecting children's sexual feelings can lead to sexual deviations that are powerful addictions. Sex is an area in which, as in so many other areas of parenting, parents must strive for an inspired balance between warning and counseling.

NATURAL CURIOSITY

Young children are naturally curious about their bodies and the ways in which they differ from others. Expressions of curiosity, such as "playing doctor," or "peek and show," are frequently innocuous situations, part of an eagerness to learn, explore, and imitate that has nothing to do with sexual deviance. Such experiences provide teaching opportunities for parents to explain sexual differences and give counsel. These specific behaviors do not mean to the child what they often mean to the parents. If inappropriate behaviors continue over a long period of time, or if there are elements of force in which young children are pressured into complying, appropriate action by parents is necessary.

It is most important at this point that the child not see parents react extremely, thereby teaching the child that this topic is emotionally charged, something to be frightened or intrigued about. Children need to receive the same matter-of-fact instruction about the sexual sphere of their lives as they do any other area. Parents may observe that what started as an innocent experience has taken on more exciting overtones for a child. The child may be curious or worried, or perhaps furtive and silent. Here the parent can help the child "talk through" the experience. If the child doesn't want to talk, parents may still have to attempt to impart an understanding through a gentle but frank lecture. The goal is to demystify the experience, to relive the memories about the experience. It is important that such events not be passed over out of embarrassment or hope that it will just go away.

Children may become involved in sex play with other, often older, children in an effort to be accepted in a social group. Although an experience like this may have been entered by the child naively and in a nonsexual way, the message taught is potentially very harmful. Children must learn that they should never have to buy or sell love and acceptance. Children should understand that their bodies are theirs, never available for someone else to "use."

Next, parents must be concerned about a possible sense of inferiority that may have prompted a child's availability in the first place. Parents may need to work toward helping the child find new friends or learn social skills to achieve greater confidence. Some parents, who may have shunned athletics themselves, have nevertheless had to practice with their children, helping them gain enough skill to feel accomplishment and an increased sense of belonging.

As children grow and mature into adolescence, true sexual feelings emerge. It is impossible, of course, for parents to completely protect or prevent their children from being exposed to unhealthy experiences. Their best weapons against the onslaught of such temptation are the bonds of love and communication that exist between them and their children. Their own healthy and mature understanding of sexuality can also be a great help. Thus children can glimpse their parents' appreciation both of the turbulence that they themselves may be experiencing and of the sacred importance of restraint that promises eternal fulfillment in marital union.

TYPICAL TYPES OF SEXUAL DEVIANCY

There are many forms of sexual deviation. Many forms are rare enough that they don't warrant specific attention here. Others, however, must be mentioned for information purposes. A very common one, homosexuality, will be dealt with more specifically.

Voyeurism, or window peeking, is usually a passive activity in which the offender secretly views others involved in disrobing or engaging in sexual activity. The offender achieves vicarious enjoyment and sexual excitement from this activity.

Obscene telephone calls are often used as a means of achieving personal sexual arousal. The caller feels successful when a strong emotional reaction is received from the unsuspecting victim.

Exhibitionism, or exposing oneself inappropriately to others, is also a way of achieving sexual arousal. When the victims react with surprise or horror the offender is able to achieve the level of sexual excitement desired.

All of these, along with many other forms of sexual deviancy, are designed for the pleasure of the offender at the expense of the victim. Children may be willing or unwilling participants as either offenders or victims.

HOMOSEXUALITY

Specific attention should be devoted to homosexuality since it is more common, more public, and of particular concern to the Church. Homosexuality is of such concern because much of the world considers it a normal activity, not a deviancy. Prophets of God have declared that such a belief is a gross error: "Satan tells his victims that it [a homosexual orientation] is a *natural way of life;* that it is normal; that [individuals with a homosexual orientation] *are a different kind of people born 'that way'* and *that they cannot change.* This is a base lie." (Spencer W. Kimball, *A Letter to a Friend,* p. 8.)

Research demonstrates there are influences, both biological and environmental, that create susceptibility to homosexual preferences. Some youth experience the beginnings of a homosexual orientation they did not choose. It is a monster or a challenge they can surrender to or choose to fight to overcome. The feeling that a homosexual orientation is more appealing or more natural than a heterosexual one does not make a person become "a homosexual." Further, having a homosexual orientation does not give one license to give up self-control and abstinence from sexual activity outside of marriage.

There is no evidence that homosexual desires are more powerful than heterosexual desires. "The so-called sex drive is mostly myth. Sexual intimacy is not an involuntary, strictly biological necessity for survival like breathing and eating. Sexual intimacy... can be delayed or even suspended for long periods of time with no negative effect. . . . Sexual powers are voluntary and controllable." (A Parents' Guide, p. 49.)

There is much evidence to suggest that indulgence in any deviant sexual activity increases the desire for further sexual activity. This is true whether the sexual activity is heterosexual, homosexual, or self-inflicted such as viewing pornography, masturbation, exhibitionism, or voyeurism.

Healthy human intimacy includes a broad range of close interactions spiritually, emotionally, socially, and physically. These interactions meet basic human needs, and are therefore natural, not addictive or progressive. Sexual intimacy is reserved exclusively for marriage. In the context of a healthy, humanly intimate relationship between a husband and wife, sexual activity and intimacy are satisfying, not addictive. So long as a couple feel emotionally, mentally, and spiritually close to each other, their sexual activity does not lead to inappropriate, deviant behaviors.

All members of the Church are expected to abstain totally from any kind of sexual activity outside of a marriage relationship. Simply claiming that one is homosexual does not give justification for indulging in sexual activity. (Normal sexual releases, such as those that occur during nocturnal emissions, or "wet dreams," do not constitute any kind of sexual deviation.)

The following are some suggestions to help parents protect their children from being overcome by problems of sexual deviancy:

1. The most important general factor in preventing the development of a homosexual orientation in children is the quality of the affectionate relationship between the mother and father.

Children need a bonding relationship with their parents, such that they can feel their parents' love and pride in each other. Hostile, emotionally cold relationships between parents can create tension, leading children to feel insecure and unsure of themselves. For instance, when a mother's emotional needs are not met in her marriage, she may transfer them to her relationship with her son to compensate. This is harmful to the son, because he is pulled into emotionally aligning himself against his father. Similarly, if the father is uninvolved, distant, or too preoccupied with his own life to emotionally "validate" his children, they may feel incomplete, as if they don't really belong with their peers. Or a punishing and authoritarian father often communicates damaging messages: "You are just not good enough to be the kind of child I want to love." (Children are often less hurt by a divorce or the death of a father than by such an attitude. They can compensate by at least believing in their value when the father is absent. His physical presence but continued emotional uninvolvement or punishment is much more painful.) The relationship of father and son is particularly important between ages seven and twelve.

2. Parents need to teach their children appropriate masculine and feminine skills. A child who is rejected by peers because they see him or her as being different will feel isolated and lonely. This opens a vulnerability to homosexual approach. Boys need to find themselves fitting in somewhere in the large definition of what boys are like—without, of course, imitating unrighteous stereotypes. In other words, when they ask themselves, "Am I a boy?" they need to be able to answer back, "Yes. I may be different from other boys in some ways, but I am definitely a boy." Feelings about femininity are equally important for girls. Some girls grow up with a distaste for or sense of inadequacy about doing "what girls do." They may define themselves outside the concept of being female.

3. Parents need to evaluate their own attitudes about sexuality. Harsh, excessive emphasis on sex as being "dirty" or sexual feelings as terrible sin can frighten children away from normal, healthy relationships and appropriate socializing.

4. Parents should take appropriate precautions to protect their children from possible homosexual encounters. In the same way that they are forewarned about inappropriate sexual advances,

children can be taught to avoid homosexual experiences. They should be supervised carefully in public places such as parks, amusement centers, and rest rooms.

5. In conclusion, if parents find that their child has been entrapped in sexual deviations, they should make every effort to love and care for him or her while they get help from the Church and from professionals with LDS values. It is critical that the individual and his or her family seek the healing, strengthening power of the Savior. In the words of a minister who once was a homosexual:

"Dear Friend:

"Like you, I have had a life-long struggle with homosexuality. I know what it means to be different, to be rejected and to cause pain to others because of your orientation. Despite what some may think we didn't just one day decide to be homosexual. Your opinion of how you became gay may differ from mine and that's okay, but I think you will agree that you didn't ask for it. We live in an imperfect world and unfair things happen. No doubt you fought a battle with homosexual impulses, then gave in and decided that you could never win, it was impossible to change, and you had to accept what you are. . . .

"Jesus saw that we couldn't help ourselves, that left alone we all self-destruct. He knew for us it was an impossible battle. This is why He called us to Himself. He said that He will walk beside us, providing the strength and the power we need to turn back to his perfect way. He did not say that we would not suffer while the changes are being made, but He did say that He will never leave us or forsake us. He will guide us throughout the difficult times." (Frank Worthen, *Steps Out of Homosexuality* [San Rafael, CA: Love in Action, Inc.], pp. 164–66.)

The healing power of the Savior is mighty to save. We must not turn away from him and try to do it on our own. He will bless us to improve our relationships as parents as well as to lift our children in their need.

SEXUAL PROMISCUITY

Sexual promiscuity is a violation of God's commandments, and disrupts the holy order of his plan. The law of chastity, unpopular though it may be in the eyes of the world, is the way to safety and true happiness.

Curiosity about the power of creation is actually God-given. It is natural for young people to have questions about the bodies of the opposite sex. This curiosity should not be condemned by parents, but discussed and controlled, like any other appetite. Youth should be taught that this curiosity does not imply a need (as do hunger and thirst, for example). It does not require immediate fulfillment. If the feelings are held in abeyance and properly nurtured, waiting for appropriate fulfillment at the proper time and place, the final satisfaction will be greatly enhanced.

The attraction of the sexes is God's earthly plan for his children. Great care needs to be taken, however, to help the attraction find proper fulfillment. Parents should teach young people that good grooming, moderate makeup, and modest dress will actually enhance sexuality, placing relationships in the proper perspective. Thoughts and actions will be on a higher plane when both parents and youth observe quality grooming standards.

Many great deeds, and some despicable ones, have been performed in the name of righteousness or honor. So it is with promiscuous sexual acts performed in the guise of love. President Spencer W. Kimball said, "When the unmarried yield to the lust that induces intimacies and indulgence, they have permitted the body to dominate and have placed the spirit in chains. It is unthinkable that anyone could call this love." (*Faith Precedes the Miracle*, p. 154.)

Some young people harbor the notion that if two people are in love, that is sufficient, and the end (eventual marriage) justifies or at least neutralizes the sting of promiscuity. The opposite is true. If two young people believe their love is genuine, obedience to God's commandments of virtue should be foremost in their minds. They should be saving themselves for their eternal mates. If they are obedient, their thoughts will dwell on planning a family and living together for eternity. If somehow this anticipated joy becomes secondary to immediate earthly satisfaction, lust, not love, is the source of their feelings. Self-gratification dulls the joy of one of life's most sacred experiences—marriage between two virtuous, righteous individuals.

Virtue is a spiritual and mental condition as well as a physical one. Promiscuous or immoral thoughts always precede immoral acts. Satan's insidious presentations of sex to youth often cause them to feel that only the actual physical act is unacceptable to God; but "out of the heart proceed evil thoughts, murders, adulteries, fornications." (Matthew 15:19.) Immoral fantasies, even if they occur only in the privacy of imagination, are harmful. Parents do well to keep wholesome, thought-provoking material continually before the minds of their children. Help "virtue garnish [their] thoughts unceasingly." (See D&C 121:45.)

Often when both parents work, an empty home is available for unwholesome experimentation. There is great wisdom in the prophetic counsel that mothers should remain in the home except in cases of emergency.

One daughter complained to her mother that it seemed like they had a lesson in Mutual on chastity and virtue every other week. A few years later she asked her mother to pass on a message to her Mutual instructor that those lessons had really helped.

Sexual promiscuity may be a form of youthful rebellion planned to embarrass parents or to get attention. Young women may become involved to gain a perceived status with popular boys, or to assure themselves of acceptability within a group. Parents whose children become involved may certainly feel frustration and heartbreak as they watch their children ignore counsel. The following suggestions may help prevent such problems from occurring:

1. Teach youth to run away from sexual temptation, in all its forms, whether mental or physical. Some cultures teach that it is less than honorable to run away from a challenge. Remember, David stood against the giant Goliath and won, but lost the battle of virtue when faced with temptation. *Youth must understand that they defeat Satan's purposes as effectively by avoiding temptation as by resisting it.* The story of Joseph and Potiphar's wife is a classic example. Because Joseph acted immediately, and ran away, he was the victor in every sense. Sometimes the practical

circumstances make physically leaving the place of temptation impractical, but wherever possible, run from temptation.

2. Rehearse with your children ahead of time some answers to requests for sexual entanglement. Teach them that it is right, preferable, even mandatory to say "No." Help them to answer the following questions in their minds before any situation presents itself:

Will I date nonmembers?

What limits on intimacy will I maintain before marriage?

What qualities must the person I date possess?

Will my thoughts follow a consistent pattern of virtue?

If youth know from the beginning that their answer to inappropriate proposals must be "No," regardless of the justification tendered, Satan will not prevail.

3. Teach children that creation is beautiful, and that it is a major reason for our being on earth. Youth look to their parents for righteous, spiritual training in matters of sex.

4. Be frank, all the while remembering discretion in communicating with youth.

5. Teach children confidentiality. Youth do infinite damage to the souls and character of those who may have been caught in sexual sin by spreading the knowledge of the act. All too often such rumors are either greatly enlarged or simply unfounded. Repentance is a quiet act among the individual, Heavenly Father, selected Church authorities, and those offended.

6. Where pregnancy results from sexual immorality, parents face a great challenge. Their love and support for the child must rise above disappointment and be manifest with assurances of family support in time of need. The young person may feel that his or her future goals, aspirations, and dreams are no longer possible. At this point parents, like Christ, must separate the person from the act.

Concerning the child to be born, it is best to seek counsel from your bishop or LDS Social Services to get proper help and advice in determining whether adoption is a viable alternative.

7. Sexual transgression, though serious—even grievous—is not the end of a youth's spiritual world. Satan would have young people believe that there is no return to Father in heaven after moral transgression. This is not true. Youth should be counseled

to begin the repentance process by going to the bishop, who holds the key to the cleansing power available through Christ's atonement.

There are times and seasons for everything—to attend school, to be baptized, to receive the priesthood, and to get married. Not only must the time be right, but individuals must be authorized to do certain things. A young man could go up and just begin passing the sacrament, or baptize his younger brother; but because the authority has not been given he refrains. Likewise, sexual involvement requires proper authorization, in the form of marriage. Divine authorization for an eternal marriage is preferable. It is neither wise nor advisable for parents to modify the Church position on sexual promiscuity based on their own experiences, or to relate any such experiences to their children.

SIBLING RIVALRY

Sibling rivalry usually refers to those quarrels and spats that occur among older children, as opposed to the very young. As brothers and sisters feel for their place in the family, they often strike out at each other. How this striking out is handled often determines the direction a solitary life within the family takes. Rivalry among brothers and sisters has been known to stretch well into adulthood, at times causing the fire of envy and jealousy to burn away all love that could have been.

One of the Ten Commandments reads, "Thou shalt not covet." (Exodus 20:17.) But it is not an easy commandment to live, especially when one is a child. There will be times, no matter how well parents try to build into their children a sense of adequacy and security, that rivalry arises. We are each given different gifts, and a child often sees another's talents and laments that they are not his or her own. Here are some things parents might do to minimize this problem:

1. Teach and demonstrate that love is like a fountain. Younger children seem to think that *all* resources in a family are scarce. They may indeed have had to compete for food and clothing, wearing hand-me-downs and getting the smallest pieces of chicken

at the table. Seeing this, it is only natural for them to feel that love also has its limits, and the time parents spend on older children often seems to verify this fact in their minds. Conversely, older children see the increased resources that are often spent on younger ones, and they somehow feel cheated. Parents must remember to show the same love and spend the same quality time with all their children. There are, however, times when a parent needs to spend special times with an individual child. If this is the case, invest the time in the one, even if it seems unfair at the moment. *Fair* does not mean *equal.* It does mean that each person's needs will be met. Parents become experts about their own children, and they will often arrive at very different solutions for each child's needs.

2. Recognize each child as an individual. Every person—even as an adult—needs to feel that he or she is in some way unique. Each child needs to feel able to make a contribution to the family that is his or her own, a special portion of the picture that only that child can fill. Parents can show this by recognizing special talents and achievements. Music or art lessons are a much better investment than new drapes or expensive furniture. Both fathers and mothers need to spend *one on one* time with each child. This must be a routine investment that comes as naturally as breathing. Ten minutes may be all the time you have to give a child each day, but this will develop the habit. Also, if each time you see a child you do something that is special just between you and that child, such as a touch on the head or a kiss on the cheek, the investment will be repaid a hundredfold.

3. Show the child how his or her unique contribution is nevertheless part of a whole. Stuart and Steve were twins identical in looks but very different in talents and gifts. Stuart was a charmer, an excellent athlete, well thought of by his classmates. Steve was good in drama and extremely thoughtful to adults. Like most brothers and sisters, they felt rivalry. Stuart had been known to avoid his brother when his football buddies were around. Steve often made fun of the "goons" on the football team when he was at play practice. Both resented being mistaken for the other in the halls at school.

Their wise father, seeing the rivalry develop, began searching for answers, and soon started a cooperation campaign in his family. At family home evening he placed a large crystal bowl on the table. Separately, each of the nine family members was given a delicious-looking piece of fruit. They were to bring those pieces of fruit to the home evening—polished and beautiful. When they were all assembled each person brought his or her piece of fruit and placed it into the crystal bowl. A lesson was then given using the bowl as a representation of the family—each member being beautifully unique with a place within the bowl. At the end of the lesson each person was invited to select a piece of fruit other than his or her own.

After this, Steve and Stuart still had squabbles. There was no magic resolution, but they called each other "goon" or "sissy" less often. Somehow the family seemed to begin to live in greater harmony together as unique parts of a beautiful whole. As the boys matured, that also helped to lessen the feelings of antagonism. Their father often felt good because he had endured the earlier squabbles with patience. In the end, over time, it all seemed to work out.

ELEVEN PRACTICAL TIPS FOR SUCCESS

1. Help younger children accept a new baby by having them help prepare for it. They could each select some of the new baby's things.

2. Toddlers usually won't share, but work with them gently and endure this stage.

3. Use the older children to help care for the younger ones— working by your side, not "slavishly" in your place. As the older children help the younger children, this helps in the bonding process.

4. Praise regularly.

5. Discipline fairly, remembering the golden rule.

6. Be cheerful and enjoy your family.

7. Teach children to say "I love you," even to each other, and say it to them.

8. Provide them with meaningful and rewarding work.

9. Do many things together while the children are young. They start to seek independence at about age fourteen. By about age seventeen children should be bonded with each other. If they are not, their future relationships and feelings for each other will

be different from what they might have been had the bonding occurred.

10. Deemphasize materialism. Teach children that true joy comes from living spiritual values.

11. Help older children understand that there will be times when their younger brothers and sisters will be obnoxious. Teach them that this is natural, and that they must work to accept it. They were obnoxious themselves once.

Remind each other often that love should be like a fountain: "Whosoever drinketh of the water . . . shall never thirst." (John 4:14.) The Savior showed the way, and we will find joy if we follow his example.

(SEE ALSO TEASING AND QUARRELING)

SINGLE PARENTS

Parenting can be like rowing a boat. Father does his share, Mother does her share, and if each oar is pulled smoothly through the water, the boat is carried toward an eternal family life. There are twists and turns, rocks and rapids, but success is attainable.

The single parent, however, seemingly is forced to travel these swirling waters without one of the oars. Such parents must row from both sides or end up going around in circles. They must assume the responsibilities of both mother and father, homemaker and breadwinner. The task is great and often appears overwhelming.

A more workable analogy for the single parent would be the kayak. A kayak is built so that it can tip completely upside down and return topside without taking in a lot of water and sinking. So it can be with the single parent. Wrapped tightly in Heavenly Father's special love, the single parent can regain a balance and victoriously complete the course. The challenge is great but the rewards are certain.

The single parent must first understand that all children are Heavenly Father's, and the Father will help. He is always willing to help. "The Lord is my helper, and I will not fear what man shall do unto me." (Hebrews 13:6.)

For single parents to deal with raising families they must quickly learn to handle their own feelings and needs. They may struggle with difficult emotions—frustration, inadequacy, stress, fear, and loneliness. Single parents don't want to be pitied or ignored. Therefore they must strengthen their own understanding of their self-worth.

Following are some suggestions for gaining a positive attitude:

1. Become humble before Heavenly Father in sincere prayer and study the scriptures faithfully.

2. Be able to laugh: laugh at yourself, laugh with others, and laugh when it sometimes would be easier to cry. A parent's attitude determines the atmosphere of the home, and a smile is contagious.

3. Have someone to talk to who is willing to really listen. There are many others in circumstances similar to yours. Sharing experiences, good and bad, and listening to others is vital and strengthening.

4. Take time for yourself. Keep well-groomed and attractive. Plan enjoyable activities with, as well as without, the children. Work on a favorite hobby, and never stop learning. No one can keep giving and giving without taking time to refill his or her own cup.

As single parents build their own self-worth, they must also think of the feelings of their children. Time is one of the hardest things to regulate. Budget it very carefully; make all time *quality time.* You may not be able to serve as many "homemade-from-scratch" meals, sew as many clothes, or always be available to "taxi" as often as you would like to, but a quick meal of canned soup and a peanut butter sandwich can still say, "I love you." Just being together to talk about the day as clothes are folded, to sing silly songs in the car, or to struggle over a homework assignment is important. Take time to soothe a scraped knee or mend a bruised ego. Being organized, with each family member having specific chores, will free some time, and it will teach children to be responsible. Having all family members together builds family solidarity. The love and support of a family together enhances a child's self-esteem and feelings of security. Bedtime can be a good quiet time with children. Family prayers and family home evenings are a must. "Organize yourselves; prepare every needful thing; and establish a house, even a house of prayer, a house of fasting, a house of faith, a house of learning, a house of glory, a house of order, a house of God." (D&C 88:119.)

The single parent must teach, mold, and discipline with love. Each of these spirits has been trusted to you. Each is very important. Children shouldn't feel of any less value because they live with only one parent. Some children may need extra reinforcement to understand this. At times they may want to be with you all the time, afraid that they might lose you too and be left totally alone. They need constant reassurance of your love, and they must be slowly taught how to establish their own independence and security.

Children are resilient, and not as fragile as we sometimes think. Natural, easy communication and mutual respect should be developed. One single mother recorded in her journal this experience with her sixteen-year-old son: "Jeff and I spent this afternoon building some storage shelves. Neither of us had done this before. As we planned and measured we talked. As we sawed and hammered we laughed. As I taught him he listened. Then as he taught me a trick or two I was a willing student and a very proud mother. At the end of the day we had constructed strong, useful shelves and a stronger respect and appreciation for one another. My joy is great!"

Single mothers without priesthood leadership in the home need to look for male role models outside the home. Single fathers need to make use of the Relief Society. The sisters of the ward or branch can teach single fathers a great deal about caring for children. The Relief Society president is available to help. Home teachers, visiting teachers, extended family members, neighbors, and friends also are available. Teach respect for the priesthood. Call priesthood holders for needed blessings for both mother and children. These can be healing and prophetic blessings.

When the father is absent from the family, the mother is entitled to inspiration directly to her concerning her family. But sometimes a single parent with a foolish pride tries to be too independent. The single parent should be willing to give someone else the pleasure and blessing of helping when it is needed. When neighbors or home teachers or visiting teachers ask what they can do, let them help. Most often they want to help but don't know what to do. Giving you a boost will also give them a boost.

As single parents paddle along these twisting curves, around gigantic obstacles, and maybe even over a waterfall or two, they need not fear if they have invited Heavenly Father along as a partner. No one is alone. "Lo, I am with you alway, even unto the end of the world." (Matthew 28:20.)

SMOKING

In 1833 the Prophet Joseph Smith initiated the School of the Prophets to prepare priesthood holders for the ministry. During the first sessions, brethren would light their pipes and chew tobacco while discussing the doctrines of the kingdom. The smoke was unpleasant to the Prophet's senses, and upon inquiring of the Lord he received the Word of Wisdom (Doctrine and Covenants Section 89), which warns that "tobacco is not for the body, neither for the belly, and is not good for man, but is an herb for bruises and all sick cattle, to be used with judgment and skill." (Verse 8.)

Of the four best known items the Word of Wisdom warns against—that is, coffee, tea, tobacco, and alcohol—only tobacco was so clearly mentioned that no interpretation is necessary. No exceptions to this rule are given. We should not smoke tobacco in any form, or use chewing tobacco.

Tobacco is a concentrated destroyer. Although there seems to be no evidence that tobacco use leads one to a life of crime, as drug abuse frequently does, or to lack of self-control, as alcohol often does, tobacco simply attacks the human body with a vengeance. "Tobacco is killing more than a million people a year in the world, and more than 350,000 a year in the United States. Over a thousand people a day are dying prematurely." (Dr. John Holbrook, member of Advisory Committee to U.S. Surgeon General on Smoking and Health, as quoted in *Ensign*, November 1986, p. 103.)

Other research indicates that "smoking tobacco is the number one preventable cause of death in all the world. It is the leading preventable cause of heart disease, lung disease, artery disease, and cancer." (William R. Pollin and R. T. Ravenbolt, *Journal of*

American Medical Association, 23 November 1984, pp. 2849–54, as quoted in *Ensign,* November 1986, p. 69.)

Even more serious, tobacco use prohibits full fellowship in the Church, thus inhibiting one's progress in the kingdom of God, depriving the user of blessings otherwise available to members of the Church.

Young people who choose to smoke or chew tobacco also choose many of their friends by default. Smokers seldom attend church meetings, not because their habit is so serious, but because its use is so evident and difficult to hide. Youth exercise this small amount of rebellion, which through their associations may lead to other things.

Some young people choose to experiment with tobacco out of curiosity and brief excursions into pseudo-macho behavior. It is important for parents to differentiate between curiosity and a determined rebelliousness. If you do discover that your child has smoked or is smoking, it may be well to discuss with the child what smoking means to him or her. Did the child smoke because friends have dared him or her to? Is it a means of gaining attention? By discovering why children have chosen to try smoking, parents can more easily help them understand its ramifications. Here are some steps they might take:

1. Take the same approach earlier recommended for alcohol abuse—that is, teach obedience because it is a commandment of our Father in heaven. (See the section in this volume titled *Alcoholism.*)

2. Point out to children the odors and messiness accompanying this habit—the ashes, burn-holes, butts, ashtrays, tobacco cannisters, pipe-cleaning equipment, tell-tale indentations in clothing, styrofoam or paper cups full of chew residue, stained clothing and teeth, tobacco juice deposits. Tobacco use is a messy, smelly habit.

3. Explain in graphic terms the weekly or monthly costs of smoking.

4. Educate children on the damage to body and mind. Years ago Elder Joseph F. Merrill said, "I have had unusual opportunities to become familiar with the many-sided tobacco problem. *The evidence now exists to show that no one who smokes can achieve the best of which he or she is capable.* Whether this be a foot

race, a prize fight, a golf game, a rifle score, writing, speaking, singing, acting, performing on violin, piano, or typewriter, attainment of health, strength endurance, beauty, glamor or any other excellence on which men and women set their hearts. It is time that those ambitious in all other lines of work should also learn the truth that tobacco harms, never helps." (Conference Report, October 7, 1951, pp. 135–36; emphasis added.)

5. Remind youth of the scriptures warning us not to defile our bodies. The body is a temple. (See 1 Corinthians 6:19.)

6. It is difficult to teach children not to smoke if parents are smoking. "Parental example is the greatest method of teaching youth what they must do to gain the promised blessings from the Lord. Young people are most fortunate if they live in a home where parents teach and observe the Word of Wisdom." (Nathan Eldon Tanner, *Ensign*, August 1981, p. 2.)

7. Finally, the best advice of all is teaching children simply to say *No!* Most adults and adolescents will understand.

STEALING

"There was a lump in my throat. Not a lump you could see or feel, but a lump of guilt that had been there for a long time — ever since that fateful day of temptation in the canyon.

"As I watched the preparations for our camp-out. . . . I saw mother pack a big blue wooden box with bedding and clothing. Knowing we should be gone a long time, she quietly slipped a sack of candy in the side for special occasions. . . .

"I often thought of the candy in the blue box and waited in great anticipation for a time when I would be alone in camp. The day finally came. And, sure enough, the candy disappeared. . . .

"The days went by. Our crops were in, and we had long since come back home. As I walked beside my father one day, he put his hand lovingly on my shoulder. As I looked into his face, he said, 'Dear, I hope you will grow up to be the kind of woman that we — Heavenly Father, your mother, and I — can be proud of.'

"I could stand it no longer, and bursting into tears I declared, 'But Daddy, I took the candy!'

"Right there on the street he stooped and put his arms around me. 'Didn't you know that we knew you took it?'

"Then the miracle happened. The lump, after all this time, was completely gone." (Enone L. Hardman, *Ensign*, July 1976, pp. 62–63.)

From this simple story we gain perspective concerning children who steal. At the same time we see how to teach them and to forgive them when they steal.

Stealing can be a very minor thing—like the candy—or it can be very serious, involving valuable items. This range of variance may be why the Lord kept this commandment so simple. He wrote in stone: "Thou shalt not steal." Four short words only. He could have said more, perhaps covering the different ways in which a person might steal, but the commandment to all is clear— we are not to take that which does not properly belong to us.

When children steal, parents often wonder *why*. Occasionally there is a true or perceived need. They may steal because of hardship, but this is rare.

Children usually steal because of greed (or covetousness), laziness, or the very young may not realize that it is wrong. They may steal for excitement, or because of peer presure. They also may suffer a sickness called kleptomania (discussed later in this section). Some children steal because they have begun to use drugs and must steal to suport their growing habit. Or, they may be crying out for help. What can parents do?

1. First, talk to your children. Teach them directly and early that it is wrong to steal; teach them what constitutes stealing. Teach that "we believe in being honest." (See Article of Faith 13.) Even small acts of dishonesty must be carefully ferreted out. Also, parents who justify dishonest acts in their own lives should not be surprised to see their children stealing. Paul asks a good question, "Thou therefore which teachest another, teachest thou not thyself? thou that preachest a man should not steal, dost thou steal?" (Romans 2:21.) Totally honest parents are the most effective teachers to their children.

2. Emphasize the golden rule. A child's heart nearly breaks if a favorite toy disappears, as does that of a youth who finds that a special sweater or skirt is missing. Help children to understand that others' feelings are like their own, and that all people feel

hurt if their things are missing. To want someone else's possessions badly enough to take them is unfeeling and selfish. Father in heaven calls this behavior "covetousness."

3. Restitution is required of those who steal. If the child still has the item that was taken, right then is an ideal time to teach the law of restitution. Have the child return the object to its rightful owner. This may humble a child and may be very difficult, but it teaches great lessons of courage and integrity. "If a child is small and simply doesn't understand the principle of honesty, our discipline may consist simply of returning the object and explaining the principle to him. If, however, he does understand that he should not steal, the consequences may have to be more severe." (Ensign, August 1985, p. 29.) If the stolen item has disappeared, like the candy, other teaching moments immediately arise. Use them to point out the seriousness of stealing.

4. Teach that the consequences of stealing may be serious. Arrests, court hearings, even jail sentences all may follow stealing. Parents may wish to allow a child of any age to suffer the consequences following a theft. If the victim is truly angry when the item is returned (or perhaps pretending to be so, in the case of another adult), let some of this emotion sink into the offender. It need not become exaggerated or physical, but may teach a good lesson for the future.

5. Constantly encourage good work habits and ambition. The righteous way to obtain what we desire is to pay the price by earning it. This approach also gives the most satisfaction to the new owner. Items obtained in this manner may be proudly displayed and openly enjoyed without any distraction from memories of dishonesty.

6. Kleptomania, literally translated, means stealing madness. There are those who have a strong desire to steal, without having a personal need or even use for the items stolen. Although kleptomania is rare, if parents' teaching efforts are not completely effective professional counseling may also help.

President Spencer W. Kimball told of some elusive monkeys who were finally captured by a box with a small hole in it and a nut inside. The hole was perfectly sized so that an empty hand could enter and grasp the nut, but a clenched fist containing the nut could not be pulled out. "And so it often seems to be with people, having such a firm grasp on things of the world—that which is telestial—that no amount of urging and no degree of emergency can persuade them to let go in favor of that which is celestial." (*Ensign*, June 1976, p. 6.)

Teach children that only eternal treasures merit their tenacious grasp.

STEPPARENTING

(SEE REMARRIAGE)

STRESS

Every day, children face situations that make them anxious, tense, and even fearful. For most, such stress is temporary. It can be caused by taking a test, going through a change at home, or anticipating any unknown situation. If allowed to go unchecked, this stress can develop into chronic pressure that can become very harmful, especially to children.

The first step in stress management is to learn that stress can be good. Some stress is required if we are to be motivated to accomplish anything or to solve problems. People often use stress to help them accept challenges, and children should have challenges.

The danger comes when excessive stress prevents a child from functioning normally. When this happens, stress should be examined, its causes determined, and ways to reduce it found.

The following scenes are all too typical in LDS homes:

"Hurry up! You always make us late for church!"

"I hope you haven't forgotten about that big exam tomorrow."

"Have you cleaned your room yet?"

Statements like these can be stressful for children, and parents at times unknowingly contribute to unhealthy stress. It is important not to push or prod children excessively, causing them discouragement or anger. Colossians 3:21 says, "Fathers, provoke not your children to anger, lest they be discouraged."

There are some stressful situations that cannot be changed. A child can't change a death or a divorce. But family arguments can be reduced or eliminated, and a child can learn to successfully complete homework and other responsibilities. The key is to change what can be changed and try to teach the child to cope with things that cannot be changed.

EXCESSIVE STRESS

How does one recognize a stressed child? Children show stress in different ways. The following may be symptomatic:
- refusal to participate in school or church activities
- excessive worry about grades
- inability to concentrate
- avoidance of friends and activities previously enjoyed
- unexplained fear or upset feelings
- prolonged nervousness or depression
- irritability and excessive anger
- abnormal demand for attention
- lying or stealing
- disturbed or excessive sleep
- frequent headaches, stomachaches, or neckaches
- nervous habits such as thumb sucking and nail biting

When these signs occur, try first to determine if there is a physical cause. Perhaps a visit to the family doctor will be necessary. Try then to create a loving and caring home environment. This can quickly reduce stress in children. Monitor your own stress level; be sure that your own anxieties and pressures are not becoming contagious. Listen to your children. Teach them to express their feelings while young. They should understand that to voice their feelings to others is all right. Then, when they do approach you, take time to listen – really listen to their concerns. You might open a conversation by saying something like, "I want to understand how you feel," or, "I remember feeling like you seem to feel." Explain that you want to understand the child's feelings and that you will always be there to help.

As parents begin to understand the fears and anxieties of a child, they can create a supportive atmosphere where problems and concerns can be talked out. One father explained: "Our daughter disliked practicing the piano. This caused a stressful situation each day for her. There were always words exchanged and some-times bitter feelings. I decided to sit down and talk to her about why practicing made her so upset.

"She explained to me that her friends asked her to play at that same time. As a result she was forced to choose between her friends and what we were asking her to do.

"With a better understanding I agreed to change the time of her practice. I asked if she would mind if I sat and listened to her play each day. Her response amazed me. She couldn't believe that it was that important to me that I would take the time to sit with her during her practice. Her attitude towards practicing improved and it became a special time together.

"Each day following her practice time we just sat and talked. Within a few days after we started spending the time together she really opened up. She told me about her friends, what her hopes and ambitions were for the future. She explained that she was extremely nervous about attending a new school next year.

"What a special time this became! By just taking a few minutes to listen to her and by making the effort to understand her, I created an opportunity for a special bond to form between us."

Even common situations that usually create stress for all family members can be changed into meaningful, positive experiences. Family members can learn to show love and to support each other. Here are some more things they can do about stress:

1. *Pray.* Try turning to the Lord and asking for his help and guidance. Let the soothing influence of the Spirit work for you. Amulek encourages us to pray for temporal and spiritual blessings: "Let your hearts be full, drawn out in prayer unto him continually for your welfare, and also for the welfare of those who are around you." (Alma 34:27.) Remind children that they can pray for help in taking a test or in any difficult situation. A father's blessing may also ease the tension and help a child to cope.

2. *Take a break.* When children show signs of stress, ask them to walk to a window with you and take a deep breath of fresh air. Or you could go for a walk together, or lead the children through some stretching exercises.

3. *Role-play.* Role-play is a simple mechanism by which the child acts out the stressful situation in a nonstressful setting. Great insight can be gained through this process. If the problem

is at school, for example, get other family members to help play the roles of those involved. Analyze all points of view. This will help the child prepare for the actual encounter.

4. *Solve problems.* As children come to understand that they can control most situations, they will gain confidence. Ask them what changes they would like to see occur. Select a goal and then brainstorm ways to accomplish the goal. Talk about the pros and cons of each suggested solution. As time passes, ask the children to evaluate their progress. Are things getting better? Should the plan be modified or changed? Problem solving and follow-through provide an avenue for a child to openly discuss stressful situations.

5. *Organize.* If disorganization is causing stress, help the child find a place to put things. Just knowing where things belong and being able to find them easily often relieves tension.

Teenagers often need help in organizing a schedule to keep track of daily activities and long-term assignments. Parents may need to look at their own schedules to see if overcrowding there may be causing some of the child's stress.

6. *Relax.* When faced with stress, children (and adults) can do some simple exercises to relax. They can learn how to tell when their bodies are tense. To relax this tension, show the children how to close their eyes and tense their toes, hold the tension for about five seconds, then relax. Continue this process by tensing calves, then knees, thighs, stomach, arms, neck, and finally face. Just going through the process relieves stress. Another relaxing exercise is deep breathing. Have the children take a deep breath, breathing in through the nose and exhaling through the mouth. Then count to two before repeating. Have the children imagine that tension is leaving their bodies with each exhaled breath. Focus on the relaxed feeling. Under stress people often breathe improperly and need more oxygen. Deep breathing and deep sighs increase oxygen intake and can release tension quickly. Breathing too rapidly causes hyperventilation, depleting the body of the correct carbon dioxide balance, causing numbness, dizziness, and disorientation—which are all symptoms of stress.

If none of the above suggestions seem to work, and the child still seems unable to cope, professional help should be sought.

King Benjamin gave wise counsel when he said: "See that all these things are done in wisdom and order; for it is not requisite that a man should run faster than he has strength." (Mosiah 4:27; see also D&C 10:4.)

As everyone in the family strives for proper balance, it will help all to cope. Parents can help children achieve this balance most quickly through love and understanding.

STUTTERING

"The hardest thing for me to say was my own name. When school started the teacher went around the room and asked each of us to introduce ourselves. When my turn came I just stuttered, but nothing came out. The teacher said she didn't hear me, and told me to say my name again. All the kids laughed and I cried and turned red and got all mad. It was horrible. I hated my name."

The above true situation indicates the level of frustration that can accompany stuttering. For some people it is hard—nearly impossible—to overcome.

In like manner, Moroni mourned that he could not write as well as he desired, and feared that the Gentiles would mock his words. The Lord's answer seems somehow to pertain to those who stutter and those who may be guilty of mocking: "And when I had said this, the Lord spake unto me, saying: Fools mock, but they shall mourn; and my grace is sufficient for the meek, that they shall take no advantage of your weakness; and if men come unto me I will show unto them their weakness. I give unto men weakness that they may be humble; and my grace is sufficient for all men that humble themselves before me; for if they humble themselves before me, and have faith in me, then will I make weak things become strong unto them." (Ether 12:26–27.) Just so, the Lord will help those who stutter.

No one knows exactly what causes people to stutter. Sometimes a combination of factors may work together to bring it on. There is, however, evidence that four major conditions have some influence in causing stuttering.

1. Many experts feel that stuttering is an inherited, genetic trait, like other traits that seem to run in families.

2. Other experts feel that, even though a person may have a

predisposition to stutter, such behavior is only activated when triggered by some form of stress or trauma within the environment. Such stresses may be present only when a person is trying to make certain sounds. Stutterers often seem more excitable, and talk faster, thus sometimes imposing the stress on themselves. Perfectionists who try to outdo themselves can find themselves stuttering. Usually several of these pressures combine to create a stressful reaction.

3. Another group believes stuttering is a psychological problem, a conditioned or learned mannerism developed in reaction to certain threats. For example, one parent remembers vividly a distraught teacher screaming at her child. So does the child. Every problem in the class seemed to be the fault of that child, at least according to the teacher. Nothing the child did seemed to please the teacher. The child was soon afraid to say anything, for fear of being scolded.

4. Still others believe that stuttering is a physical problem that prevents sound from being formed properly. In some cases, experts think a block, such as a chemical imbalance, may exist that prevents the proper signal from being transmitted to the voice box from the brain. In other cases, the voice box may "lock up" in a spasm. Some experts have the idea that improper air flow and faulty air pressure from the lungs are the culprits that cause stuttering.

Parents of children who stutter could try the following:

1. Be very helpful and supportive when a child begins to stutter. Focus your attention on what the child is trying to say rather than on how it is being said.

2. Listen to the child carefully. Don't express any alarm or react negatively. Just as a child may stumble or be clumsy when learning to walk, he or she may also be awkward putting sounds together. Words and sentences are even harder.

3. Don't panic. It is natural for a child to hesitate. Practice sounds aloud with the child.

4. Let each child learn at his or her pace.

5. Avoid labeling any child as a stutterer.

6. Don't keep correcting or rushing the child.

7. Attend to and give credit for the child's thoughts and ideas. Value the child's decisions.

8. Make eye contact with the child, as well as loving physical contact. This may help simplify the communication process, and the temporary nonfluency may soon disappear as mysteriously as it came.

Many young children go through a stuttering stage, and time will be all that is necessary for them to become fluent. At other times it may be useful to involve a professional speech specialist or pathologist to help correct stuttering. Most schools, health clinics, or hospitals can suggest trained people.

Many stutterers are extremely intelligent and come from very successful families who have high expectations for their children. This often leads to a demand for perfection, either by the parents or from within the child. Such pressures to overachieve are not healthy. The scriptures teach patience, long-suffering, and a time and a season for all things.

Sometimes so much frustration builds up during the day that the stutterer may come home and unload pent-up anger on the family at night. Family members may be the only people the child feels safe with, the only ones who can be trusted to listen to him or her. When this happens, let the child have the unhurried time needed to express feelings and say the words he or she needs to say. As children start to develop confidence and feel secure in the private family setting, they will carry that sense of security into their public lives, and will have more courage to speak in situations that have previously caused embarrassment and fright.

Children should be allowed time to participate openly and freely in family discussions, conversations and private talks. Let the whole family, even the ward family, help. Participation in Church activities, speaking assignments, and group discussions will help one who stutters to feel more secure. One boy who stuttered was concerned with his ability to be a successful missionary, but had the faith to accept the call when it came. In a letter to this boy's parents, one convert wrote: "The thing which first attracted my wife and I to the gospel was the fact that your son was willing to bear his testimony to total strangers under such difficult circumstances. We decided that if his church meant so much to him that he was willing to be ridiculed for even trying to talk about it, then we should find out more about it."

As important as it is for people to learn how to communicate with fluent speech, it is more important that we remember who we are, and that we have divine worth. Every person can make a contribution in building up the kingdom of God on earth.

We should never give up and quit trying to improve ourselves. Moral values are of greater worth to God than fluent speech. All are agents to choose for themselves whether they will have control over their lives, or whether they will submit. Every person must deal with reality as it occurs in his or her own life.

The Apostle Paul had to live with his infirmity. "There was given to me a thorn in the flesh . . . lest I should be exalted above measure. For this thing I besought the Lord thrice, that it might depart from me. And he said unto me, My grace is sufficient for thee: for my strength is made perfect in weakness. Most gladly therefore will I rather glory in my infirmities, that the power of Christ may rest upon me." (2 Corinthians 12:7–9.)

Many individuals have become great by sheer perseverance in an area in which they desired to improve, including speaking. The Lord expects each person, regardless of individual problems, to trust in him, keep his commandments, and do his will. His grace will then be sufficient to make up for any mortal deficiencies.

TEASING AND QUARRELING

"He made a face at me!"
"She called me a name!"
"He took my place!"
"She won't let me play with her!"

These exclamations and many others like them commonly resound through homes where children are present. Teasing has often been described as one of children's favorite indoor (and sometimes outdoor) sports! And quarreling is closely related, as one often leads to the other. Teasing varies from mild forms of name calling to vicious and cruel taunting.

The suggestions below can help parents deal with teasing and quarreling among children under the age of twelve. Usually, as children move into adolescence, the kind of behavior described here tends to decrease and there is more harmony and cooperation between siblings.

Teasing in childhood usually occurs because children are in many ways rivals as they grow up together. They feel jealous when another child is honored or praised. And, no matter how fair a parent tries to be, there will be times that one child will get more attention than another. "Low-level teasing and kidding can be a healthy way for the 'slighted' child to get his concern off his chest. Permit it. Respond with humor. This is healthy and necessary, but you do have to draw the line if the teasing becomes deeply hurtful and destructive." (Victor B. Cline, *How To Make Your Child a Winner*, p. 153.)

Teasing also occurs when children become bored. Many parents have observed an increase in teasing when the television has been on too long, when too much free time is available without planned work or play activities, or when the same children have been together too long. Teasing and quarreling also increase when children are tired, hungry, or unwell.

Parents are usually the key to harmony in the home. Quarreling and fighting may be a reflection of how the parents relate to their children. If parents are always complaining, verbally attacking, and being negative, the emotional climate in the home may encourage disrespectful and uncooperative behavior. Children will imitate their parents.

Teasing and fighting among children will often increase when marital problems exist. If children frequently hear parents using insults, sarcasm, and criticsm, they will use these methods of communicating as well. Also, children may try to draw negative attention to themselves as a way of reducing marital conflict between their parents.

Lack of leadership may also encourage teasing and quarreling. Without rules, the family lacks security and unity. The home is full of chaos, and the children feel selfish and insecure. Everyone seems to be fending for himself or herself. Children want and need rules and positive, consistent discipline to guide them.

One of the first steps necessary to change teasing behavior is an evaluation of the problem. A couple could sit down together regularly, perhaps each Sunday, to evaluate how they are doing as parents. After thinking carefully about each child, parents could set goals to work on together for the next week. These goals might be discussed with the children in family home evening. End these evaluative sessions by kneeling in prayer.

The following scripture may also be a good starting point: "And ye will not suffer your children that they go hungry, or naked; neither will ye suffer that they transgress the laws of God, and fight and quarrel one with another, and serve the devil, who is the master of sin, or who is the evil spirit which hath been spoken of by our fathers, he being an enemy to all righteousness.

"But ye will teach them to walk in the ways of truth and soberness; ye will teach them to love one another, and to serve one another." (Mosiah 4:14–15.)

Try first to discern the reasons for the teasing, and then seek specific solutions. Some of the following suggestions may be helpful:

1. Consider age characteristics. Some teasing can be accounted for by the children's differing growth stages. If this is so, relax and be patient. Children will outgrow these stages.

2. Prevent harmful behavior. Do not allow teasing that becomes vicious and hurtful for a child, physically or emotionally. The child who is causing the problem should be removed from the situation, and firmly but lovingly told why the behavior is unacceptable. If the disturbing behavior continues, ask the child to go to his or her room or another appropriate area separate from others. Indicate that the child may return to be with the other children in five minutes if he or she can behave kindly. Then watch for ways to praise the disciplined child when he or she behaves cooperatively and lovingly.

Sometimes it is difficult to tell who is "to blame" for the teasing and fighting that occurs. Some parents have found it helpful to send all the children involved to their rooms with a statement such as: "In our family we do not hurt each other with words or actions. When you decide you want to be a cooperative member of this family you may come out of your room."

3. Let children work things out themselves. If children are constantly tattling on siblings and seeking out parents to referee their fights, parents can encourage the children to solve their own conflicts with a simple statement like: "The two of you can work it out together." Parents should avoid becoming involved in chil-

dren's conflicts unless they feel a child may be injured physically or emotionally, or unless the quarreling is seriously disrupting the feeling in the home.

4. Avoid comparing children. Parents should avoid comparisons, which show favoritism and cause children to be jealous of each other.

5. Help children to be involved in enriching and rewarding work and play activities, both with others and alone, so that boredom will not lead to teasing and quarreling.

6. Set an example by treating others with politeness, love, and concern in everyday life. Teach children ways of expressing their anger with words that describe why they feel angry rather than words that lash out and accuse or hurt others. They could say, for example: "I feel mad when you won't let me play the game with you!" rather than, "You are a big, dumb, idiot and I hate you!"

7. Do not provoke children. Parents have been known to tease, sometimes viciously. Such teasing may have harmful side effects. One father put a snake in the glove compartment of a car and then told his child there was a present there. The harmful effect proved almost irreversible. Calling children uncomplimentary names (even in jest) or teasing them about their faults, fears, or anxieties may seem harmless to an adult, but children are sensitive and usually believe everything a parent says about them. Children enjoy some playful teasing from parents, when they joke together and the children know they are not being made fun of. For example, some parents have said: "Are you sure one and one aren't three?" or, "You swim so well I think you must be a fish—are you a fish?" This gentle teasing conveys subtle compliments rather than accusations—children can tell the difference.

8. Talk together. Use family home evenings, family councils, and mealtimes to teach and encourage loving relationships among brothers and sisters. Talk to children about what to do when someone starts teasing them. Share stories and examples, role-play situations, ask questions for discussion of ideas, praise children's positive behaviors, discuss concerns, ask for the children's help in solving problems, and bear testimony of the importance of striving to have the Lord's spirit in the home.

9. Sometimes a child may be a bully, or the child may be

having trouble with a bully outside of the home. Comfort the child and listen to his or her explanation of what happened. Children can be encouraged to ignore most teasing, but in some situations it may be helpful to teach the child some assertive skills, including things to do and say when confronted by bullies. If your child is a bully, help him or her see the unacceptability of the behavior by talking directly from other children's points of view.

10. Take children as they are. Fill your children's lives with an abounding and nurturing love so that they know they are wanted, cared for, and accepted just the way they are.

11. Seek the Spirit for an understanding of how to guide children toward Christlike behavior.

Though some mild teasing may be acceptable and normal during childhood, the Lord has admonished his children to love one another and to live in peace. Parents should take heart in the realization that, though teasing and fighting among young children seem now so emotionally draining, this time will pass. As children are taught and as they mature, these behaviors will tend to decrease, and parents will remember the rewards and joys of parenthood rather than the teasing and quarreling.

TELEVISION

(SEE MEDIA INFLUENCES)

TEMPLE MARRIAGE

(SEE PLANNING FOR THE FUTURE)

THUMB SUCKING

Many parents dislike having their babies suck fingers or thumbs. Yet thumb sucking is part of an instinctive need, and it starts almost at birth. Some babies even suck their thumbs in the womb. This sucking instinct fulfills two purposes: (1) it allows a baby to receive nourishment from the breast or bottle, and (2) it fulfills a baby's need for comfort and relaxation. If parents can accept these functions as necessary, and if they will develop a more relaxed attitude toward thumb sucking, it usually will not become a problem for the babies.

Many babies find their thumbs at about six to eight weeks of age. Studies indicate that babies who suck their thumbs, fingers, or pacifiers usually cry less, sleep more easily, and get through the teething process more comfortably. Colicky babies will often quiet down when permitted to suck their thumbs or pacifiers.

Generally this sucking need will subside by around two to two-and-a-half years of age, though there will be some children who will continue to suck their thumbs until age four or five, or even longer.

Because thumb sucking is viewed as a natural way for children to receive comfort and security in the early years, it is not recommended that parents try to keep their children's thumbs out of their mouths by restraining devices. Putting mitts on a baby usually only makes the baby more frustrated and unhappy. The only known method of stopping thumb or finger sucking without upsetting a baby is to give the child a pacifier before the thumb-sucking habit is established.

Babies who use pacifiers rarely become thumb suckers, and usually children will spontaneously give up a pacifier at about age two when the need for sucking has subsided. If a child continues to want the pacifier past this time, you can begin a gradual weaning process by limiting the use of the pacifier to nap and bedtime, eventually taking it away altogether. If you choose to use a pacifier, get a safe one that meets safety standards, and sterilize it if it is used often. If a child continues to be fussy, comfort him or her and check out all other possible reasons for the fussiness. Do not use a pacifier as a "plug" every time a child cries, nor as a substitute for loving and comforting.

Holding a baby in your arms during feeding time gives the baby a warm, secure feeling. Merely propping a bottle or having the baby hold it sometimes encourages thumb sucking because the warmth and security of parents' arms are not felt. Babies who are nursed often need thumbs and pacifiers less than bottle-fed babies because they are allowed to suck longer.

As stated before, the need to suck for comfort and relaxation usually stops at about two, but this need may return if a child feels anxious, tense, or embarrassed. Parents who are worried about thumb sucking in children over two can usually prevent it by lessening stress, providing comfort and attention, arranging for a nap, or giving the child a little snack. Just keeping track of when thumb sucking occurs can be helpful.

Sometimes, even after you have spent time with your children and tried to meet their needs, there will still be those who continue to suck their thumbs. One little girl said, "I just like to!"

Part of the loving and nurturing process is patience. Don't make thumb sucking a problem by putting too much emphasis on it. If a child reaches age five and begins school still sucking his or her thumb, some feel it is time to take a firmer stand. However, around age five children tend to be quite cooperative, and they will usually be willing to try to give up their thumb sucking. It is a good approach to say, "You are so big now that you are going off to school, and you probably don't need your thumb anymore."

Make the child an ally, with the problem itself being the enemy. You might ask the child directly: "Do you think this is a problem?" Develop a plan together. Be on the child's team.

Little girls will often stop sucking their thumbs if their fingernails are painted with polish. Some children respond to a chart or calendar that they can put stars on. Work toward a small reward or activity of their choosing. Give lots of praise and encouragement during this time.

Some parents have found it effective to paint a strong-tasting substance (found in stores and labeled for this purpose) on the thumb or place a bandage or piece of adhesive over the thumb. Sometimes a dentist will advise placing an attachment in the child's mouth inside the upper teeth that makes thumb sucking impossible. This is done when the dentist feels that the child's teeth and jawline are not developing properly because of the thumb sucking.

Scolding, shaming, or slapping a child's hand are not effective ways to stop thumb sucking. Often children will continue to suck their thumbs when no one is watching or in the privacy of their rooms to prevent parents from seeing them, but they will not give up the habit.

As parents realize how much their nurturing love and attention count for in their children's lives, and as they seek the Lord's help through prayer, they will develop the insight and patience necessary to guide their children in each aspect of their development.

TOILET TRAINING

As children enter their second year of life, they continue to be confronted with new tasks to be learned and mastered. This is the process of growing up, and a time when parents have an excellent opportunity to give supportive love and guidance.

One of these tasks is learning to use the toilet. Most children will be ready to begin toilet training at about eighteen to twenty-four months, but as is usually true some will be ready sooner and others later. Learning proper use of the toilet comes gradually. Most research suggests that an average child achieves daytime control at about two-and-a-half to three years of age, and nighttime control between the third and fourth birthday. Usually boys take longer to gain control than girls do. By watching for signs of readiness, parents can often spare a child the pressure and humiliation of starting too early and meeting with disappointment.

It is most important to handle children with respect and patience, encouraging them all through the process. If this happens, both parent and child can have a positive experience. Remember that a child must be physically, mentally, and emotionally ready to be toilet trained. When this stage is reached, the task becomes quite simple. Forcing children before they are ready generally leads to a traumatic experience for both parent and child.

When is a good time to start toilet training? Before a child can control bowels or bladder, certain muscles and parts of the nervous system must mature to the point where they can be consciously controlled.

Parents can begin looking for signs that indicate children's

readiness when they are about one year old. The usual signs are:
(1) walking by themselves, (2) interest in the toilet and an awareness of what it is used for, (3) some regularity in bowel movements,
(4) staying dry for longer and longer periods of time, and (5) letting
parents know that a diaper is wet or that a bowel movement has
occurred. Some children may even go into closets or behind furniture and doors when they are about to have a bowel movement.
This does not mean they are trying to hide; it can be, however,
an indication that the child knows what he or she is about to do.
The parents can then calmly and gently remind the child to use
the toilet.

Children usually develop bowel control before bladder control.
Some move their bowels every day, others every second or third
day. Observe the normal cycles. Children should not be urged to
go more frequently than they need to. Laxatives, enemas, or sup-
positories should not be used without a doctor's advice.

There are some times to avoid beginning training. For example, do not try to train a child during or soon after a change
of residence. Also, if a new baby has come into a home, training
may be difficult. An illness or any other stressful situation may
cause the same hesitance in the child. Make toilet training a time
of nurturing, a time of positive encouragement. Children need to
feel good about progress they are making.

When the child is ready, show him or her the toilet and explain
in simple words what it is used for. Set the child on the seat for
a few minutes at the time a bowel movement usually occurs. Tell
the child calmly and lovingly what you want him or her to do. A
child who protests and wants to get off is probably not ready. Wait
a week or two. Give praise if the child does eliminate; if not,
simply and cheerfully say, "Okay, we'll try again later." Help
children learn to wipe themselves and wash their hands each time
they try to use the toilet. Habits of cleanliness and modesty can
be best reinforced during toilet training.

Parent's own views about changing diapers and elimination
will become their children's views. It is good to approach both of
these with the attitude that this is a natural part of life, not
something that is "dirty" or "messy" or "stinky." Here are a few
more suggestions that may prove helpful:

1. A patient, warm, casual approach to toilet training can

prevent problems and frustrations for parent and child. Always use a positive approach and give the child lots of praise.

2. Let children know that they are loved and that you have confidence in them. If frustrations develop, reassure them that they will soon be able to use the toilet on their own. If frustrations arise for the parent, evaluate why—perhaps the child is not ready or too much is expected too soon.

3. Teach appropriate and correct words for elimination. Avoid teaching "babyish" words that would be inappropriate to use in later years.

4. Be consistent with the child as training begins. Follow through to set the child on the toilet every few hours when he or she is first learning.

5. Children will need to be reminded to use the toilet as they begin mastering this task. Sometimes they are not aware of their need to use the toilet if they are engrossed in an activity.

Toilet training cannot be rushed! Children who are pushed too soon and meet with repeated failure may lose confidence and stop trying—the pressured child will often take longer to train. Try to avoid competing with other parents to see who has trained their child by the youngest age. When one wise father heard another father tell how his child was trained before the age of one, the first father jokingly replied, "My child was trained before he was twenty!"

Accidents will happen during this training time. Children may wet their pants when they are excited, tired, ill, engrossed in an activity, or under too much pressure. Never scold, shame, embarrass, or punish a child for an accident. Such situations require support rather than disapproval.

If a child has not achieved day and night bladder control, with only occasional accidents, by the time he or she is four years old, parents will probably want to discuss the situation with their doctor. This may be an indication of a physical or emotional problem the child is having.

As children achieve bowel and bladder control, their sense of independence and security increases. Their confidence is reinforced as they see the exciting evidence of their growth. And the patient and loving "teamwork" between parent and child that has been experienced during this toilet-training process will be a model for other experiences that lie ahead on the road to growing up. Once again, this is a prime opportunity to nurture children and reaffirm their great worth and their parents' abiding love for them.

VANDALISM

Vandalism is not the accidental defacing or destruction of property, but damage that is maliciously and willfully done. Why does it occur? Vandalism generally denotes a lack of respect or a kind of rebellion. Many people vandalize to get other people to acknowledge and pay attention to them.

Respect is something that must be acquired. Having a deep appreciation and respect for objects and people must come from effort. A person can only feel true appreciation for a thing of beauty if he or she has become involved with it. Chapels and homes take on a new meaning for those who help maintain them. Cemeteries become hallowed if youth know about their ancestors and life beyond the grave. Names, dates, and places are important if one has done temple work for those ancestors. Could a struggling artist, agonizing to create the image in his or her mind, ever destroy the beauty another has placed on canvas or in stone?

Parents need to spend time teaching their children a love for the rights of others. When children understand that *their* tithing helped to build the meetinghouse, and that *their* taxes helped build and preserve natural resources and public shrines, they begin to respect those objects and what they stand for.

Two young men spray-painted a message on a railroad bridge. The bridge had not been exactly beautiful before, but after the painting it became ugly. To restore it meant great effort and expense, but the parents insisted that their youth do the job. Thereby, these parents taught the youth how much greater effort is required to restore, compared to the few moments it takes to deface. When it was over they asked their youth, "Was it worth it?"

In another instance, chopping down the community Christmas tree in the center of town got a great deal of attention. Some laughed, some cried, some were outraged when they saw the forty-foot pine on the ground. The village elders called all together and counted the rings in the tree. This count showed the tree to be sixty-five years old. All who watched as the elders counted learned that respect comes from knowing what is required to create.

In another example, a mountain cabin was a middle-aged man's dream. It was paneled with native wood, had a fireplace made of the stones from a nearby stream, and although not lavish it was comfortable and serene. After an extended absence the man returned to find all the windows and the door shattered; bottles of fruit, jam, and kerosene thrown on the walls; honey poured onto the bed and mixed into the covers, along with the broken glass; pictures and dishes smashed. A young person who had helped create this cabin would not have done this. Perhaps the most important thing we can do to curb vandalism is to teach our children to create, to build, to cherish.

Vandalizing an object is perhaps even worse than stealing it. Though it may still be there, the beauty, majesty, and even the usefulness has been stolen away. Only the dead relic remains.

While some acts of vandalism (like painting the railroad bridge) can be fully erased, others cannot. Priceless historical relics almost never return to be as they were.

Children need to be *told* by parents what is expected of them. Parents who assume that their children know and understand their heritage and values may be disappointed unless some early, gentle teaching is done. This is not always easy, but it pays dividends.

WORD OF WISDOM

(SEE ALCOHOLISM; DRUG ABUSE; SMOKING)

WORK

(SEE HOUSEHOLD CHORES; RESPONSIBILITY)

ZEITGEIST

The challenges and rewards of parenting are summed up well in the word *zeitgeist,* which is defined as "the spirit of the time; the intellectual and moral tendencies that characterize any age or epoch." (*Funk and Wagnalls Standard Encyclopedic College Dictionary* [New York: Reader's Digest, 1968], p. 1561.) The spirit of our time is an exciting one, but it is fraught with perils, particularly as "intellectual and moral tendencies" swing to favor worldly views over God's commandments. Majority opinion must never become an excuse for unrighteous behavior. (See D&C 88:35.)

As Latter-day Saint parents, ours is the challenge to guide our children intellectually, morally, and spiritually so that the spirit of the time can be one of preparation for the second coming of the Savior.